Nonpr[illegible] Sanctions

Richard H. Speier

Brian G. Chow

S. Rae Starr

Prepared for the Office of the Secretary of Defense

RAND

National Defense Research Institute

Approved for public release; distribution unlimited

The research described in this report was sponsored by the Office of the Secretary of Defense (OSD). The research was conducted in RAND's National Defense Research Institute, a federally funded research and development center supported by the OSD, the Joint Staff, the unified commands, and the defense agencies under Contract DASW01-01-C-0004.

Library of Congress Cataloging-in-Publication Data

Speier, Richard.
Nonproliferation sanctions / Richard H. Speier, Brian G. Chow, S. Rae Starr.
p. cm.
"MR-1285-OSD."
ISBN 0-8330-2940-1
1. Nuclear nonproliferation. 2. Weapons of mass destruction. 3. Sanctions (International law) 4. Economic sanctions, American. I. Chow, Brian G. II. Starr, S. Rae. III. Title.

JZ5675 .S69 2000
327.1'17—dc21

00-051841

RAND is a nonprofit institution that helps improve policy and decisionmaking through research and analysis. RAND® is a registered trademark. RAND's publications do not necessarily reflect the opinions or policies of its research sponsors.

© Copyright 2001 RAND

All rights reserved. No part of this book may be reproduced in any form by any electronic or mechanical means (including photocopying, recording, or information storage and retrieval) without permission in writing from RAND.

Published 2001 by RAND
1700 Main Street, P.O. Box 2138, Santa Monica, CA 90407-2138
1200 South Hayes Street, Arlington, VA 22202-5050
RAND URL: http://www.rand.org/
To order RAND documents or to obtain additional information, contact Distribution Services: Telephone: (310) 451-7002; Fax: (310) 451-6915; Internet: order@rand.org

PREFACE

The proliferation of nuclear, biological, and chemical weapons and missiles for these weapons' delivery is a major threat to international security. This study examines the United States' use of sanctions against foreign entities to prevent such proliferation. This report should be of interest to analysts, lawyers, public-interest groups, and government officials working on sanctions issues.

In the 1970s, Congress passed laws requiring sanctions against acts contributing to nuclear proliferation. These laws remained fairly unchanged until 1990, when Congress began passing many laws requiring sanctions against all forms of proliferation. By the mid-1990s, a backlash had developed against a broad range of unilateral U.S. economic sanctions. This backlash, appropriately or not, may affect nonproliferation sanctions.

This study begins with a review of the objectives and provisions of the various U.S. nonproliferation sanctions laws. The legal provisions are compared at each step of the sanctions process. The study then reviews the history of the application of sanctions against proliferation, and the problems revealed by the experience. It then explores alternatives for dealing with these problems—including possible actions by both Congress and the Executive Branch, and concludes with recommendations. An Appendix provides the text of all major nonproliferation sanctions laws and other relevant materials as of 1997.

The Indian and Pakistani nuclear tests in 1998 triggered automatic and severe nonproliferation sanctions. Congress and the Executive Branch reacted with new laws reducing the scope and broadening the flexibility of these sanctions. Unfortunately, the official compilation of laws—the U.S. Code—lags behind legislation by some two years. So, rather than wait to update the laws, the authors extracted the sanctions passages from laws as of 1997 and present them in the Appendix. The body of this study and Section A–I.D of the Appendix describe the law changes in 1998.

This research was sponsored by the Office of Nonproliferation Policy, Office of the Assistant Secreatry of Defense for Strategy & Threat Reduction. It was conducted within the International Security and Defense Policy Center of RAND's National Defense Research Institute, a federally funded research and development center sponsored by the Office of the Secretary of Defense, the Joint Staff, the unified commands, and the defense agencies. The views expressed in this report are those of the authors and do not necessarily reflect the opinions or policies of their affiliated organizations or of their research sponsor.

CONTENTS

SUMMARY

In pursuing international issues, sanctions offer a middle ground between diplomacy and the use of military force. Sanctions are retaliatory international measures, most often involving trade or financial restrictions. This study looks at their use to prevent the proliferation of nuclear, biological, or chemical weapons (NBC weapons) or missiles for these weapons' delivery.

The first U.S. nonproliferation sanctions law was enacted in 1974. It was targeted at India for its "peaceful nuclear explosion." More general nuclear nonproliferation sanctions were enacted from 1976 through 1978. Thereafter, nonproliferation sanctions laws remained mostly unchanged for 12 years. But, beginning in 1990, Congress passed many sanctions laws against the proliferation of all NBC weapons and missiles.

By the mid-1990s, there was a backlash against a broad range of laws requiring U.S. unilateral economic sanctions. This study takes account of the criticisms being aired in this backlash—to the extent that they apply to nonproliferation sanctions.

In 1998, Indian and Pakistani nuclear tests led to automatic and severe sanctions. Laws were enacted in late 1998 to reduce the severity and to increase the flexibility of these sanctions. This study describes these changes. However, it does not analyze their legal texts in as much detail as it does the law that existed in 1997, because the most usable form of the law, the U.S. Code, did not reflect the recent changes at the time (April 1999) that the legal data for this study were last revised.

OBJECTIVES AND PROVISIONS OF THE SANCTIONS LAWS

Four objectives of sanctions are (1) *action,* to demonstrate that something is being done in response to outrageous foreign behavior; (2) *deterrence,* to dissuade both the sanctionee and onlookers from repeating such behavior; (3) *constraint,* to use economic or technological restrictions to interfere with the continuation of the behavior; and (4) *coercion,* to lead to improved behavior in the future.

U.S. bilateral relations with any given government cover a range of issues. Sanctions in pursuit of nonproliferation can interfere with the pursuit of other international objectives.

Sanctions can lead to collateral damage, not only to the handling of other foreign policy issues, but also to domestic economic interests on which the trade or financial restrictions fall. Minimizing such collateral damage can be an objective that limits the sanctions process.

The sanctions process, as established by law and practice, includes nine elements:

Triggering events may be dramatic actions such as a nuclear detonation or the use of chemical or biological weapons. Triggers are most frequently quiet transfers of hardware, materials, or technologies relating to NBC weapons or missiles. Such quiet episodes accounted for all of the nonproliferation sanctions imposed from the late 1970s until the spring of 1998, when sanctions were triggered by Indian and Pakistani nuclear tests.

Targeted entities may be individuals, subnational organizations, governments, or entire countries. In more than half of the sanctions laws, the sanctions fall exclusively on governments or countries. The rest of the sanctions laws are aimed at foreign persons or corporations. The wide scope of targeted entities often poses a major foreign policy dilemma for the imposition of sanctions, making collateral damage to other issues and interests a prime concern.

A *determination of sanctionability* is the process by which the President decides that, in a specific episode, the triggering event and the targeted entity meet the legal requirements for the imposition of sanctions. The result of an undefined determination process is that the clash of nonproliferation objectives with other goals may lead to long delays in the process.

A *certification of nonsanctionability* is the reverse of the previous process. With certifications, sanctions or equivalent restrictions exist at the outset and can only be lifted by Presidential "certification" that the sanctionable condition does not exist or has ended. The certification process means that, in the absence of Presidential action, sanctions continue.

Waivers are instruments with which sanctions can be avoided by means of a Presidential assertion that the national interests override nonproliferation concerns. Waivers do not require the President to certify good behavior on the part of the targeted entity.

The *design of a specific sanction* varies from law to law, from far-reaching measures against entire nations to import prohibitions against specific firms or individuals. The measures are often inflexible and may or may not promote the objectives of sanctions in a particular situation. Moreover, the sanctions generally do not deal with security motivations but, rather, with trade or finance.

Implementation of a sanction can be delayed by provisions set out in the law or, as noted above, by a dragging out of the determination process. Moreover, Executive Branch treatment of the details of the sanction can greatly affect its impact.

Multilateral support to reinforce U.S. sanctions is urged in some laws. However, there is no formal process for exploring or securing such multilateral support—except in the Chemical Weapons Convention, by which sanctions are imposed by an international administrative body and, in the most serious cases, can be referred to the United Nations Security Council.

Incentives are positive inducements that may be offered by the United States in negotiations associated with the sanctions process. Incentives can increase the likelihood of improved foreign behavior, but they also offer opportunities to "game the system."

To these nine elements can be added a process that, while not a formal part of sanctions legislation, can dominate the effectiveness of sanctions. This is the *sanctionee response.* The targeted entity or his government or other supporters may not remain static as sanctions are imposed. The sanctionee may engage in countermeasures to evade the sanctions, campaigns to have the sanctions mitigated, or negotiations or behavioral improvement to have the sanctions waived.

HISTORY AND PROBLEMS ASSOCIATED WITH SANCTIONS

This study has found 24 instances in which sanctions were imposed under the nonproliferation laws. Of these, only seven sanctions had enough of an effect on the sanctioned party to lead to negotiations. In most cases, sanctions were imposed on parties that did little business with the United States or against which the United States already had an embargo. For example, in a 1993 case the Department of Commerce reinterpreted the coverage of the sanction to reduce its economic impact by 90 percent. Before 1998, the last sanction with a substantial economic impact—missile proliferation sanctions against Russia and India—had been imposed in 1992. In 1998, substantial sanctions were imposed against India and Pakistan for their nuclear tests.

Whatever the direct effects (or the lack thereof) from the imposition of sanctions, sanctions laws may have had a deterrent or coercive effect in cases in which sanctions were *not* imposed. Unfortunately, it is difficult to document these cases from the public record. The evidence of cases where sanctions were not imposed is often one of delays, perhaps indefinite, in the determination process as a result of conflicting objectives within the U.S. government. In such conflicted cases, a government official may be led to fudge the process or to behave like a defense attorney to undermine the evidence, indicating that a sanctionable transfer has taken place.

The leverage that U.S. sanctions have on foreign proliferators has changed its character over time. The U.S. weight in international financial institutions is declining. And membership in nonproliferation regimes—which under some laws may exempt the member government from sanctions—is increasing. But the U.S. role—or potential role—as a trade partner is increasing. Meanwhile, as more governments make it their policy to observe international nonproliferation restrictions, the profits increase for the fewer remaining parties willing to transfer items that contribute to proliferation. This trend makes ever more appropriate one of the most succinct statements of the objectives of nonproliferation sanctions: "To take the profit out of proliferation."

ALTERNATIVES

This study explores four broad alternatives to the existing policy on nonproliferation sanctions:

Reducing reliance on unilateral sanctions involves such measures as increased reliance on incentives, diplomacy, and multilateral support. It may also involve strategic planning and monitoring to ensure that the sanctions process does not go out of control. This approach appreciates the dynamic (time-phased, measures/countermeasures) nature of the sanctions process. But by weakening the deterrent and constraining values of sanctions, this approach threatens to undermine the diplomacy that it promotes as an alternative.

Improving the existing sanctions process involves standardizing the best provisions of existing law, such as timetables for determining sanctionability and for conducting international negotiations before imposing sanctions, improving the formulation of laws in such areas as determining sanctionability and applying sanctions to members of regimes, and disciplining the sanctions process with greater congressional involvement. This approach may lead to greater clashes between the Legislative and Executive Branches. However, there is room for compromise. And this approach has the practical value of introducing incremental changes in procedures that have evolved over the years.

Targeting and calibrating sanctions more precisely involves giving the President discretionary authority to make the punishment fit the crime—as long as he imposes sanctions that are at least as effective as sanctions required by existing law (with effectiveness evaluated with respect to the objectives of the law), creating an Incentives and Sanctions Analysis Staff to design more precisely targeted, country- or individual-specific sanctions and to analyze and monitor each ongoing sanctions episode; minimum standards for sanctions to ensure that they "take the profit out of proliferation"; and an expansion of sanctions instruments to include security and incentives measures (and perhaps compensation of sanction-damaged domestic parties). This approach might promote many of the objectives of sanctions, but it represents a major departure from existing practice. It might be "gamed" within the U.S. government and by domestic parties seeking compensation.

Fashioning more powerful sanctions would entail leveling up existing legislation to include more of the stronger measures, apply them to members of existing regimes, and place more emphasis on the certification process; making advance preparations for multilateralizing sanctions; and broadening sanctions into areas such as incentives, existing Presidential authorities, military involvement, and expulsion from international nonproliferation regimes. This approach runs the highest risk of damaging U.S. bilateral relationships but would maximize the deterrent and constraining effects of sanctions.

RECOMMENDATIONS

We recommend detailed, as well as more fundamental, changes to the sanctions process. The detailed approach would include the alternatives for "improving the existing sanctions process" and "targeting and calibrating sanctions more precisely (except the compensation provision)." Elements of "fashioning more powerful sanctions" and even of "reducing reliance on unilateral sanctions" could complement these detailed approaches.

For more fundamental changes, we recommend a new set of three principles for sanctions:

1. *A "worse-off" criterion* for the design of sanctions. This criterion entails finite economic or security-related penalties on the target entity so that the costs imposed by the sanctions exceed the benefits of the sanctionable activity.
2. *Automaticity* in the imposition of sanctions. This is a recommendation to tighten up the determination process, eliminate waivers altogether, and require Presidential certifications of improved behavior before lifting continuing sanctions prescribed by Congress.
3. *Specialized staff* to design and oversee the implementation of sanctions.

The intent of these fundamental changes is to substantially increase the effectiveness of nonproliferation sanctions while minimizing collateral damage to competing interests.

ACKNOWLEDGMENTS

This study encountered surprising difficulties. The first was finding the nonproliferation sanctions laws themselves. There was no single place to turn for the relevant texts. Fortunately, Jason Robach, a summer intern at the Office of the Secretary of Defense, was working with OSD's Office of General Counsel to compile the sanctions laws when this study began. Mr. Robach's work set this study on its way.

There remained many bits and pieces of the law to be assembled. This could not have been done without the help of Randy Rydell, on the staff of the Senate Committee on Governmental Operations until a few years ago. Dr. Rydell maintained some of the best files on nonproliferation sanctions. He made these files available for this study and worked with Congressional Research Service staff to fill in remaining gaps.

After Dr. Rydell retired from the U.S. government, Dianne Rennack of the Congressional Research Service came to the assistance of RAND's researchers. She supplied her publications on nonproliferation sanctions and updated them to cover the intense period of sanctions legislation in late 1998.

The raging debate over U.S. unilateral economic sanctions involves many individuals and organizations. J. Daniel O'Flaherty of the National Foreign Trade Council and Mark McConnell of the law firm of Hogan and Hartson led the authors to concepts, documents, and other individuals involved in this debate.

Among the many individuals working in non-governmental organizations, Leonard Spector, Greg Koblenz, and Virginia Foran—in

1997, all with the Carnegie Endowment for International Peace—were particularly helpful in sharing their own work on sanctions laws and on the interaction of incentives with sanctions.

In May 1997, one of the authors had the good fortune to attend a conference, "The Strategy of Sanctions," held at the Cantigny Estate outside of Chicago. The conference generated thought-provoking interactions between many of the most prominent advocates and critics of U.S. unilateral economic sanctions.

A number of officials of the Executive Branch assisted throughout this study in providing historical data and insights to maintain relevance to policy concerns.

Lynn Davis—now retired from government—and Randy Rydell provided detailed comments on the draft of this study. The authors accepted some, but by no means all, of their suggestions.

Our project officer, Gerald M. Fitzgibbon, Deputy Director of the Office of Nonproliferation Policy, Office of the Assistant Secretary of Defense for Strategy & Threat Reduction, gave us free rein to explore new approaches while still keeping our efforts relevant to the policy world.

The authors thank all of these people for their assistance. However, this does not necessarily imply that they agree with us on our assessments and recommendations.

ACRONYMS

ACDA	Arms Control and Disarmament Agency
AECA	Arms Export Control Act
BW	Biological weapons
CBW	Chemical and biological weapons
CIA	Central Intelligence Agency
COCOM	Coordination Committee
CSIS	Center for Strategic and International Studies
CTBT	Comprehensive Test Ban Treaty
CW	Chemical weapons
CWC	Chemical Weapons Convention
DOE	Department of Energy
EAA	Export Administration Act
EU	European Union
ExImBank	See Eximbank
Eximbank	Export-Import Bank
FMS	Foreign Military Sales
GNP	Gross National Product

GPO	Government Printing Office
IAEA	International Atomic Energy Agency
IEEPA	International Emergency Economic Powers Act
ILAS	Iran-Libya Sanctions Act
ISAS	Incentives and Sanctions Analysis Staff
KEDO	Korean Peninsula Energy Development Organization
MTCR	Missile Technology Control Regime
NBC	Nuclear, biological, or chemical (weapons)
NDAA	National Defense Authorization Act
NNPA	Nuclear Nonproliferation Act
NNWS	Non-nuclear-weapon states
NPPA	Nuclear Proliferation Prevention Act
NPT	Treaty on the Non-Proliferation of Nuclear Weapons
NRC	Nuclear Regulatory Commission
OSD	Office of the Secretary of Defense
TNT	Trinitrotoluene
UK	United Kingdom
UN	United Nations
USC	United States Code
USCA	United States Code (Annotated)
WMD	Weapons of mass destruction

Chapter One

SOMEWHERE BETWEEN DIPLOMACY AND WAR

When it comes to pursuing some international issues, diplomacy is too little and war is too much. Sanctions help fill the gap.

Proliferation of nuclear, biological, and chemical (NBC) weapons and missiles is one such issue. Some governments contribute to proliferation for their own or their allies' security. But for some individuals, organizations, and governments, there is money to be made in proliferation. Diplomatic agreements against proliferation bind governments concerned with international security. But others see an opportunity to take advantage of such restraint by gaining new business. To discourage or limit such proliferators, there is a value to punitive actions—notably, sanctions.

At first approximation, sanctions may be considered to be retaliatory international measures involving trade or financial restrictions. The United States has employed sanctions for most of two centuries. Perhaps the first proposal for nonproliferation sanctions appeared in 1946 as part of the Marks-Acheson-Lilienthal-Baruch Plan for international control of atomic energy. To prevent violations of the plan, Bernard Baruch insisted on a system of "condign punishments . . . as immediate and certain in their execution as possible."[1] The first U.S. nonproliferation sanctions law was enacted specifically to punish India for its 1974 "peaceful nuclear explosion." In 1976–1977, important laws of global scope were passed to discourage the transfer of nuclear enrichment and reprocessing technology. More sanctions

[1]Bernard Baruch, presentation to the United States Atomic Energy Commission, June 14, 1946; online at http://www.nuclearfiles.org/docs/1946/460614-baruch.html.

against nuclear proliferation were enacted in 1978. For the next 12 years, until 1990, the U.S. nonproliferation sanctions laws went mostly unchanged. Then, following Iraq's invasion of Kuwait, Congress and Presidents George Bush and William J. Clinton approved a cascade of new nonproliferation sanctions laws. This study examines the use of these most recent sanctions to prevent the proliferation of NBC weapons, or weapons of mass destruction (WMD), or missiles for these weapons' delivery.

WHAT ARE SANCTIONS AND THEIR OBJECTIVES?

Defining *sanctions* is far more than an academic exercise. Current critics of unilateral economic sanctions omit from their definition the use of economic retaliation in opening up foreign markets, on the grounds that economic diplomacy for economic purposes is different from economic diplomacy for political purposes.[2] Yet the same critics include export controls in their definition, leading to estimates of annual sanctions costs to the U.S. economy of more than $15–$19 billion—estimates that are arguably an order of magnitude too high for the monetary effects of sanctions as they are considered in this study.[3]

---

[2]"The Strategy of Sanctions" Conference sponsored by the McCormick Tribune Foundation, the Strategic Studies Institute of the U.S. Army War College, the American Bar Association Standing Committee on Laws and National Security, and the National Strategy Forum, Cantigny Estate, Wheaton, Ill., May 8–9, 1997, hereafter called the "Cantigny Conference." A Summary of Proceedings of this conference is published in the *National Security Law Report* (American Bar Association Standing Committee on Law and National Security, Washington, D.C.), Vol. 19, No. 5, September 1997.

[3]Gary Clyde Hufbauer, interview with one of the authors, May 8, 1997. Also, see G. C. Hufbauer, J. J. Schott, and K. A. Elliott, *Economic Sanctions Reconsidered,* 2nd ed., Washington, D.C.: Institute for International Economics, 1990, pp. 6, 38, 81, 125–130, which treats the Coordinating Committee (COCOM) export controls as sanctions. The $15–$19-billion figure appears in The President's Export Council, *Unilateral Economic Sanctions: A Review of Existing Sanctions and Their Impacts on U.S. Economic Interest with Recommendations for Policy and Process Improvement, Executive Summary,* Washington, D.C., June 1997; hereafter called *Unilateral Economic Sanctions.* It should be noted that most U.S. export controls are global in scope, in contrast to sanctions imposed against specific entities in response to specific actions. Many nonproliferation export controls are administered according to the rules of multilateral regimes, restricting the transfers of items ranking from Minuteman missiles to flash X-ray machines to anthrax spores. Other export controls, restricting the transfer of items in short supply, are administered solely for economic reasons. A critique of some of Hufbauer, Schott, and Elliott's analysis appears in Robert A. Pape,

Even more far-reaching concepts of sanctions have been proffered. Blockades and acts associated with war are sometimes included.[4] Indeed, one *Webster's New Collegiate Dictionary* definition of *sanction* is "a coercive measure, usually by several nations in concert, for forcing a nation violating international law to desist or yield to adjudication, as by withholding loans or limiting trade relations or by military force or blockade."[5]

More than 50 years after the first proposal for nonproliferation sanctions, a system of nonproliferation sanctions, if not "condign punishments," is in place. The objectives of these later sanctions can be inferred from reams of official statements and scholarly analyses as including the following:

Action, "to placate domestic groups who insist that the U.S. government 'do something' to address foreign misdeeds"[6]

Deterrence of the sanctionee and of onlookers from contributing to proliferation

Constraint of the sanctionee through economic or technological restrictions to reduce his ability to make further contributions to proliferation

Coercion, to secure improved behavior on the part of the sanctionee to reduce the contributions to further proliferation.

The advocates of sanctions argue that these objectives are fully suited to an international security policy as vital as nonproliferation. Nonproliferation sanctions are most frequently triggered by international transfers. The buyers and sellers in those transfers are creating third-party consequences: reduced security for the rest of the world. It is, therefore, fully appropriate for the third parties—or at least the United States—to weigh into the transaction. Indeed, given the money-making character of many sanction-triggering events, the objectives of sanctions might sometimes be formulated in quanti-

---

"Why Economic Sanctions Do Not Work," *International Security,* Vol. 22, No. 2, Fall 1997.

[4]Hufbauer, Schott, and Elliott, 1990.

[5]G. & C. Merriam Co., *Webster's New Collegiate Dictionary,* Springfield, Mass., 1956.

[6]G. C. Hufbauer and E. Winston, "'Smarter' Sanctions: Updating the Economic Weapons," paper presented at the Cantigny Conference, Wheaton, Ill., May 8–9, 1997.

tative terms. In the frequently repeated words of Senator John Glenn, the objective of such sanctions is "to take the profit out of proliferation."[7]

The critics of sanctions have an answer. They point out that sanctions, too, have third-party consequences. When the United States acts against a foreign sanctionee, it interferes with voluntary international commerce between the United States and the sanctionee. Voluntary exchange improves the lot of both the buyer and the seller. Sanctions that interfere with such voluntary exchange will hurt not only the foreign sanctionee but also its U.S. trade partner.

Moreover, U.S. foreign policy officials have increasingly added another concern: The effects of nonproliferation sanctions, they fear, threaten other foreign policy goals, including international security cooperation with the targeted nation. Every U.S. foreign policy agency has both a regional desk and a functional desk. The functional desk worries about such global matters as international security and becomes agitated about the slippery-slope consequences of allowing exceptions to international rules. The regional desk worries about relations with individual governments and frets about the consequences of allowing one issue to interfere with the resolution of other issues with that government. Almost every sanctions case brings to the fore this clash of objectives between functional and regional desks.

Congress often has another objective in prescribing sanctions: to tie the hands of the Executive Branch so that strong enforcement of nonproliferation policy cannot be evaded.

All parties acknowledge the importance of nonproliferation. So the clash of objectives is muted. But that clash may be decisive for the functioning of the sanctions process.

Much of the current criticism of unilateral economic sanctions appears to be directed toward a type of economic coercion that might be termed "GNP wars," in which the power of the U.S. economy is used to devastate the economy of a targeted nation. The

---

[7]Senator John Glenn, "Senate Passes Major Nuclear Non-Proliferation Bill," news release, Washington, D.C., April 9, 1992.

criticism is that this type of sanction, because of its broad scope, causes wide collateral damage—to the handling of other foreign policy issues, to domestic economic interests on which the trade or financial restrictions fall, to the innocent in the targeted nation, and to a broad spectrum of U.S. economic interests.[8]

THE FOCUS OF THIS STUDY

This study examines a different type of sanction. Nonproliferation sanctions most frequently are directed at specific industrial sectors, firms, or even individuals in the targeted nations. Their objective is rarely to bring a national economy to its knees, but usually to stop specific programs for NBC weapons or missiles and, most frequently, to stop international transfers that contribute to such programs.

The critics of unilateral economic sanctions recognize this difference and frequently disclaim any intent to weaken nonproliferation sanctions.[9] Indeed, "arms embargoes and export controls are classic targeted trade controls," constituting a desirable type of sanction: "smarter sanctions."[10] But the rhetoric against sanctions often gains a life of its own, and nonproliferation sanctions are threatened not so much on their own merits as by the generalized attacks on sanctions.

Nonproliferation sanctions, their effectiveness, and future alternatives are the focus of this study. In this study, *nonproliferation sanctions,* as commonly used among the nonproliferation community within and outside the government, do not include export controls of indefinite duration. Export controls are a long-term component of U.S. national security policy. By contrast, the imposition of nonproliferation sanctions is usually triggered by a specific event, and the sanctions themselves are of limited duration.[11]

---

[8] Hufbauer and Winston, 1997.

[9] Cantigny Conference, 1997.

[10] Hufbauer and Winston, 1997. Also, see http://www.smartsanctions.ch

[11] The language of U.S. laws does not always make it easy to distinguish nonproliferation sanctions from "GNP wars." For example, see the Iran and Libya Sanctions Act, Section A–V.D in the Appendix, which is broad in its scope yet justified largely for nonproliferation reasons. This is, however, an atypical example of "nonproliferation sanctions," if it is that at all.

To make the study manageable, and to pay particular attention to the controversial aspects of nonproliferation sanctions that call for the most attention, this study generally passes over the sections of nonproliferation sanctions laws that apply to "domestic persons." The domestic application of sanctions laws is closely related to the enforcement of export controls and is not particularly controversial.[12] This study also focuses on sanctions laws with future applications, as opposed to *ex post facto* laws against India and Iraq.[13]

The triggering event for the imposition of nonproliferation sanctions can be a rare and dramatic event, such as the detonation of a nuclear device or the use of chemical or biological weapons, or a more frequent and quieter event, such as a transfer of items to another nation's NBC program. This study focuses much of its discussion on the latter, sanctions triggered by transfers, because—except for the important sanctions episodes triggered by the 1998 Indian and Pakistani nuclear tests, which are discussed in Chapter Three—the application of sanctions to transfers has caused the most controversy in recent years and is likely to be a continuing source of difficulty. The Appendix contains the texts of laws in place in 1997, regardless of the type of event triggering the imposition of sanctions.

This study treats sanctions as closely related to instruments of certifications and incentives. Certifications require a positive action by the Executive Branch before sanctions can be lifted, rather than a positive Presidential determination before sanctions can be imposed. This difference has attractions to Congress in compelling the use of sanctions. Incentives and sanctions are often used together, and the imposition of sanctions is often the withholding of incentives rather than just interference with customary trade and financial relations.[14]

---

[12]See Section A–I.A in the Appendix for more discussion of this point.

[13]Sanctions against India followed its 1974 "peaceful nuclear explosion," and those against Iraq followed its 1990 invasion of Kuwait and UN Security Council Resolutions calling for an embargo. Both involved U.S. legislation passed after the triggering events.

[14]For a discussion of the role of sanctions in the array of foreign policy instruments, see John C. Baker, *Non-Proliferation Incentives for Russia and Ukraine,* Oxford, UK: Oxford University Press, Adelphi Paper 309, May 1997.

OBJECTIVE AND ORGANIZATION OF THIS REPORT

The years since the mid-1990s have seen a backlash against a broad spectrum of unilateral economic sanctions. Some industry groups and academicians fear that the use of sanctions has gone too far, with indiscriminate and counterproductive effects on foreign and domestic entities. A major study commissioned by the White House concluded as follows:

> The most important economic impact of unilateral economic sanctions is the cumulative weakening of U.S. competitiveness in friendly third-country markets, including those of our largest trading partners.[15]

On the other hand, some in Congress and the nonproliferation community have complained in recent years that the United States has been insufficiently active in imposing nonproliferation sanctions. An illustrative statement of this theme is the following:

> The Committee is particularly concerned that nonproliferation imperatives have at times been subordinated to such other considerations as trade and commercial benefits . . . . The Committee will expect the Secretary of State to put national security objectives ahead of economic considerations . . . .[16]

This study attempts to sort through these issues as they apply to nonproliferation sanctions, and to examine options for formulating and using such sanctions in the future. This study focuses on sanctions against transfers by foreign persons to other foreign

---

[15]*Unilateral Economic Sanctions,* 1997. Other important recent critiques of sanctions include two statements by Stuart E. Eizenstat, Under Secretary of State for Economic, Business and Agricultural Affairs, in Remarks before the North American Committee of the National Policy Association, Washington, D.C., January 7, 1998, and Testimony Before the Lott Bipartisan Senate Task Force on Sanctions, Washington, D.C., September 8, 1998. Center for Strategic and International Studies (CSIS), *Unilateral Economic Sanctions: Interim Report of the Steering Committee of the CSIS Project on Unilateral Economic Sanctions,* Washington, D.C., June 10, 1998; Richard N. Haass, ed., *Economic Sanctions and American Diplomacy,* New York: Council on Foreign Relations, 1998; and the publications of the group USA Engage, online at http://www.usaengage.org.

[16]U.S. Senate, Committee on Foreign Relations, *Foreign Affairs Reform and Restructuring Act of 1997,* Washington, D.C.: Senate Report 105-28, June 12, 1997.

persons. It does not examine export controls in general, the application of sanctions to domestic persons, or sanctions laws, nor does it dwell extensively on sanctions against rare and dramatic proliferation events.

This study examines the functioning of the sanctions process, in Chapter Two; looks at the historical record of sanctions and the lessons to be derived from them, in Chapter Three; pinpoints problems that have arisen from these sanctions, in view of the historical record and the objectives of sanctions, in Chapter Four; delineates alternatives for dealing with the range of objectives involved, in Chapter Five; and recommends three principles for the formulation of sanctions, in Chapter Six.

Chapter Two

THE SANCTIONS PROCESS

The process of imposing and lifting sanctions involves a number of elements, which we have drawn from the U.S. sanctions laws through 1997, relevant texts of which appear in the Appendix. We categorize these elements as follows:

- *Triggering events.* These most often are the marketing or actual transfers of hardware, material, and technology prohibited by international treaties, agreements, and policies—although conspiracy to commit these acts is covered by some laws. Triggering events also include actual nuclear detonations or the use of chemical or biological weapons.
- *Targeted entities.* Those against whom the sanctions are leveled, the sanctionees, can range from governments to industrial sectors, specific firms, or individuals.
- *Determination of sanctionability.* This critical step involves a decision by the Executive Branch that a triggering event and a targeted entity meet the legal tests for the imposition of sanctions.
- *Certification of nonsanctionability.* In some laws, the Executive Branch must take a positive step to terminate sanctions or to lift a congressionally imposed restriction that is equivalent to a sanction. To do this, the President must certify to Congress that the target of the sanctions is not (or is no longer) engaging in proscribed behavior.
- *Waivers.* Some laws provide room for exceptions—for withholding the imposition of sanctions even after the President

makes a determination of sanctionability. The President can grant a waiver of sanctions by citing a higher consideration that outweighs the importance of the sanctions process.

- *Design of a specific sanction.* In some cases, the law gives the Executive Branch discretion in formulating the actual sanction to be imposed, including its duration and conditions for lifting it.
- *Implementation.* This step specifies the myriad elements involved in the actual operation of the sanction.
- *Multilateral support.* Congress sometimes encourages the Executive Branch to seek the reinforcement of unilateral U.S. sanctions with actions by other governments.
- *Incentives.* As an alternative to sanctions, the sanctions process often involves attractive offers to the targeted nation if its behavior improves.

A full discussion of the sanctions process must also include the *sanctionee response,* which can lead the sanctions process onto unanticipated paths.

Because all of these elements except the last are grounded in law, it is important to understand the limitations of this study's discussion of sanctions legislation. The implementation measures and the sanctionee response can overlay the sanctions process with a lengthy time dimension, within which resolves can weaken.

A CAUTION: THE LAW

As with most areas of law, sanctions legislation is complex. As one observer put it, there are many problems in applying the law,

> the first of which is figuring out precisely what the law is. Statutes can run on for hundreds of pages of details and are enforced by volumes of convoluted administrative regulations and even greater piles of interpretations, guidelines and exceptions. It is often

> impossible for anyone to fully know the law, even with the best of intentions.[1]

The authors of this study have found that every compilation of nonproliferation sanctions law that they have consulted has contained errors of omission or commission—even the recent study commissioned by the White House, Unilateral Economic Sanctions.[2]

Lawyers often discover subtle aspects of the law that have been overlooked or misinterpreted by other lawyers. We discovered a sanctions law that was unknown to key nonproliferation officials during whose tenure it was passed. But such surprises are not the only difficulties. In addition, the law cannot be discovered completely by reading texts; it must also be seen as it is administered by officials and adjudicated by courts. And the law is always changing, with time lags in the publication and the codification of the changes.[3]

For these reasons, the reader should not assume that the Appendix to this study includes all legislation relevant to nonproliferation sanctions through the 1997 cutoff date, nor that the legal summaries and interpretations of this chapter are immune to challenge. None of the authors of this study is a lawyer. However, the Appendix does include the major pieces of sanctions legislation before the 1998 Indian and Pakistani nuclear tests.

---

[1]J. V. DeLong, "Just What Crime Did Columbia/HCA Commit?" *The Wall Street Journal*, August 20, 1997, p. A15. Although this article does not apply explicitly to sanctions legislation, it explicates the difficulties of many legal areas, including sanctions laws.

[2]*Unilateral Economic Sanctions*, 1997, Appendix I, section II.E.1., summarizes missile sanctions as applying to trade that "contributes to the production of missiles . . . ." The Arms Export Control Act was amended, however, to require sanctions for transfers contributing "to the *acquisition*, design, development, or production of missiles. . . ." (See Section A–III of the Appendix to this study.) The important addition of "acquisition" provided for sanctions whereby entire missiles, and not just their production capabilities, were transferred. "Acquisition" does not, however, appear in the missile sanctions provisions of the Export Administration Act—highlighting the complexity of the law. *Unilateral Economic Sanctions* also omits mention of the NBC transfers to Libya that trigger sanctions; mistakenly, it claims that all UN–prohibited transfers would trigger U.S. sanctions.

[3]See the Appendix, Section A–I, for a discussion of such limitations.

This chapter, the authors believe, is a reliable summary of the major elements of the sanctions process. For details, the reader is encouraged to refer to the Appendix for the full text of legal provisions summarized and discussed in this chapter—but to do so with a realization that pieces may be missing and that later legislation will further change the picture.[4]

The following sections list elements of the sanctions process law-by-law, in the order in which the laws appear in the Appendix.

TRIGGERING EVENTS

The laws themselves have already imposed certain sanctions, or conditions equivalent to sanctions—for instance, against China, Iran, and Iraq. The additional triggering events set down by law are the following:

NNPA (Nuclear Nonproliferation Act).[5] In non–nuclear-weapons states (NNWS), detonation of a nuclear device; termination or abrogation of IAEA safeguards; material violation of International Atomic Energy Agency (IAEA) safeguards agreement; or certain activities of direct significance for nuclear explosives. In any nation, material violation of an agreement for cooperation with or other commitments to the United States regarding nuclear items; assistance, encouragement, or inducement of an NNWS to engage in certain activities of direct significance for nuclear explosives; or an agreement to transfer, to an NNWS, reprocessing items or technology, except in connection with an international evaluation or agreement in which the United States participates.

Nuclear nonproliferation controls.[6] Delivering or receiving nuclear enrichment items or technology to or from any other country, unless they are under multilateral auspices and management (when available) and all of the recipient country's nuclear fuel and facilities

[4]The Appendix also includes a United Nations General Assembly resolution to show the attitude of this body toward sanctions, in Section A–V.M.

[5]Initial provisions enacted in 1978.

[6]Initial provisions enacted in 1977 as Symington and Glenn amendments to the International Security Assistance Act.

are under IAEA safeguards. Delivering or receiving nuclear reprocessing items or technology to or from any other country unless they are associated with an international evaluation of alternatives in which the United States participates. In an NNWS, exporting (or attempting to export) illegally from the United States items or technology of significance for the manufacture of a nuclear explosive. Transfer of a nuclear explosive, or important components or design information "known" to be for a nuclear explosive, to an NNWS. If an NNWS, detonation of a nuclear explosive, or receipt of a nuclear explosive or components or design information intended for a nuclear explosive.

Enforcement of nuclear agreements.[7] If an NNWS, termination, abrogation, or material violation of IAEA full-scope safeguards. For any nation, material violation of a nuclear nonproliferation agreement with the United States.

NPPA (Nuclear Proliferation Prevention Act).[8] "Materially and with requisite knowledge," contributing through exports or directly contributing or attempting to contribute through financing to efforts by any individual, group, or NNWS to acquire unsafeguarded weapon-usable material or use, develop, produce, stockpile, or otherwise acquire a nuclear explosive.

Eximbank Act.[9] Violating IAEA safeguards; materially violating, abrogating, or terminating an agreement for cooperation with the United States; for NNWS, detonating a nuclear explosive; or "willfully aid[ing] or abet[ting]" an NNWS to acquire a nuclear explosive or unsafeguarded weapon-usable material.

Missile Technology Controls.[10] "Knowingly" exporting, transferring, or otherwise engaging in the trade of any Missile Technology Control Regime (MTCR) equipment or technology that contributes to the acquisition [in the Arms Export Control Act (AECA) but not the Export Administration Act (EAA)], design, development, or produc-

---

[7] Initial provisions enacted in 1981 and 1994.

[8] Enacted in 1994, amending earlier legislation.

[9] Export-Import Bank (Eximbank) Act; initial nuclear provisions enacted in 1977.

[10] Initial provisions enacted in 1990.

tion of missiles in a country that is not an MTCR adherent and would be, if the transfer were of U.S. origin, subject to U.S. jurisdiction; conspiring or attempting to engage in such an act; or facilitating such an act by any other person.

Chemical and biological weapons (CBW) transfers.[11] "Knowingly and materially" contributing through exports from the United States of U.S.–jurisdiction goods or technology, or through exports from any other country of goods and technology that would be subject to U.S. jurisdiction if they were from the United States, to efforts by any foreign country, project, or entity—which has used or made substantial preparations to use chemical weapons (CW) or biological weapons (BW) in violation of international law or, with lethal weapons, against its own nationals or supports international terrorism or is otherwise designated by the President—to use, develop, produce, stockpile, or otherwise acquire CW or BW.

Chemical and biological weapons use.[12] A foreign government making substantial preparations to use or having used CW or BW in violation of international law or, with lethal weapons, against its own nationals.

CWC (Chemical Weapons Convention).[13] Activities prohibited by the Convention, or a State Party failing within a specified time to fulfill a request by the Executive Council to redress a situation raising problems with regard to its compliance.

IEEPA (International Emergency Economic Powers Act).[14] Any unusual and extraordinary threat—which has its source in whole or substantial part outside the United States—to the national security, foreign policy, or economy of the United States.

Iraq sanctions.[15] A government or its officials assisting Iraq to improve its rocket technology or NBC weapons capability.

---

[11]CBW amendments enacted in 1991.

[12]Enacted in 1991.

[13]Ratified by the United States and entered into force in 1997.

[14]Initial law enacted in 1977.

[15]Initial provisions enacted in 1990.

Iran and Libya sanctions.[16] Making certain large investments that directly and significantly contribute to Iran or Libya's ability to develop their petroleum resources. Toward Libya, with "actual knowledge," exporting, transferring, or otherwise providing goods, services, or technology prohibited by the UN and significantly and materially contributing to Libya's ability to acquire NBC weapons or destabilizing numbers and types of advanced conventional weapons, or enhancing Libya's military or paramilitary capabilities, or contributing to Libya's development of its petroleum resources or to its maintenance of its aviation capabilities.

Iran-Iraq Arms Non-Proliferation Act.[17] Transferring goods or technology to contribute "knowingly and materially" to Iran or Iraq acquiring NBC weapons or destabilizing numbers and types of advanced conventional weapons.

Ukraine assistance limitations.[18] Government of Ukraine engaged in military cooperation with the Government of Libya.

This list of triggering events places in quotation marks (". . .") phrases that include the terms "known," "knowledge," or "knowingly." These terms have caused problems, which will be discussed in later chapters.

Two broad categories of triggers can be distinguished on this list. One set of triggers consists of dramatic events, such as a nuclear detonation, a violation of an IAEA safeguards agreement or a U.S. agreement for cooperation, or the use of CW or BW. These triggering events are likely for the most part to be clear-cut and undeniable. They are likely to be committed by governments. But—except for the 1998 Indian and Pakistani nuclear tests—they have apparently never occurred in a manner that could result in the imposition of sanctions (although the section "Trends and Implications" in Chapter Three discusses a close call with respect to India).

---

[16]Enacted in 1996.

[17]Enacted in 1992.

[18]Initial provisions enacted in 1996.

The other set of triggers consists of transfers or acts associated with transfers. Often subtle and quiet actions, difficult to detect and sometimes ambiguous, these triggers are not necessarily committed by governments; indeed, the responsible governments may not even be aware of them. Such triggers have resulted in all the nonproliferation sanctions that have been imposed. They have also led to most of the controversies over the further application of sanctions.

An anomalous subset of triggering events consists of transfers contributing to Iranian and Libyan petroleum resources. In the Iran and Libya sanctions laws, the sanctionability of such transfers is justified for nonproliferation reasons. Such transfers can enhance Iran and Libya's ability to finance NBC and missile programs (as well as terrorism). But they are indirect, rather than direct, in their effects on proliferation.

Because transfers are the key sanctions triggers from the point of view of policy dilemmas, this study focuses on them.

TARGETED ENTITIES

The above list of triggering events often refers to an NNWS, "any country," or "a government" that must be the actor in order to trigger sanctions. But the "foreign persons" on whom sanctions are imposed are even more specifically defined, as follows:

NNPA, nuclear nonproliferation controls, and enforcement of nuclear agreements. Any NNWS for some triggering actions; any nation or group of nations for others.

NPPA. A *foreign person* (defined as an individual or nongovernment entity, such as a corporation).

Eximbank Act. Any country or countries for most triggering events; any *person* (defined as a natural person, nongovernmental entity, or governmental entity operating as a business) for "aiding and abetting."

Missile technology controls. A foreign person not authorized in his trading activity by the laws of an *MTCR adherent* (a country participating in the MTCR or in an equivalent international understanding to which the United States is a party), or who obtained authorization from such an adherent through misrepresentation or fraud, and who is not processed by judicial or other enforcement action by such an adherent. A *person* is defined as a natural person as well as any other nongovernmental entity or any governmental entity operating as a business. In the AECA (Arms Export Control Act) but not the EAA (Export Administration Act), a *person* in a non-market economy (excluding former Warsaw Pact nations) means all government activities relating to the development or production of missile equipment or technology, electronics, space systems or equipment, and military aircraft. In the EAA but not the AECA, a *person* in a country where it is impossible to identify a specific government entity, means all government activities described in the previous sentence plus those related to the development or production of civilian aircraft.

Chemical and biological weapons transfers. A *foreign person* (defined as an individual, corporation, partnership or other entity).

Chemical and biological weapons use. A country, or—in the case of bank loans, diplomatic relations, and aviation—the government of that country.

CWC. A State Party.

IEEPA. Any property in which any foreign company or a national thereof has any interest.

Iraq sanctions. In addition to Iraq, any country whose government or government officials are assisting Iraq's rocket or NBC weapons capabilities.

Iran and Libya sanctions. In addition to Iran and Libya, a *person* (defined as a natural person, nongovernmental entity, or any governmental entity operating as a business).

Iran-Iraq Arms Non-Proliferation Act. In addition to Iran and Iraq, a *person* (defined as an individual, partnership, corporation, or other form of association) or a country.

Ukraine assistance limitations. The Government of Ukraine.

Certification requirements. The nation for which a certification is required.

A noteworthy aspect of this list of targeted entities is the fact that, in more than half the cases listed, the entire country or government is the exclusive target. The Eximbank Act, Missile Technology Controls, Chemical and Biological Weapons transfers, IEEPA, Iran and Libya sanctions, and the Iran-Iraq Arms Non-Proliferation Act have greater or lesser coverage of governments in addition to non-governmental entities. The NPPA, one of the most recent pieces of sanctions legislation, may seem to be the only one that targets non-governmental entities exclusively. But the nuclear nonproliferation controls and the enforcement of nuclear agreements legislation, revised by the NPPA, do treat countries as the exclusive targets.

Given that many of these laws are triggered by transfers, which may or may not involve governments, the expansion of sanctions to entire governments increases the consequences. Such an escalation of consequences is often intended by Congress to serve as an incentive for foreign governments to control transfers under their jurisdiction. But it can reduce the likelihood of any U.S. action at all. Deciding on such broad sanctions can create major conflicts within the U.S. government, where many issues besides nonproliferation are at play with any foreign government.

Such conflicts influence the process of determining formally whether a triggering event has occurred.

DETERMINATION OF SANCTIONABILITY

The text of the nonproliferation sanctions laws on the determination process is usually simple:

NNPA. ". . . found by the President to have . . . ."

Nuclear nonproliferation controls. "the President determines . . . ."

Enforcement of nuclear agreements. ". . . is found by the President to have . . . ." and ". . . the President has determined . . . ."

NPPA. With respect to exports that contribute to proliferation, ". . . the President determines in writing that . . . ." With respect to financing or attempted financing that contributes to proliferation, ". . . the President determines, in writing after opportunity for a hearing on the record, that . . . ."

Eximbank Act. "... the Secretary of State determines that ...."

Missile Technology Controls. ". . . the President determines that . . . ." In the AECA but not the EAA, there is a "rebuttable presumption" that a transfer is for use in a missile if the transfer is of any item on the Missile Technology Control Regime (MTCR) Annex and "the President determines" it is to a country "the government of which the Secretary has determined," under provisions of the EAA, supports international terrorism. There is no stated process for rebutting the presumption.

Chemical and biological weapons transfers. ". . . the President determines ...."

Chemical and biological weapons use. "Whenever persuasive information becomes available to the executive branch . . . the President shall, within 60 days after the receipt of such information by the executive branch, determine whether ...." The law specifies matters that "the President shall consider" in making his determination.

CWC. In cases of failure to redress problems with compliance, "The Conference may, *inter alia,* upon the recommendation of the Executive Council, restrict or suspend . . . ." In cases of activities prohibited by the Convention, "the Conference may recommend . . . ."

IEEPA. "... the President declares a national emergency ...."

Iraq sanctions. Other than the sanctions on Iraq itself, ". . . the President determines ...."

Iran and Libya sanctions. Other than the sanctions on Iran and Libya, "... the President determines that ...."

Iran-Iraq Arms Non-Proliferation Act. No determination process has been specified for transfers by persons. With respect to transfers by governments, "... the President determines that ...."

Ukraine assistance limitations. "... the President determines ...."

In all of these cases, except for the CWC, the ultimate determination authority is the President. Even where no determination process is specified, the facts are likely to be established by the intelligence community, which is a part of the Executive Branch.

Congress has done little to define the determination process. Only one law, that regarding chemical and biological weapons use, gives a time limit for the determination and sets out factors to be considered. Otherwise, the Executive Branch has broad discretion for *not* making a determination. The tactics for not acting can include nit-picking intelligence information that almost invariably has loose ends, adjusting the criteria for certainty of intelligence information based upon bilateral political considerations, delaying indefinitely the processing of information, failing to put reports of a potentially triggering event on a formal agenda, failing to send such reports up the line to the President in a formal process, using "fact-finding" negotiations to delay determinations, and insisting—in the words of former Under Secretary of State Lynn Davis—"to hold a very high standard in making sanctions determinations."[19]

Congress has used two instruments to try to force the determination process. The first is to require Executive Branch reports on matters about which determinations should be made. These reporting requirements are included in the Appendix.

The second is to turn the determination process on its head by assuming that a sanctionable condition exists unless the President makes a positive certification that it has ended. Under the certification process, inaction by the Executive Branch cannot prevent the use of sanctions. And action to make a positive certification cannot be taken quietly but, rather, throws the Executive Branch's views on the issue of sanctionability out into the open.

CERTIFICATION OF NONSANCTIONABILITY

Certifications should not be confused with waivers (which are discussed in the next section). Unfortunately, waivers are sometimes called certifications.

---

[19]B. Gertz, "Limits to Be Loosened on Supercomputers, Clinton Waits on Sanctioning China," *The Washington Times*, October 5, 1995.

The certification process starts with sanctions (or equivalent restrictions) already imposed and requires a positive action by the Executive Branch to remove them. The *positive action* is a certification that a sanctionable condition does not exist or has ended. This is the opposite of the determination process, which requires a positive action to impose sanctions.

Because inaction is always easier than action, it is fairly easy for the Executive Branch not to make a determination, and thereby avoid imposing sanctions. But with the certification process, inaction means that sanctions continue. From the point of view of sanctions advocates in Congress, certifications are effective sanctions instruments. Several, but not all, of the sanctions laws discussed above have certification provisions:

NPPA. To terminate sanctions, Presidential certification in writing to Congress is required to the effect that the sanctioned person has ceased the triggering activity and that the President has received reliable assurances that the person will not engage in the activity in the future.

Eximbank Act. The sanctions process is delayed if the Secretary of State certifies that corrective action is being taken. Sanctions will not be applied if the Secretary certifies that corrective action has been taken and the President certifies in writing that reliable information indicates that the sanctionable action has ceased and that steps have been taken to prevent its resumption.

China certification requirements. No nuclear cooperation with China will occur until 30 days of continuous congressional session after the President certifies to Congress that China has undertaken certain nonproliferation arrangements and policies, and is not in violation of certain provisions and until the President certifies to Congress that China "has provided clear and unequivocal assurances to the [United States] that it is not assisting and will not assist any [NNWS], either directly or indirectly, in acquiring nuclear" explosives or their materials or components.

Pakistan provisions. Limits on U.S. military assistance and transfers to Pakistan unless the President certifies to Congress in writing that Pakistan does not possess a nuclear explosive and that the proposed

U.S. military assistance will reduce significantly the risk of Pakistan's possessing a nuclear explosive.

Chemical and biological weapons transfers. To terminate sanctions, Presidential certification to Congress that the foreign person has ceased to aid and abet any foreign efforts to acquire CW or BW.

Chemical and biological weapons use. To avoid additional sanctions, Presidential certification in writing to Congress that the government has ceased CW or BW use that would trigger sanctions, has provided reliable assurances that it will not do so in the future, and is willing to allow on-site inspections. To remove sanctions, Presidential certification to Congress of reliable assurances against and lack of preparations for future use that would trigger sanctions, willingness to allow on-site inspections—or the existence of other means—to verify nonpreparation for use, and restitution to victims by the sanctioned government.

Russia certification requirements. Limitation on funds for Cooperative Threat Reduction until the President certifies to Congress that Russia is, among other things, in compliance with the Biological Weapons Convention and is making substantial progress to facilitate the CWC.

Iraq sanctions. To waive sanctions on Iraq, Presidential certification to Congress that, among other things, Iraq is not acquiring, developing, or manufacturing, and has forsworn first use and is taking steps to destroy or dispose of, NBC weapons and ballistic missiles.

Iran and Libya sanctions. To terminate all sanctions, Presidential certification to Congress that Iran has ceased certain proliferation activities and has been removed from the terrorism list compiled under the EAA, and Libya has fulfilled the requirements of certain UN resolutions. To terminate sanctions in an individual case, Presidential certification to Congress that the person is no longer engaging in sanctioned activities and that the President has received reliable assurances that the person will not in the future engage in such activities.

Cooperative Threat Reduction certifications. To authorize assistance to any independent state of the former Soviet Union,

Presidential certification to Congress that the state is, among other things, complying with all relevant arms control agreements.

The laws cited here that involve specific nations—China, Iran, Iraq, Libya, Pakistan, and the former Soviet Union—in effect have Congress imposing sanctions by requiring certifications before certain cooperation, transfers, or assistance can begin. The other laws cited here, and Iran and Libya sanctions against individual persons, come into play only after the President has made a sanctions determination—at which time the certifications serve to delay, limit, or terminate sanctions. All of the certifications require a Presidential finding of good behavior.

But there is a way to avoid sanctions without such a finding of good behavior. That is the waiver process.

WAIVERS

In contrast to the certification process, the waiver process starts with an admission that bad behavior has occurred. A waiver, citing some level of the national interest, is necessary to withhold the imposition of sanctions.

The waiver process is complex. It would not serve the purposes of this study to relate in detail each law's waiver provisions. The reader is referred to the Appendix for those details.[20] However, the general waiver provisions of each law are as follows:

NNPA. Presidential determination that a sanction would be "seriously prejudicial" to nonproliferation or would "jeopardize the common defense and security"—with provision for a congressional override of this determination.

Nuclear nonproliferation controls. For enrichment transfers, Presidential certification that sanctions "would have a serious adverse effect on vital [U.S.] security interests" and that he has reli-

---

[20]One congressional staffer, frustrated with the criticism of "inflexible" sanctions, listed "250 loopholes, waivers, and other exemptions" in the U.S. nonproliferation sanctions laws.

able assurances that the country will not acquire or develop nuclear weapons or assist other nations in doing so—subject to congressional override. For reprocessing transfers, Presidential certification that sanctions "would be seriously prejudicial to the achievement of [U.S.] nonproliferation objectives or otherwise jeopardize the common defense and security"—subject to congressional override. For nuclear explosive transfers and detonations, a Presidential certification that, without a 30-day delay of sanctions, sanctions "would be detrimental to the national security"; this certification must be approved by Congress, and approval may be followed by a Presidential waiver of all sanctions upon "certification" that they "would be seriously prejudicial to the achievement of [U.S.] nonproliferation objectives or otherwise jeopardize the common defense and security."

Enforcement of nuclear agreements. To lift most sanctions, the same waiver language as for nuclear nonproliferation controls may be used, without explicit provision for congressional override. However, as long as a material breach continues with respect to an agreement with the United States, there is no waiver provision to lift the embargo on arms sales.

NPPA. Waivers of sanctions for transfers permitted with respect to the procurement of defense articles or services or, after the sanctions have run for 12 months, if the President "certifies in writing" to Congress that continued imposition "would have a serious adverse effect on vital [U.S.] interests." Waivers of sanctions for financing are permitted if the President "certifies in writing" to Congress that continued imposition "would have a serious adverse effect on the safety and soundness of the domestic or international financial system or on domestic or international payments systems."

Eximbank Act. Waiver permitted if the President determines "it is in the national interest" to avoid sanctions—subject to opportunity for congressional review.

Missile Technology Controls. Waiver permitted if the President notifies Congress a certain number of days in advance that such a waiver is "essential to the national security." Waiver or nonimposition permitted if the President determines, among other things, that the sanction would block products or services essential to the national defense, security, products, or production.

Chemical and biological weapons transfers. Non-imposition permitted if the President determines, among other things, that the sanction would block products or services for the military or those essential for the national security, products, or production. Waiver permitted at the end of 12 months if the President certifies to Congress that it is "important to the national security interests."

Use of chemical and biological weapons. Waiver permitted if the President gives Congress specified advance certification that it is "essential to the national security interests" or that there has been a fundamental change in the leadership and policies of the sanctioned country.

Iran and Libya sanctions. Non-imposition permitted for procurement of defense articles or certain other items. Waiver permitted 30 days after the President reports to Congress that it is "important to the national interest."

Iran-Iraq Arms Non-Proliferation Act. Waiver permitted 15 days after the President reports to Congress that it is "essential to the national security interest."

As the language of some of these waiver provisions indicates, there is occasionally a thin line between "certifications" and "waivers." The difference remains, however, that *certifications* assert good behavior on the part of the sanctioned entity and are necessary to end sanctions or sanctions-type restrictions. By contrast, *waivers* make no assertion of good behavior and can be used to withhold the imposition of sanctions.

It should be noted that many of the waiver and non-imposition provisions have complex rules pertaining to contract sanctity and the role of the sanctions in otherwise blocking U.S. military or civilian programs.

However, the *essence* of all the waiver provisions is the same: The President determines that a triggering event has occurred, but he cites overriding interests to avoid imposing sanctions.

The publicity associated with the waiver process can potentially damage relations with another government and, in some cases, cause a furor that would lead to a congressional override of the waivers. But, as is discussed in the next chapter, it is possible that classified waivers have been used to avoid this publicity.

DESIGN OF A SPECIFIC SANCTION

The punishments imposed by the sanctions laws are sometimes highly specific about type and duration, and are sometimes open to the discretion of the President. They are as follows:

NNPA. No exports of nuclear material and equipment or sensitive nuclear technology.

Nuclear nonproliferation controls. For enrichment or reprocessing transfers or illegal exports, no economic or military assistance. For nuclear explosive–related transfers, no economic assistance (except humanitarian, food, or agricultural aid); no military assistance, arms sales, or export licenses; no U.S. public or private financial credits (except when humanitarian, food, etc.); and U.S. opposition to international financial institution loans or assistance (except for food or agriculture).

Enforcement of nuclear agreements. No economic assistance. In addition, for material breach of agreements with the United States, no arms sales.

NPPA. For transfers, no U.S. government procurement from the sanctioned person for at least 12 months. For financing, a ban on certain dealings in U.S. government finance and on operating new lines of business or new locations of business in the United States for at least 12 months.

Eximbank Act. No Eximbank credit participation in exports to the sanctioned country.

Pakistan provisions. Ban on military assistance applies to F-16 deliveries but not to certain types of assistance (e.g., narcotics control, peacekeeping, antiterrorism) or to other assistance under contracts or cases predating October 1, 1990. However, EAA missile sanctions remain in effect.

Missile technology controls. If the sanctioned transfer was Category II on the MTCR Annex [generally dual-use components or technology], then a ban on U.S. government contracts relating to missiles [in the AECA but not the EAA] and on exports of MTCR-controlled items for two years. If the sanctioned transfer was Category I [large missiles or their major components or technology], then a ban on all U.S. government contracts [in the AECA but not the EAA] and all licensed exports for not less than two years. If the President determines that the sanctioned transfer "has substantially contributed to the design, development, or production of [MTCR-class] missiles in a country that is not an MTCR adherent," then a prohibition of imports from the sanctioned person for not less than two years. There are certain exceptions to the import bans involving such matters as defense articles, contract sanctity, spare or routine items, essential components or information or technology.

Chemical and biological weapons transfers. No U.S. government procurement from and no importation of products produced by the sanctioned person for at least 12 months. There are exceptions similar to those of the missile sanctions laws.

Chemical and biological weapons use. As initial sanctions: termination of foreign assistance (except for food, agriculture, and urgent humanitarian items), arms sales, export licenses for munitions and other national-security-controlled items, foreign military financing, and all other U.S. government credits and financial assistance. After three months (absent a Presidential certification), at least three of the following: opposition to loans or assistance from international financial institutions, prohibition of bank credits except for food and agriculture, prohibition of all remaining licensed exports except for food and agriculture, import restrictions, downgrading or suspension of diplomatic relations, and suspension of air carrier rights in the United States. There are exceptions with respect to existing contracts (see, for example, Section A–IV.A of the Appendix).

CWC. Suspension of a State Party's rights and privileges, and recommendations for collective measures.

IEEPA. As the President may prescribe, prohibitions on foreign-exchange transactions, credit transfers, importing or exporting of currency or securities, or dealing in any property subject to

U.S. jurisdiction. Exceptions involve communications, donations, information, and transactions incidental to travel.

Iraq sanctions. With respect to countries assisting Iraq's NBC or rocket programs, denial of licensing for supercomputer exports.

Iran and Libya sanctions. For at least two years (or, with a Presidential certification, at least one year) a prohibition on two or more of the following: Eximbank assistance, export licenses, loans exceeding $10 million in 12 months except to relieve human suffering, certain dealings in U.S. government finance, U.S. government procurement, and—in accordance with the IEEPA—imports.

Iran-Iraq Arms Non-Proliferation Act. With respect to sanctioned persons, a two year ban on U.S. government procurement and export licenses. With respect to sanctioned countries, a one-year suspension of U.S. assistance, opposition to loans or assistance from international financial institutions, suspension of military codevelopment or coproduction, suspension of technical exchange agreements that do not directly contribute to U.S. security and suspension of technology exports, and a ban on munitions export licenses. In addition, at the discretion of the President, a use of IEEPA authority on sanctioned countries, except with respect to urgent humanitarian assistance.

Ukraine assistance limitations. A ban on FY 97 export and investment assistance.

Some of these sanctions give the President broad discretion, particularly those authorized by the IEEPA.

But some of the sanctions are predetermined, regardless of the specifics of the episode. For example, in missile and chemical/biological transfer sanctions, there are bans on imports and on U.S. government procurement; and the NPPA imposes the latter sanctions. As will become apparent in the next chapter, these bans may not affect foreign persons doing business with the Third World rather than with the United States. As another example, the export-licensing sanctions for Category II missile-related transfers apply only to missile-related items, which keeps the sanctions in the missile arena. However, they may or may not be the most appropriate measure to affect the sanctioned person. Finally, some sanctions have enormous consequences for the entire sanctioned nation, regardless of whether the government of that nation was responsible for the triggering event. The nuclear nonproliferation control sanctions are examples.

"Inflexibility" is one of the chief criticisms of the sanctions process. The concept of "inflexibility" is, however, an omnibus criticism, embracing sanctions that are (1) *automatic*, without a great deal of discretion as to whether to impose them, (2) *predetermined,* not necessarily appropriate in scale or targeting, and (3) *draconian,* too severe in their effects.

As noted earlier in this chapter, there are reasons for such "inflexible" provisions. By minimizing Presidential discretion, they are intended to force the Executive Branch to take action. By prescribing huge and widespread consequences, they are intended to force other governments to get control of their exporters. But the "inflexibility" has another side: It runs the risk of sanctions' having no effect on the sanctioned person or the risk of sanctions' having such a devastating effect on bilateral relations that the Executive Branch will want to avoid the necessary Presidential determination. Alternatives for dealing with this dilemma—and the different considerations applicable to the different aspects of "inflexibility"—are discussed in Chapter Five.

There is one other noteworthy aspect of these sanctions. Except for the sanctions provided in the CWC and for certain military assistance and export limitations, the sanctions generally do not deal with security. Nations seeking NBC weapons or missiles—and some nations supplying them—are motivated in many cases by security considerations (see the discussion of Pakistan in Chapter Three). Sanctions relating to trade or finance may hurt these nations, but they may be irrelevant to these nations' primary motivations. Trade and finance sanctions may, on the other hand, be just the right disincentive for suppliers when it is necessary to "take the profit out of proliferation." Again, the inflexibility of sanctions may lead to some inappropriate actions.

Even with inflexible sanctions, the process of imposing them is not necessarily cut and dried. The next section describes that process.

IMPLEMENTATION

A few laws provide for time lags and negotiations before sanctions are imposed:

Nuclear nonproliferation controls. For nuclear-explosive transfers and detonations, the President may delay imposition of sanctions for 30 days, as is described in the "Waiver" section of this chapter.

NPPA. Congress urges the President, after he makes a determination of sanctionability, to consult immediately with the government with jurisdiction over the person to be sanctioned. To this end, the President may delay imposition of sanctions for up to 90 days, and for an additional 90 days if he certifies in writing to Congress that the foreign government is in the process of taking action—including imposing appropriate penalties—to terminate the involvement of the foreign person in sanctionable activities.

Eximbank Act. In the case of sanctions against a *person* (ranging from a natural person to a governmental entity operating as a business), but not against a *country,* the law provides for the same delays for negotiations with the foreign government as in the NPPA.

Chemical and biological weapons transfers. The law authorizes the same delays as in the NPPA.

Chemical and biological weapons use. The three-month delay between the initial and additional sanctions allows time for negotiations that could lead to a Presidential certification of assurances of no further use and on-site inspection.

CWC. A State Party with compliance problems is given a specified time to redress the situation.

Iran and Libya sanctions. The law authorizes the same delays as in the NPPA.

There are other ways that the Executive Branch can delay implementation of sanctions. As noted in the discussion of determinations, the determination process can usually be delayed by bureaucratic action. Moreover, the Executive Branch can attempt to justify negotiations with a foreign government as part of a fact-finding process for a determination or for a decision on a waiver or certification.

But even when sanctions are imposed, the Executive Branch can attempt to widen its discretion. When missile sanctions were imposed on China in 1991, the Executive Branch included exports of space satellites for launch by China in the export-licensing ban. However, shortly after the same sanctions were imposed in 1993, the Commerce Department ruled that satellites were not covered by the ban—effectively reducing the dollar impact on China by some 90 percent.

MULTILATERAL SUPPORT

The critics of unilateral economic sanctions have argued that the United States should attempt to multilateralize sanctions—both in order to increase their effectiveness and to avoid unfair advantages for foreign competitors.[21] In the Iraq sanctions law, the Iran and Libya sanctions law, and the Iran-Iraq Arms Non-Proliferation Act, the President is "urged" by Congress to seek multilateral reinforcement of U.S. sanctions.

However, with the exception of the CWC (which is a treaty and, therefore, the law of the land) and sanctions imposed by the United Nations, no law integrates multilateral support with the imposition of sanctions. Nor does any of the laws provide for a delay in the imposition of sanctions while the United States seeks such support. The market power of the United States and Congress' desire for action make the use of unilateral sanctions understandable.

By contrast, the CWC, by working the sanctions process through a multilateral organization, automatically multilateralizes the process. And, likewise, the nonproliferation sanctions imposed on Iraq by the United Nations as part of Resolution 687 have multilateral application. This study, which examines what the law has to say about the future application of sanctions, does not deliberate on the sanctions already imposed against Iraq.

---

[21] *Unilateral Economic Sanctions, Executive Summary,* 1997, recommends "the exhaustion of diplomatic efforts to obtain multilateral cooperation" as a means of establishing a context for the justification of unilateral sanctions.

INCENTIVES

Negotiations with governments subject to sanctions have often featured possibilities not included in the sanctions laws—positive outcomes, or incentives, beyond the absence of imposed sanctions.

Incentives may range from membership in nonproliferation organizations, which may facilitate access to technologies, to specific commercial deals, to security commitments. In some cases, without any explicit link, erasing a sanctions episode from the slate may unblock other issues, allowing a foreign government to shake off its pariah status and giving access to international trade, credits, and technical cooperation.

The incentives process can be abused. Ordinarily, no government would want to precipitate the imposition of sanctions on itself. However, if by undertaking and then ceasing bad behavior a government can win incentives and emerge better off, there is a game to be played. North Korea is often suspected of playing this game. Policies of engagement can generate costly side effects and can ultimately fail, just as sanctions can.

Some examples of the use of incentives—and of the other elements of the sanctions process—appear in the next chapter.

SANCTIONEE RESPONSE

The sanctions process is rarely static. In most cases, the entity targeted by sanctions will react, forcing the United States to respond to the reaction. If the sanctions have a significant impact, the sanctionee may try to evade them—for example, with U.S. export cutoffs, by searching for other suppliers. If the United States is conflicted about the imposition of the sanctions, the sanctionee may seek the support of domestic U.S. groups for an easing of the sanctions. If the sanctions can be terminated by a waiver, the sanctionee may seek to show that he has mended his ways or that other elements of the U.S. national interest are jeopardized by the continuation of sanctions.

This measures-countermeasures process tests the U.S. commitment to staying the course, not only for the individual sanctions episode but—with onlookers who need to be deterred—for the broader process of nonproliferation sanctions. In the next chapter, we discuss the history of this experience.

Chapter Three

HISTORY AND LESSONS LEARNED

This chapter examines the historical experience with nonproliferation sanctions. The historical discussion is broken into two sections: one on the actual imposition of sanctions, which is publicly documented; and one on the threat or non-imposition of sanctions, which requires some artful use of such public information as exists. We end the chapter with observations on larger trends and implications. The chapter does not attempt to be a comprehensive history. Many histories are already available.[1]

IMPOSITION OF SANCTIONS

Until 1998, nuclear nonproliferation sanctions had been imposed under current laws[2] in only one case: Pakistan.

Pakistan's receipt of enrichment technology resulted in a mandated cutoff of U.S. economic and military assistance in 1979. After the

[1]For histories of economic sanctions in general, see Hufbauer, Schott, and Elliott, 1990, and E. Day, *Economic Sanctions Imposed by the United States Against Specific Countries: 1979 Through 1992,* Washington, D.C.: Congressional Research Service, Report No. 92-631F, August 10, 1992. Day is currently updating the report for the Department of Defense. For a history of nuclear nonproliferation sanctions, see Rodney W. Jones et al. (The Carnegie Endowment for International Peace), *Tracking Nuclear Proliferation: A Guide in Maps and Charts, 1998,* Washington, D.C.: The Brookings Institution Press, 1998. For a nearly complete history of missile nonproliferation sanctions, see D. A. Ozga, "A Chronology of the Missile Technology Control Regime," *The Nonproliferation Review* (Monterey Institute of International Studies, Monterey, Calif.), Winter 1994, pp. 66–93. This chapter draws on these publications or their drafts, supplemented by press reports.

[2]See Chapter One, footnote 13, for the *ex post facto* sanctions imposed on India.

Soviet invasion of Afghanistan, Congress modified the law to allow for a waiver if the President certified a waiver to be in the national interest. President Ronald Reagan made this certification for the first time in 1982.[3] In 1982, Pakistan also became subject to sanctions because of reprocessing transfers, and these sanctions were also waived. In 1985, the Pressler Amendment required that, for U.S. economic assistance and military sales to continue, the President certify that Pakistan did "not possess a nuclear explosive device and that the proposed U.S. assistance program will significantly reduce the risk that Pakistan will possess a nuclear explosive device." These certifications were made through 1989, after which time Pakistan apparently had fabricated pits for nuclear weapons—leading to the refusal of the President to make the certification. The last "national interest" waiver, allowing military credits and loans, was made in 1990 and continued in effect until 1991. Later legislation allowed limited military cooperation with Pakistan.[4]

In the context of this study, the Pakistan experience has two noteworthy aspects. First, even with massive sanctions involving economic and military assistance and arms sales, Pakistan could not be dissuaded from pursuing a course that it considered essential to its security. Second, the U.S. President was unwilling to make certifications that were grossly inconsistent with intelligence information.

The difficulty for a President to make certifications (even though sanctions are technically not being imposed) was highlighted in another case: China. A 1985 Joint Resolution[5] required a Presidential certification of China's nuclear nonproliferation policies and behavior before the United States could engage in nuclear cooperation with China. Twelve years later, with new Chinese export controls and stated policies in place, the Administration decided that it could make that certification.[6]

---

[3]See Pakistan provisions in the Appendix, Section A–II.G, for a history of waivers.

[4]For a comprehensive history of these sanctions against Pakistan through 1997, see the chapter on Pakistan in Jones et al., 1998.

[5]See the China certification provisions in the Appendix, Section A–II.F.

[6]The White House, Office of the Press Secretary, "Text of a Letter from the President to the Speaker of the House of Representatives, the President of the Senate, and the Chairmen of the Senate Committee on Foreign Relations and the House Committee

On May 11, 1998, India announced that it had detonated three nuclear devices. Two days later, India announced the tests of two more devices. On May 13, the President imposed sanctions required by the Arms Export Control Act provisions of the NNPA as expanded by the NPPA.[7] These sanctions included termination of all but humanitarian assistance, termination of military sales and financing, opposition to loans by international financial institutions, prohibition of U.S. loans except for the purchase of agricultural commodities, and prohibition of the export of specific goods licensed by the Department of Commerce. The United States was not alone. Japan, Germany, Canada, Australia, Sweden, and Denmark also imposed sanctions. The effect of the U.S. sanctions was substantial. On May 14, the rupee dropped to a record low. By the next day, however, some business executives were warning that the sanctions could have a broader effect on American interests in India than on the Indian economy itself. And there were limits to the multilateral support that the United States could organize. The G-8 condemned the tests but refused to impose sanctions (although four of its members did), and the United States could not block (although it did delay) World Bank loans to India.

Meanwhile, the problem was to dissuade Pakistan from detonating its own nuclear devices. On May 14, two senators, with White House support, introduced legislation to repeal the Pressler Amendment prohibition of military assistance to Pakistan if Pakistan would refrain from a nuclear test. The Administration began an intense series of security consultations with Pakistan to attempt to dissuade it from a test. And Japan threatened economic sanctions against Pakistan if it tested.

Nonetheless, Pakistan announced nuclear detonations on May 28—claiming that five devices has been tested simultaneously. The United States and the other major countries that had imposed sanctions on India immediately followed suit with Pakistan. The sanc-

---

on International Relations," letter dated January 12, 1998, Washington, D.C., January 15, 1998.

[7]For a discussion of these sanctions and their aftermath, see Randy J. Rydell, "Giving Nonproliferation Norms Teeth: Sanctions and the NPPA," *The Nonproliferation Review*, Vol. 6, No. 2, Winter 1999; and Daniel Morrow and Michael Carriere, "The Economic Impacts of the 1998 Sanctions on India and Pakistan," *The Nonproliferation Review*, Vol. 6, No. 4, Fall 1999.

tions were predicted to have a far greater impact on Pakistan than on India because foreign assistance counted for twice as large a fraction of Pakistan's economy as India's and because Pakistan's economy was generally reckoned to be far weaker than India's. There were even predictions that the government of Pakistan could collapse as a result of the loss of aid. Pakistan nonetheless announced the test of a sixth device on May 30.

But at this point the direction of events started to shift. On the day of Pakistan's first tests, Deputy Secretary of State Strobe Talbott announced that the U.S. goals were to have India and Pakistan renounce further testing, sign the Comprehensive Test Ban Treaty (CTBT), take decisive steps to reduce tensions between each other, join negotiations for the cutoff of fissile material production for military use,[8] and undertake not to weaponize or deploy ballistic missiles. The next day, the White House Press Secretary announced that the United States was "willing to examine" a reduction of sanctions if India and Pakistan would take the steps suggested by the United States. The United States settled for a G-8 agreement to "postpone" aid from international financial institutions, deferred cutoffs of private loans, and delayed its implementation of Department of Commerce sanctions by issuing what an assistant secretary of Commerce called "an initial and minimal response."

By early June, some members of Congress were criticizing the severity of the sanctions, legislation to exempt U.S. credits for wheat sales was headed for passage, and the Secretary of State was calling for "flexibility." And some individuals began calling for U.S. assistance to the Indian and Pakistani nuclear weapon programs to make the devices "safer." On June 25, the World Bank resumed loans to India for a broad range of "humanitarian" purposes. By early July, with Pakistan's rupee devalued by 4.4 percent and Pakistan threatening to renege on its international debt payments, the Administration called for legislation to allow the sanctions to be waived. The exemption for agricultural sanctions was enacted in mid-July. In late July, the United States announced that it would not veto any new International Monetary Fund assistance for Pakistan, and several

---

[8]For a discussion of the limitations of this proposed treaty, see Brian G. Chow et al., *The Proposed Fissile-Material Production Cutoff: Next Steps,* Santa Monica, Calif.: RAND, MR-586-1-OSD, 1995.

bills had been introduced in Congress to limit the use of any economic sanctions in foreign policy.

By September, India and Pakistan had declared moratoria on further nuclear tests and had announced their willingness to sign the CTBT during the coming year, but linked the offer to the lifting of sanctions. In October, President Clinton signed legislation giving him authority to waive most sanctions against India and Pakistan for up to 12 months.[9] The President lifted some of the sanctions on November 7.[10] Six days later, the Department of Commerce finally issued a list of Indian and Pakistani entities covered by export restrictions under the sanctions laws. In December, the United States announced a deal to reimburse Pakistan for F-16 aircraft, the delivery of which had been blocked in 1990. By February 1999, the United States was offering to lift its objections to the remaining World Bank loans to India in return for India's early signing of the CTBT.

How effective were the sanctions in response to India and Pakistan's nuclear tests? They clearly inflicted substantial economic losses on both nations—falling relatively more heavily on Pakistan. And they clearly brought both governments to the bargaining table.

But the motive for nuclear tests is not basically an economic one. Is the security of either country worse off as a result of the sanctions? In the early 1980s, India and Pakistan signed a little-noticed treaty to refrain from attacking each other's nuclear facilities. The United States, in the aftermath of a 1981 Israeli attack on an Iraqi nuclear reactor, endorsed the India-Pakistan treaty. It could be argued that this no-attack treaty made it safe for both countries to develop their nuclear weapon programs without worrying about destruction over the following 1-1/2 decades. Except for the threat that the Indian and Pakistani programs pose to each other (a threat that is not part of U.S. sanctions law) and some residual limitations on U.S. exports, there appears to be no security penalty for the nuclear tests.

It should also be noted that, given the short period during which most sanctions were imposed, more time-limited economic sanc-

---

[9]See the Appendix, Section A-I, for a list of the relevant legislation.

[10]The White House, Office of the Press Secretary, "Easing of Sanctions on India and Pakistan," statement, November 7, 1998.

tions could have had the same financial effect. This U.S. experience with "draconian" nonproliferation sanctions demonstrates the difficulty of maintaining broad and open-ended penalties. The law itself lacked specific provisions for terminating the sanctions—a gap that the Administration filled with its five goals (and terminating most of the sanctions after India and Pakistan had promised to fulfill two of the goals—moratoria on nuclear tests and willingness to sign the CTBT).

With respect to missile nonproliferation sanctions, the State Department has listed nine instances in which sanctions mandated by law were imposed for missile-related transfers.[11] The narrative, after the statement of the date and target of the sanctions, is supplied by the authors, not by the State Department:

- June 1991 against Chinese and Pakistani entities. Among other export cutoffs, U.S. satellite exports to China for launch by Chinese space launch vehicles were suspended by the sanction, threatening the Chinese rocket industry with a major financial loss. Five months later, Secretary of State James Baker announced a verbal agreement that China would observe the MTCR "guidelines and parameters," an unusual formulation that left open the question of whether China would only control exports of complete missiles or also their components and technologies as required by the MTCR. After China delivered its agreement in writing, sanctions against it were waived in March 1992; those against Pakistan expired two years after they were imposed.
- September 1991 against a South African entity, with no trade partner cited but widely regarded as being Israel, with which the United States had concluded an agreement making it an MTCR adherent exempt from sanctions. These sanctions expired two years later, a period during which negotiations with South Africa led to the abandonment of their large rocket program and their acceptance into the MTCR in 1995.

---

[11]In addition to the State Department list, other "determinations" (no further information given) have been announced in the *Federal Register*. See a discussion of these later in this chapter.

- March 1992 against North Korean entities, with no trade partner cited but reported as being Egypt or Pakistan. The sanctions against North Korea had no effect because the United States already prohibited all significant trade with that nation.
- May 1992 against Russian and Indian entities. These sanctions blocked the prospect for Russian space cooperation with the United States, leading to intense negotiations with Russia. In 1993, the United States announced a tentative agreement with Russia under which, in return for Russian agreement to observe the MTCR and to limit the sanctioned transfer to India, the United States would lift sanctions. It was widely reported that this agreement was linked to a lucrative incentive—a space-cooperation agreement for U.S. aid to the Mir space station project and U.S. permission for Russia to enter the market to launch satellites containing U.S. components. Sanctions on Russia and India nevertheless went their full term of two years, reportedly because the United States had remaining concerns about Russian missile-related transfers. Russia was admitted by consensus (i.e., including U.S. approval) to the MTCR in 1995, but later reports aver that Russia continued, deliberately or inadvertently, to make missile-related transfers to Armenia, China, Iran, Iraq, and Syria that would have resulted in sanctions if Russia were not an MTCR adherent.[12]
- June 1992 against North Korean and Syrian entities. Again, these sanctions had no effect, because U.S. law prohibited significant trade with the sanctioned nations.
- August 1993, again against China and Pakistan. Shortly after these sanctions were imposed, the Commerce Department interpreted them as not applying to U.S. transfers of satellites for launch by China, reducing the economic effect of the sanctions by 90 percent. In contrast to the 1991 sanctions, which blocked Chinese launches of U.S. satellites and which led to a Chinese

---

[12] A. A. Pikayev, L. S. Spector, E. V. Kirichenko, and R. Gibson (International Institute for Strategic Studies), *Russia, the U.S. and the Missile Technology Control Regime,* New York: Oxford University Press, Adelphi Paper 317, 1998. Also, R. H. Speier, "Russia and Missile Proliferation," statement before the U.S. Senate, Subcommittee on International Security, Proliferation, and Federal Services of the Committee on Governmental Affairs, Washington, D.C., June 5, 1997.

agreement within five months, the 1993 case took nearly three times as long for the Chinese to reach an agreement that led the United States to lift sanctions. This agreement reaffirmed the 1991 Chinese pledge, adding a technical improvement covering range/payload trade-offs and a further Chinese pledge not to export MTCR-class "ground-to-ground missiles." The agreement left open the Chinese policy toward other types of missiles of MTCR class, as well as the continuing questions of whether their observation of MTCR "guidelines and parameters" covered components and technology. Sanctions against China were waived in November 1994, but the sanctions against Pakistan ran their full two-year term.

- May 1996 against North Korean and Iranian entities, again without effect because of preexisting U.S. embargoes.
- August 1997 against North Korean entities with no trading partner identified. Again, these sanctions added nothing to preexisting embargoes.
- March 1998 against three Egyptian firms for Category II transfers presumably involving Scud technology from North Korea.
- April 1998 against a North Korean trading corporation and the Khan Research Laboratories of Pakistan for Category I transfers, presumably involving the Pakistani development of the Ghauri missile, based on North Korean Nodong missile technology. The sanctions were imposed 11 days after Pakistan's first test of the Ghauri missile, although the United States had been reviewing "a growing body of evidence about the possible sources of the missile-parts supply to Pakistan" for at least two months before.[13] As with the 1991 and 1993 missile sanctions on

---

[13]Syed talat Hussain, "US Sanctions Against KRL Raise Old Issues," *The Nation* (Islamabad, Pakistan), May 5, 1998; available as FBIS-TAC-98-125, May 5, 1998.

Pakistani entities, which expired after two years, these sanctions did not visibly lead to negotiations to restrain Pakistan's missile program. However, such negotiations were part of the diplomacy following India's and Pakistan's nuclear tests in May.

In sum, the last strongly effective missile sanctions mandated by law were imposed in 1992. The 1993 sanctions against China were reinterpreted to greatly reduce their impact, and later missile sanctions had no practical effect. Starting in 1993, the *Federal Register* recorded the fact that "determinations" had been made regarding missile sanctions, but that the names and nationalities of the entities were withheld on grounds that publication would be "harmful to the national security." Press reports suggest that at least some of these entities were Brazilian, Chinese, and Russian.[14]

In July 1998 and again in January 1999, the United States did impose sanctions on Russian entities for missile (and to some extent nuclear) cooperation with Iran, even though these sanctions were not mandated by law. Earlier in 1998, Congress had passed a bill, the Iran Missile Proliferation Sanctions Act of 1998, mandating sanctions for missile-related transfers to Iran. The President vetoed the bill. But as a veto override vote approached, the President, on July 28, 1998, amended Executive Order 12938 to authorize many of the sanctions in the bill. Sanctions—including a cutoff of U.S. government assistance to and a ban on procurement and imports from the sanctioned entities—were immediately imposed on seven of nine entities being investigated by the Russian government for missile transfers to Iran.[15] In January 1999, the sanctions were extended to three more Russian entities. The issue of assistance by Russian entities to Iran's ballistic missile program had been the subject of U.S., Russian, and Israeli diplomacy for some two years before the imposition of sanctions. Diplomacy on the matter continues to the time of this writing. The State Department has announced that the United States is using

[14]Pikayev et al., 1998.

[15]Richard Speier, "Iran Missile Sanctions," *Proliferation Brief* (Carnegie Endowment for International Peace Non-Proliferation Project, Washington, D.C.), Vol. I, No. 10, August 27, 1998.

the threat of reduced quotas for Russian launches of U.S. satellites as a lever to secure greater Russian restraint.[16]

These sanctions on Russian entities were the second example of nonproliferation sanctions being imposed by policy but not by law. In 1977, President Jimmy Carter had cut off assistance to Pakistan without being required to do so by law.

The State Department has also supplied a list of 11 instances in which sanctions were imposed for chemical and biological weapon transfers. Note that these sanctions, under the law, apply only to suppliers—not, as in the case of missile sanctions, to both suppliers and recipients:

- February 1994 against Thai entities
- July 1994 against entities of unspecified nationality
- August 1994 against an Italian individual
- November 1994 against Swiss entities
- November 1994 against Australian, Austrian, and German individuals
- February 1995 against entities of unspecified nationality
- May 1995 against Austrian and German entities
- November 1995 against a Russian individual
- May 1997 against Chinese entities
- September 1997 against German entities
- February 1998 against a fugitive from justice last known to be in Lebanon.

Note that these sanctions prohibit only imports into the United States or procurement by the U.S. government from the sanctioned entities. It is not clear how dependent these entities are on sales to the United States. In fact, according to a National Security Council staff member, the first nine sanctions listed here were imposed on a

---

[16]Associated Press, "U.S. Raises Ante Against Russia," January 14, 1999.

"motley crew" that did not export to the United States.[17] But these sanctions are targeted at individuals and businesses, so their effect even on friendly governments can be minimal.

This study has found no sanctions imposed under what the Appendix describes as the "combined weapons nonproliferation" sanctions laws, although sanctions imposed on Iraq by the UN in the wake of the Gulf War may or may not be considered to be imposed under U.S. law.

Not counting the 1974 India sanctions, the Iraq sanctions, the Russia-Iran sanctions imposed by Executive Order, or the China certification requirements described above, the public record indicates that legally mandated nonproliferation sanctions have been imposed 24 times. Of these 24, seven instances led to publicly reported negotiations (the early Pakistan nuclear sanctions, the two China missile episodes, South African missile sanctions, Russian missile sanctions, and the Indian and Pakistani sanctions following their nuclear tests), and 17 had little effect (North Korean missile sales, all of the chemical weapons sanctions).

The arithmetic of sanctions' effectiveness is sensitive to the precise concept of "sanctions" that is used. Moreover, pressure, brought quietly to bear to prevent proliferation, may or may not be considered a sanction. We now examine cases in which sanctions were not imposed but were threatened.

NON-IMPOSITION OF SANCTIONS

In the mid-1990s, shortly after the Eximbank Act was strengthened through a provision of the 1994 NPPA, press stories reported that India might be preparing for a second nuclear detonation (the first having occurred 20 years earlier). The press later reported that India, having discovered that a detonation would now lead to a cutoff of Eximbank financing, had backed off from its preparations.

---

[17]Remarks by Gary Samore, Special Assistant to the President and Senior Director for Nonproliferation and Export Controls, National Security Council, at a panel discussion on "Using Sanctions to Support Non-Proliferation," Conference on Nuclear Non-Proliferation: Enhancing the Tools of the Trade, sponsored by the Carnegie Endowment for International Peace, Washington, D.C., June 9, 1997.

Were the two related? It is difficult to establish cause and effect even when two historical events are fully recorded. It is even more difficult when one is a non-event or when important records are shrouded in diplomatic confidentiality.

Most records of diplomatic discussions are classified at least at the CONFIDENTIAL level to permit fairly frank discussions between governments. So, when sanctions are threatened but not imposed (or are waived), the public record is likely to be sparse.

The most extensive case of non-imposition of sanctions involved Pakistan's nuclear weapons program. Beginning in 1982, Congress created eight Presidential waiver authorities exclusively on Pakistan's behalf, and five of these were exercised. The initial concern was to avoid discouraging Pakistan from playing its vital role in opposing Soviet involvement in Afghanistan. But the result was a fairly unimpeded Pakistani weapons program that led to nuclear tests in 1998.

Beyond the Indian and Pakistani episodes, there are two widely reported, long-term transfer activities in which missile sanctions must have at least lurked in the background but were not imposed—at least until recently.

The first involves North Korean Scud missile assistance to Egypt. This has been reported in the press since 1987, was publicly admitted by President Hosni Mubarak in 1996, and has been described in increasing detail in recent months by the Director of Central Intelligence.[18] The specifics of the transfers are not public, so it is difficult to know whether or when a triggering event occurred that met the letter of the sanctions law. But Egypt is the only one of North

---

[18]From the Director of Central Intelligence, *Report of Proliferation-Related Acquisition in 1997,* Langley, Va., September 17, 1998: "During 1997, Egypt continued to obtain ballistic missile components and associated equipment from North Korea. According to information obtained in 1997 from a North Korean Army defector, Egypt and North Korea are partners in joint missile development." From the Director of Central Intelligence, *Unclassified Report to Congress on the Acquisition of Technology Relating to Weapons of Mass Destruction and Advanced Conventional Munitions,* Langley, Va., February 9, 1999: "During the first half of 1998, Egypt continued to obtain ballistic missile components and associated equipment from North Korea. This activity is part of a long-running program of ballistic missile cooperation between these two countries."

Korea's known missile customers never to have been cited until 1999—long after the facts had been reported—in any sanctions imposition. Even then, the sanctions announcement did not mention Egypt but only "certain entities in the Middle East," and additional research was required to determine the location of the entities.[19] Egypt, of course, is a particularly close friend of the United States.

Missile sanctions determinations have from time to time been reported in the *Federal Register* without the relevant parties being named. And, under the missile technology controls legislation, the President can waive sanctions by notifying certain congressional committees—committees that are cleared for classified information. So, in spite of press complaints of inaction,[20] it is conceivable that the sanctions process was in play with respect to the North Korean–unknown country transfers. The North Korean–Egyptian Scud cooperation has, presumably, only after many years, led to the imposition of sanctions on both parties. But does this mean that action was never taken until recently? Missile sanctions were imposed on North Korea in 1992 and again in 1997, without any customer being named. What is known publicly is that the United States has discussed, or attempted to discuss, missile sales with North Korea since 1996.[21]

In October 1998, Congress strengthened the Administration's bargaining power with respect to North Korea by conditioning the release of funds for the Korean Peninsula Energy Development Organization on a prior Presidential certification (subject to waivers) relating to progress on the dismantling of the North Korean nuclear weapons program and impeding of North Korea's development and export of ballistic missiles. To date, in nuclear discussions, North Korea has agreed to allow inspection of a suspect underground

---

[19] *Federal Register*, Vol. 64, No. 73, April 16, 1999, p. 18957.

[20] For instance, "Turning a Blind Eye," *Defense News*, September 8–14, 1997, p. 26.

[21] The March 1999 sanctions on the Egyptian entities did not have the immediate effect of halting missile cooperation with North Korea. The U.S. intelligence community reported, with respect to proliferation-related activity in the second half of 1999, "Egypt continues its effort to develop and produce ballistic missiles with the assistance of North Korea." See Director of Central Intelligence, "Unclassified Report to Congress on the Acquisition of Technology Relating to Weapons of Mass Destruction and Advanced Conventional Munitions, 1 July Through 31 December 1999," August 9, 2000; online at http://www.cia.gov/publications/bian/bian_aug2000.htm.

facility—in conjunction with an increase in Western food shipments. In missile discussions, North Korea has been willing only to offer to stop its ballistic missile exports, not its development program—and on the condition that it be compensated for the lost revenue. To be sure, since its 1988 Taepo-Dong ballistic missile test, North Korea has suspended its flight tests of ballistic missiles. This is generally ascribed to the incentive of better relations with the United States and other nations.

The second illustration involves China—widely cited by Administration officials as having a history of troubling exports to Pakistan and Iran. Chinese and Pakistani entities were sanctioned for missile cooperation in 1991 and again in 1993.

But since the 1980s, there have been reports of nuclear weapon–related cooperation between China and Pakistan. In May 1996, China pledged not to assist unsafeguarded nuclear facilities; however, this pledge came in the midst of a debate over a $70,000 sale by a Chinese firm of critical ring magnets to Pakistan's unsafeguarded enrichment program. This sale could have triggered a cutoff of Eximbank financing for exports to China. Under Secretary of State Lynn Davis went to China six months later and reported that "senior leadership in China had no knowledge" of the transfer—referring to the provisions of the Eximbank Act requiring that triggering activities be undertaken "willfully" or "knowingly." Under Secretary Davis also stated that discussions had established "that, in the future, transactions such as the ring magnets transactions would not go forward"—referring to the provision of the Eximbank Act allowing for the withholding of sanctions upon corrective action reported by the Secretary of State.[22] The Eximbank reportedly held up financing during the period of these negotiations, but—other than this temporary measure—sanctions were never imposed. Would China's behavior have been as strongly affected if the escape clauses of the law were not invoked and sanctions were imposed? On the one hand, the credible threat of powerful sanctions may have been as effective as—or conceivably more effective than—their imposition. But, on

[22]Press conference by Dr. Lynn E. Davis, Under Secretary of State for Arms Control and International Security Affairs, Beijing, China, November 5, 1996.

the other hand, the failure actually to impose sanctions may weaken their deterrent effect.

China has also been reported to be engaged in missile cooperation with Iran over many years. In late 1996, U.S. defense officials revealed that China had transferred supersonic C-802 anti-ship cruise missiles to Iran, straining the ability of U.S. forces to defend shipping in the Persian Gulf and potentially triggering sanctions under the Iran-Iraq Arms Non-Proliferation Act. But the Act requires that the transfer be of "destabilizing numbers and types." Nearly a year later the Administration still claimed

> It's a fine call, in terms of what constitutes destabilizing, because, you know, at this point the military, the U.S. Navy, tells us that despite the increased threat from the sale of cruise missiles, it can continue to operate and carry out its mission in the Persian Gulf. And so even though they're exceedingly unhappy with this new development, it is not, on the face of it destabilizing at this point . . . if you define it as overturning the ability of the United States to operate in the Persian Gulf.[23]

The question again is whether such exculpatory interpretations weaken the deterrent effect of sanctions. "At this point" at least leaves a threat open to impose sanctions in the future.

The threat may have had its effect. In January 1998, the Chinese President gave assurances that China would halt all new sales of anti-ship cruise missiles to Iran and end transfers of related technology. But an incentive may also have been in play. In April 1998 the U.S. Secretary of State renewed an offer to let American satellite manufacturers buy more rocket-launching services from China in exchange for tougher missile-technology controls.

The effect of the quiet U.S. diplomacy with China has been limited. Over the year before this writing, reports had appeared of Chinese missile assistance to Libya and North Korea, as well as to its traditional customers in Iran and Pakistan. High-level U.S. teams traveling to Beijing discussed the matter as recently as November 1998 and

---

[23]Testimony by Stanley Roth, Assistant Secretary of State, East Asian and Pacific Affairs, before the U.S. Senate, Foreign Relations Committee, September 17, 1997.

July 2000. But the diplomacy has remained quiet, and sanctions have not been imposed.[24]

The last undeniably powerful imposition of missile sanctions occurred in 1992, on Russian and Indian entities. In the intervening years, the press has increasingly reported transfers by North Korea, China, and Russia. Is this a result of increased press attention or of an actual increase in sanctionable activity? If the latter, is it encouraged by the hiatus in the imposition of powerful sanctions? Or is the threat of sanctions, not backed up by the occasional use of sanctions, enough to deter?

A less-promising example of the non-use of nonproliferation sanctions came in 1998, with respect to the Iran-Libya Sanctions Act (ILSA). On May 18, 1998, the Administration announced that investment by French, Malaysian, and Russian firms in Iran's oil and gas industry constituted sanctionable activity.[25] However, in return for such achievements as "an EU commitment to give high priority to proliferation concerns regarding Iran," and "closer coordination of diplomatic efforts to stem technology exports by other countries to proliferators, including Iran," the Administration waived the sanctions. The result was a rapid unraveling of the ILSA sanctions against energy investments, first in Iran and more recently in Libya. Such investments now appear to be unconstrained by the threat of sanctions.[26]

---

[24]The U.S. intelligence community assesses that, in the last half of 1999, Chinese missile-related exports to Pakistan actually increased; and "firms in China provided missile-related items, raw materials, and/or assistance to several countries of proliferation concern—such as Iran, North Korea, and Libya." See Director of Central Intelligence, 2000.

[25]The White House, Office of the Press Secretary, "Fact Sheet on Cooperation on Non-Proliferation and Counterterrorism," Washington, D.C., May 18, 1998.

[26]Bhushan Bahree, "European Oil Majors March Back to Iran," *The Wall Street Journal,* March 10, 1999. Bloomberg News, "European Oil Companies Plan Expansions in Libya," *The New York Times,* April 6, 1999. The unraveling of ILSA sanctions was part of a rush in early 1999 to ease a variety of sanctions on Libya. With respect to the results of some of these sanctions suspensions, the Director of Central Intelligence, 2000, reported, " We expect that the suspension of UN sanctions last year [i.e., in 1999] will allow Libya to expand its [ballistic missile] procurement effort. Libya remains heavily dependent on foreign suppliers for precursor chemicals and other key CW-related equipment. Following the suspension of UN sanctions in April 1999, it wasted no time in re-establishing contacts with sources of expertise, parts, and precursor chemicals abroad, primarily in Western Europe."

TRENDS AND IMPLICATIONS

After India's 1974 "peaceful nuclear explosion," Congress passed a law requiring that the United States vote against assistance to India in the World Bank.[27] At the time, the United States did not seek to multilateralize its mandated vote against India. However, the United States and three or four other large donors had enough weighted voting power in the World Bank to block the 50 percent required for loan approval.

Times have changed. The United States would now need the support of the eight next-largest donors—or a greater number of smaller donors—to block a loan.[28]

So, while some potential sanctions levers are diminishing in effectiveness, others are growing. With the end of the Cold War, unilateral trade and financial levers are far more effective with China, Russia, and—prospectively—North Korea than they could have been a few decades ago. Both China and Russia acted quickly when the United States used the space-launch-services market as a sanction and/or incentive in the early 1990s.

There is another trend worth noting. Membership is growing in the international nonproliferation regimes. This growth has both positive and negative effects. The positive effect is that the rules of nonproliferation are assuming the status of international norms. Fewer governments have policies allowing themselves to contribute to proliferation. And sanctions—especially future attempts to multilateralize them—can benefit from this growing legitimacy.

But the negative effect is that some governments may take advantage of the situation. In general, membership in a regime facilitates access to U.S. technology and reduces exposure to U.S. sanctions.[29] For example, once it is in the MTCR, a government is exempt from

---

[27]As with other retroactive sanctions, this study does not treat this law in detail. Other, proactive, legislation now serves the same function. However, *ad hoc* sanctions are discussed in Chapter Five.

[28]The eight are Canada, China, France, Germany, Italy, Japan, Saudi Arabia, and the United Kingdom.

[29]See, in the Appendix (Section A–III.B), the provisions of the EAA favoring regime members and penalizing nonmembers.

U.S. missile sanctions—as long as it authorizes exports in question, which makes it far easier for otherwise-sanctionable transfers to occur to, from, or among regime members.

And as the number of governments observing nonproliferation norms increases, the potential profits of the few willing to flout the rules also increase.[30] Most of the accounts of proliferation now focus on suppliers in China, Russia, and North Korea—suppliers who have the market almost to themselves. But there are indications of a growing second tier of suppliers.[31]

To deal with the increased profits to be realized from proliferation, the deterrent power of sanctions needs to be greater than ever before. This need sharpens the issues of whether sanctions should be downplayed in favor of diplomacy, whether they should be withheld in favor of a "high standard of proof," and whether they should be used in a manner that has minimal impact on the target of sanctions.

There are reasons why these are statements of issues and not merely rhetoric. The next chapter examines these reasons in the context of problems with the current sanctions laws and process.

---

[30]In the case of missile exports, see Brian Chow, *Emerging National Space Launch Programs: Economics and Safeguards,* Santa Monica, Calif.: RAND, R-4179-USDP, 1993, pp. 41–42.

[31]"Among those countries of concern to the U.S., commerce in ballistic missile and WMD technology and hardware has been growing, which may make proliferation self-sustaining among them and facilitate their ability to proliferate technology and hardware to others." Rumsfeld Commission, *Report of the Commission to Assess the Ballistic Missile Threat to the United States, Executive Summary,* Washington, D.C.: U.S. Government Printing Office, July 15, 1998, p. 17.

Chapter Four

PROBLEMS WITH SANCTIONS

The history in the preceding chapter brought into relief the need for changes in sanctions. In this chapter, we review the difficulties with nonproliferation sanctions in light of the historical experience and in terms of the four objectives outlined at the beginning of this study: action, deterrence, constraint, coercion.

ACTION

Action is dramatic retaliation in response to inexcusable behavior. Congress has demonstrated time and again in its sanctions legislation that it wants such action. This is why some sanctions legislation is "inflexible": automatic, prescribing predetermined sanctions, and in many cases draconian. The legislation is meant to tie the hands of the Executive Branch.

But "inflexible" laws can create problems for many elements of the foreign policy system. In the words of the Director of the CIA's Nonproliferation Center,

> In the view of some in the Executive Branch, the sanctions laws provide little flexibility to policymakers because, once a determination that a transfer has taken place, they must either impose sanctions or grant a waiver. In their view, often neither of these options is in the best interests of the U.S., for it limits negotiating flexibility. The imposition of sanctions may also undermine other policy initiatives in other areas. This presents a dilemma for policymakers. One option is to challenge the veracity of the intelligence case that a transfer of concern actually occurred. This can lead a decision-maker to behave like a defense attorney working to undermine the

> evidence indicating a transfer has occurred or that the transferring nation knew that the transfer involved WMD-related items. This can place the intelligence community at odds with its important customers over important, high visibility issues.[1]

After retiring from the CIA, the same individual expanded on the Executive Branch's insistence on "high standards" of evidence for sanctionable activities. He accused policymakers of using "almost any measure" to block intelligence judgments confirming Chinese transfer of 34 M-11 missiles to Pakistan, judgments that could lead to a determination to impose Category I sanctions. "One of the easier outs on this is to say that the intelligence information doesn't quite meet their high standards," he said.[2]

President Clinton himself had already confirmed the tendency to "fudge" evaluations that could lead to the imposition of sanctions. He said,

> What always happens if you have automatic sanctions legislation is it puts enormous pressure on whoever is in the executive branch to fudge an evaluation of the facts of what is going on. And that's not what you want. What you want is to leave the President some flexibility, including the ability to impose sanctions, some flexibility with a range of appropriate reactions.[3]

The most formidable "inflexibility" in the sanctions laws is that most of the laws target the sanctions on entire governments or nations (see Chapter Two). There is not necessarily an intractable problem here, but a problem of formulation of sanctions laws and processes: *how to permit actions to be scaled and targeted appropriately while ensuring that strong action is taken.*

---

[1]G. Oehler, "Detection and Interdiction of Weapons of Mass Destruction: Intelligence Community Support to U.S. Policy Objectives," undated remarks, approximately spring 1996.

[2]Bill Gertz, "U.S. Helped China Beat Sanctions, Witness Says," *The Washington Times,* June 12, 1998.

[3]Elaine Sciolino, "Clinton Argues for 'Flexibility' Over Sanctions," *The New York Times,* April 28, 1998.

DETERRENCE

Deterrence results from a negative consequence, such as a sanction, being both likely and painful. This is an easy prescription when the targets of sanctions are unimportant "persons" or, if important persons, persons who are pariahs. But—when China or Russia is a seller or Egypt, India, Pakistan, or Saudi Arabia is a buyer—the U.S. government is faced with a conflict between the priority espoused by the regional desk and that espoused by the functional desk.

The easiest bureaucratic solution is to "split the difference" in the deterrence formula that calls for consequences to be likely and painful. Painful sanctions become unlikely; wrist slaps can be administered with near certainty.

To force more-effective action by the Executive Branch, it is possible for Congress to try to tighten up the letter of the law. The next chapter looks at such possibilities. But the result could just as well be a measures/countermeasures battle between the Executive and Legislative Branches. Moreover, some weakening of deterrence occurs—not because of Executive Branch inaction, but because of laws that prescribe predetermined and inappropriate sanctions. The cutoff of U.S. trade with an entity that trades only with the Third World is not a painful sanction and does not create deterrence. The cutoff of all foreign assistance to Russia is not an effective deterrent to actions by a subnational Russian entity, because the sanction will be resisted by the Executive Branch. The cutoff of assistance to Pakistan was not an effective deterrent, because Pakistan was motivated by its national security. The prescribed sanction did not adequately address security motivations.

The basic problem behind all of these complications needs to be addressed: *how to find sanctions that work on the motives of the sanctioned entity without destroying important international relationships.* The next chapter examines some alternatives.

CONSTRAINT

Constraint results from U.S. actions, prescribed by some sanctions laws, that, ideally, will reduce the ability of the sanctioned person to continue his offenses. Whether or not it is an effective deterrent or punishment for the missile sanctions laws to restrict, preferentially, exports controlled by the MTCR, such restrictions have a chance of retarding the technological abilities of the sanctionee. The Iran and Libya sanctions, justified largely by concerns about proliferation, target an industrial sector that, on its face, has nothing to do with proliferation: the petroleum industry. But, of course, petroleum provides the financing for the proliferation activities in Iran and Iraq.

The difficulty is that these sanctions do not always work. They may be evaded if they are not multilaterally enforced. Or the sanctionee may simply outwait the sanctions, which often expire after one or two years. There are draconian ways of dealing with this difficulty, but such measures—for reasons described above—reduce the likelihood that sanctions will be employed at all.

Moreover, permanent damage to the sanctionee can redound on other parties. This study has cited the concerns of the current critics of sanctions that the disruptions resulting from sanctions can damage U.S. industry as well as innocents in the sanctioned nation.

The problem is: *how to reduce the sanctioned person's ability to continue to contribute to proliferation without causing unacceptable damage to innocent bystanders, and still preserve a sanctions process that will be used.*

COERCION

Coercion is to improve behavior on the part of the sanctioned "person" or, especially, his government. Indeed, several sanctions laws allow for the mitigation or termination of sanctions once the President certifies that behavior has improved.

This painful aspect of sanctions can serve as a goad to improved behavior, but it can also be counterproductive. On the one hand, it can harden government positions and even leave the sanctionee with nothing to lose. On the other hand, a U.S. willingness to accept future promises and to avoid inflicting a painful experience can lead to promises that are either vague or ultimately broken. Depending on who interprets such experiences, the objective of improved behavior may conflict with the objectives of action, deterrence, and constraint.

Sanctions are often treated as a one-shot process, like a massive air strike at the beginning of a war. But sanctions, like wars, are continuing processes. The dynamics of sanctions—of actions and reactions between the United States, the sanctioned party, and the onlookers—makes sanctions a complicated process that plays out over time. One of the strong themes of the Cantigny Conference was the contrast between planning for sanctions and planning for war. War takes enormous staff work and advance consideration of many contingencies. Sanctions often are imposed with much less contingency planning and are sometimes treated in the law as an action against an unreactive opponent.

The military analogy goes far. Fred C. Iklé entitled a book *Every War Must End.* B. H. Liddell Hart drove home the statement, "The object in war is a better state of peace." Every sanction must also end. And the object of sanctions is a more secure world.

The problem is: *how to structure the sanctions process so that it helps achieve worthwhile outcomes while still preserving the deterrent and constraining effects of sanctions.*

It is important to make clear that this study is not searching for "perfect" sanctions. The requirements for sanctions can be overstated, for example:

> Historically, economic sanctions have worked only when they have been universal and comprehensive, consistent, and credible—in short, leakproof.[4]

A more operational, if limited, statement of at least some of the objectives of sanctions is Senator John Glenn's, "Our goal is to take the profits out of proliferation."[5] There are ways to accomplish the specific objective of inflicting costs on the sanctionee that exceed the benefits of his inappropriate actions.

There are other, more limited or technical problems with sanctions: They include possible legal loopholes, such as "willfully" or

---

[4]J. Amuzegar, "Adjusting to Sanctions,"*Foreign Affairs,* May/June 1997, pp. 31–41.

[5]Senator John Glenn, "Senate Passes Major Nuclear Non-Proliferation Bill," news release, April 9, 1992.

"knowingly"; the looseness of most of the determination processes; the possibly bewildering variety of triggers, waiver conditions, duration, etc.; and the increasingly important exemptions for regime members. In the next chapter, we examine alternatives for dealing with these problems.

Chapter Five

ALTERNATIVES

Both critics and advocates of the sanctions process provide many elements to be examined in formulating alternatives to the current sanctions process, as do two recent presentations by Administration nonproliferation officials,[1] and possibilities generated by this study itself. There are a vast number of permutations and combinations of specific elements. Some are mutually exclusive. Some are complementary. To highlight the major differences in approach, we combine these elements into four major alternatives:

1. Reducing reliance on unilateral sanctions
2. Improving the existing sanctions process
3. Targeting and calibrating sanctions more precisely
4. Fashioning more-powerful sanctions.

ALTERNATIVE 1: REDUCING RELIANCE ON UNILATERAL SANCTIONS

The critics' justification for reducing reliance on unilateral sanctions is not to challenge the importance of nonproliferation. Rather, it is that, whatever the theoretical value of sanctions, sanctions do not

[1]Remarks by Ambassador Thomas E. McNamara, Assistant Secretary of State, Political-Military Affairs, at a panel discussion on "Unilateral Sanctions/Restrictions on U.S. Defense Trade," 14th Annual International Conference of the National Security Industrial Association, Arlington, Va., February 25, 1997; and remarks by Gary Samore, 1997.

always work very well in practice. Critics argue that the history of nonproliferation sanctions is discouraging. Moreover, sanctions may well hurt the United States more than they hurt the sanctioned person—by tying up the nonproliferation bureaucracy in sanctions debates, hamstringing U.S. diplomacy, and damaging U.S. industry (through the immediate loss of trade as prescribed in the sanction and through the longer-term loss of a reputation for reliability).

The following measures would contribute to reducing reliance on such sanctions:

1. Place increased reliance on incentives as the first resort and not just as a supplement to sanctions.
2. Make sanctions contingent on the exhaustion of diplomatic efforts with the government of the sanctionable person.
3. Make unilateral U.S. sanctions contingent on the exhaustion of efforts to obtain multilateral sanctions.
4. Strengthen the contract sanctity provisions of the sanctions laws.
5. Place increased reliance on high-profile and highly targeted non-economic sanctions, such as the refusal of the International Cricket Association to admit South African teams into international competition.[2]
6. Require review points for ongoing sanctions, and an exit strategy for extricating the United States from sanctions confrontations in which the United States has failed.[3]

The problem with this approach is that it reduces the deterrent and constraining values of sanctions—both threatened and imposed. The result may be to weaken the very diplomacy on which this approach seeks to rely. The increased use of incentives could lead some countries to game the system.

The value of this approach is that it attempts to look realistically at the dynamic aspects of the sanctions process—the time-consuming working of diplomacy and the need for reassessments over time—

---

[2]Hufbauer and Winston, 1997, p. 9.

[3]See *Unilateral Economic Sanctions*, 1997, for additional recommendations.

and at the role of additional parties—other governments that can reinforce the sanctions and U.S. firms that may suffer more than the sanctionee. And the regional desks of the U.S. government would undoubtedly add that this approach gives them more flexibility to prevent nonproliferation from sidetracking other bilateral efforts.

ALTERNATIVE 2: IMPROVING THE EXISTING SANCTIONS PROCESS

The justification for this approach is that it is readily implemented by making incremental changes in existing laws and procedures—and that it can be tried before departing further from the existing process. Moreover, this approach minimizes reliance on theory. It attempts to correct the defects in instruments and procedures that have evolved over the years.

The following measures might improve the existing process:

1. Standardize some of the best provisions of existing law by applying them to other sanctions legislation. These include

   —the 60-day timetable from the availability of persuasive information to the Executive Branch to a Presidential determination of sanctionability (as in the sanctions for chemical and biological weapons use)

   —a test for "knowingly" consistent with domestic criminal law (as in the Foreign Corrupt Practices Act,[4] used as the standard in the FY 97 National Defense Authorization Act (NDAA) amendment to the nonproliferation provisions of the Eximbank Act)

   —a 90-day timetable (renewable once) for international negotiations after a determination of sanctionability has been made (as in the NPPA and some other sanctions laws)

---

[4]See 15 USC 78dd-2(h)(3). The test of "knowingly" involves a person being "aware that" or having "firm belief that" a circumstance exists. The test may be met if a person is "aware of a high probability of the existence of such circumstance." The test is designed to avoid circumvention by a person willfully "burying his head in the sand."

—the possibility of reporting Presidential determinations and waivers to Congress on a classified basis (as apparently is permitted in the missile sanctions), at least for the duration of the 90–180-day negotiation process

—uniform provisions for similar sanctions, as between the AECA and EAA versions of the missile sanctions

—deletion of the provisions triggering nuclear sanctions by "seeking" nuclear-explosive-related items and missile sanctions by "conspiracy" to buy or sell, so that the triggers for sanctions are uniformly limited to overt acts

—more nearly uniform duration and termination provisions for sanctions across all sanctions laws.

2. Improve the formulation of sanctions legislation with such features as

—a "preponderance of evidence" test for determinations of sanctionability, to prevent the process from becoming sidetracked with an impossibly "high standard of proof"

—application of sanctions to persons whose government is a member of existing regimes, on the condition that the President (1) certify that such sanctions are "not inconsistent" with U.S. obligations under the regime and (2) take account of the role of the foreign government if the sanctionable activity was approved by that government

—Presidential certification, before the United States votes in favor of a new regime member, that it has an established track record of nonsanctionable behavior and a demonstrated willingness and ability to observe the requirements of the regime[5]

—a change in the "rebuttable" presumption provision of the AECA version of missile sanctions to apply to items "contributing to" a missile and not just "designed for use in" such a missile, as well as removing the word "rebuttable" to

---

[5]See The Nonproliferation Policy Education Center, "Nonproliferation Policy Reform: Enhancing the Role of Congress," Washington, D.C., June 1996.

eliminate the suggestion that the presumption can easily be swept away

—conformance, as much as possible, of the definitions for activities triggering sanctions to the terminology of the international nonproliferation regimes[6]

—urging the President to seek, within the 90–180-day timetable for diplomacy (see above), multilateral support for that diplomacy and for sanctions if they are imposed.

3. Discipline the sanctions process with greater congressional involvement in specific cases by means of

—follow-up letters and hearings in instances in which the observance of the spirit of the law is in doubt

—as a last resort, *ad hoc* legislated sanctions.

The shortcoming of this alternative is that some of its measures may exacerbate clashes between the Legislative and Executive Branches. But some of the measures, such as a timetable for diplomacy to work and greater conformity of statute language to the terminology of regimes, are exactly what the Executive Branch is seeking. And this alternative requires no revolution in the U.S. approach to sanctions.

ALTERNATIVE 3: TARGETING AND CALIBRATING SANCTIONS MORE PRECISELY

There are three major justifications for this approach. First, it is more likely that sanctions will be imposed if there is less collateral damage to domestic and foreign parties from the imposition of sanctions against a specific foreign person. The most devastating collateral damage to foreign parties occurs when entire governments or nations are routinely the target for sanctions (see Chapter Two). But the Executive Branch has shown, time and again, its reluctance to let a single issue jeopardize other aspects of important bilateral ties.

---

[6]The missile technology controls legislation; for example, it prescribes different sanctions according to whether the triggering transfers are Category I or Category II, as defined by the Missile Technology Control Regime. Some of the most important requirements of nonproliferation treaty regimes are "not in any way to assist . . . ."

Second, more precisely targeted sanctions are not only more likely to be imposed but can also be designed more specifically and made more damaging to the sanctionee—both of which features tend to increase the deterrent and constraining values of sanctions.

Third, sanctions that are specifically designed and precisely targeted can more readily be complemented by incentives, without losing control of incentives by offering them to others on a global basis.[7]

This alternative could include the following measures:

1. New legislation to permit the President discretionary authority over the target, type, and severity of sanctions to be imposed—subject to the essential requirement that they promote U.S. nonproliferation objectives in a manner "at least as effective as" the sanctions required by existing law (with effectiveness evaluated with respect to the objectives of the law), and providing for notification of and possible override by Congress on the specific sanctions that the President chooses to impose. To be sure, this formula has a potentially troublesome subjective element. But, the legislation would allow the President to devise discriminating and effective sanctions that take advantage of the proliferator's unique vulnerabilities.
2. The creation in the Executive Branch of an Incentives and Sanctions Analysis Staff (ISAS), featuring

   —a charter to design and monitor sanctions specifically tailored to the sanctioned person and meeting the "at least as effective as" test

   —a capability to assess economic and other impacts of sanctions alternatives

   —membership consisting of staff from the intelligence community and other agencies concerned with the sanctions process

---

[7]For example, sanctions involving the threatened cutoff of U.S. exports to Russian space organizations were reinforced by an offer to permit U.S.–origin satellites to be launched by Russia if the offending behavior was permanently stopped.

—financial expertise, including that of the drug interdiction community, to analyze the sources of revenue and the location of assets belonging to the sanctioned person

—a capability to analyze the dynamic (time-phased measures/countermeasures) aspects of the sanctions process and to recommend modifications to that process as a specific sanctions episode unfolds.

3. Within the limits of the law, a minimum standard of punishment for trade and financial sanctions. For example, when a foreign person realizes a financial profit, the sanction could be required to inflict losses on the sanctioned person of at least, say, 10 times his gains—with a minimum loss of $10 million (which may lead to bankruptcy). In some instances, multilateral sanctions may be necessary to reach this standard.

4. An expansion of optional sanctions instruments, beyond trade and finance, to include measures reducing the security of nations engaged in sanctionable activities. These instruments could include not only reduced arms-related sales to the sanctioned nation but also increased arms sales and security assurances to potential regional adversaries. They could also include the withdrawal of U.S.–recognized security guarantees with respect to armed conflict resulting from the act of proliferation, so that the world is not made "safe for proliferation" by arrangements such as those of the Indian-Pakistani treaty prohibiting attacks on each other's nuclear facilities.

5. Targeted incentives designed and monitored by the ISAS, to complement the diplomacy associated with the sanctions process.

6. Consideration of legal provisions allowing the Executive Branch to compensate domestic parties for actual damages resulting from the sanctions and not associated with normal business risks in their lines of work.[8]

---

[8]See, in the Appendix, the Agricultural Improvement and Reform Act (Section A–V.J) for an example of such legislation. Compensation can reduce the collateral damage from sanctions. However, it is a hazardous business because it can expand out of all proportion.

This alternative has the great liability that many of its approaches are untried. Weak implementation, or gaming of some of these approaches by the Executive Branch or by domestic parties who consider themselves to be damaged by sanctions, could lead to substantial difficulties.

The advantage of this alternative is that it meets the repeated Executive Branch calls for "flexibility" and "proportionality" in sanctions, without sacrificing the objectives of the process. Effectively implemented, this alternative could be terrifying to proliferators and economically devastating to suppliers, and could undercut the security objectives of nations seeking NBC weapons and missiles. It could result in sanctions that would be imposed because they would minimize collateral damage to bilateral relations and to domestic parties. And this alternative could "take the profit out of proliferation," whether that profit is measured in dollars or security.

ALTERNATIVE 4: FASHIONING MORE-POWERFUL SANCTIONS

The justification for this approach is that it promotes the objectives of sanctions by increasing their impact on the sanctioned person or government. The previous approach consisted of sanctions measures on a targeted, discriminating basis, which had the disadvantage of a number of novel elements. This approach works more closely with the existing elements of the sanctions process.

This alternative could include the following measures:

1. "Leveling up" of existing sanctions legislation to include more of the stronger measures (e.g., the cutoff of Eximbank credits) in more sanctions and to augment the less-ineffective sanctions such as those for chemical and biological weapons transfers.
2. Legislation prescribing an increased minimum duration for sanctions.
3. The application of sanctions to members of nonproliferation regimes—with changes in legislation as necessary.

4. A reorientation of sanctions legislation to place more emphasis on Presidential certification[9] of good nonproliferation behavior before trade and financial cooperation can take place—as opposed to the present system oriented toward requiring a Presidential determination of bad behavior before sanctions are imposed.
5. A standard policy of withdrawing incentives given (as in the 1993 space cooperation/missile nonproliferation deal with Russia) in return for good nonproliferation behavior—if nonproliferation behavior has turned bad.
6. Greater use of the President's IEEPA authority to freeze assets, especially individual or corporate assets, and otherwise impose a broader range of financial sanctions.
7. Initiatives by both the Legislative and Executive Branches to promote advance preparations for the multilateralization of sanctions, including

   —the exploration of coalitions in international financial institutions

   —coordinated and reinforcing national sanctions by like-minded governments

   —agreements with other governments at least not to undercut each other's nonproliferation sanctions of specific types

   —expanded use of sanctions against parties who are undercutting sanctions.
8. New types of sanctions, such as

   —undercutting the security of the sanctioned nation (see previous alternative)

   —expulsion of foreign students in technical areas related to the type of proliferation[10]

---

[9]It is extraordinarily difficult for Presidents to make certifications in suspect situations. See, for example, the talk of a "partial certification" in Reuters Ltd., "United States Sees Possible Okay for China Nuclear Deals," September 18, 1997, 8:42 p.m.

[10]See M. Leitenberg, "The Desirability of International Sanctions Against the Use of Biological Weapons and Against Violations of the Biological Weapons Convention,"

—expulsion from international nonproliferation regimes

—covert or overt destruction of prohibited items in sanctioned nations

—military interdiction of certain types of prohibited traffic to sanctioned nations.

These are strong measures, and they are certain to be resisted by many regional desks. Legislation embodying some of these measures may face a veto. To be sure, these measures will increase the deterrent and constraining effects of sanctions; but they could damage many elements of bilateral U.S. relationships.

However, in the absence of progress with other sanctions alternatives—or after another dramatic proliferation event—it may be necessary to turn to some of these measures. Stronger measures are not always reckless measures. For instance, the multilateralization of sanctions is widely advocated. Given the mixed history of the imposition of nonproliferation sanctions and the likelihood that sanctionable activities are increasingly profitable, there is good reason to increase the forcefulness of sanctions.

The Monitor (Center for International Trade and Security of the University of Georgia, Athens, Ga.), Summer 1997, pp. 23–27.

Chapter Six

RECOMMENDATIONS

A subject as complex as nonproliferation sanctions can drown the reader in details. Legal and operational details are vital; they determine how sanctions will actually function. And this study has attempted to address the details. But the details can be incomplete and contradictory—as they are in much of the current sanctions legislation. It is possible to reduce these gaps and inconsistencies if there are a few major principles from which the details can be derived.

This chapter briefly sums up the authors' preferences from among the detailed alternatives discussed the Chapter Five. Drawing from the discussion of the most vexing problems identified in the previous chapters, it then lays out principles from which improved nonproliferation sanctions might be derived.

PREFERRED ALTERNATIVES

From the alternatives in Chapter Five, we prefer Alternatives 2 and 3 (except for the compensation provision, Item 6, under Alternative 3, which, as discussed, has a substantial potential for abuse). These alternatives include detailed measures for improving the existing sanctions process and for targeting and calibrating sanctions more precisely. The authors believe that these measures are realistic and would improve the effective use of sanctions for nonproliferation objectives. These measures would not prejudge subsequent, more-controversial steps.

Some elements of Alternative 1 and Alternative 4 could complement these approaches. The discussion in Chapter Five suggests which elements offer the greatest promise.

But the nonproliferation sanctions process will be a patchwork of approaches, even with the alternatives of the last chapter. To make the process more effective, we recommend that it be unified by addressing the three most salient issues from the previous chapters: the objective of sanctions, waivers, and the management of the sanction process. To that end, the authors propose three principles: a "worse-off" criterion, automaticity, and specialized staff.

THREE PRINCIPLES GUIDING AN IMPROVED SANCTIONS PROCESS

(1) A "Worse-Off" Criterion

Senator Glenn's criterion for sanctions, "to take the profit out of proliferation," offers operational guidance for sanctions against suppliers motivated by economic gain. If U.S. sanctions policy can create a reliable expectation that sanctionable transfers will lose money, there will be no economic motive for such commerce.

Predetermined sanctions cannot guarantee this result. They may hit the wrong target or employ an ineffective measure against the right target. A case-by-case design of the sanctions, performed by a specialized staff as recommended below, is the way to ensure that a supplier ends up economically worse off. The sanctions may be unilateral or multilateral as each case-by-case analysis dictates.

Many sanctionable actions are motivated not by economic gain but by security concerns. Here, again, the criterion for sanctions should be to make the target of sanctions "worse off." Unfortunately, there is no way of quantifying "worse off" when it comes to security. But there are ways of making sensible judgments in applying the criterion. A specialized staff can weigh alternatives of unilateral and multilateral sanctions—including cutoffs or reductions of munitions and dual-use supplies, military training, cooperation in military-related technology, and financial assistance for all of these. The same staff can weigh alternatives of reducing security commitments to the targeted entity and of aiding regional rivals. In some cases, such as North Korea today, the withholding of civil trade such as fuel shipments may make the target's security worse off.

A "worse-off" criterion implies a scale of sanctions that fits the offense and the offender. On the one hand, it avoids predetermined sanctions that are no more effective than a wrist slap. On the other hand, it does not require that the target of the sanctions be made infinitely worse off. "Taking the profit out of proliferation" will not necessarily entail draconian sanctions that penalize entire governments or nations. A "worse-off" criterion also contains its own exit strategy. For one-time triggering events, such as a sanctionable transfer, there should be a finite sanction and—consequently—a beginning, middle, and end to the sanctions process.

What is an example of a "worse-off" sanction? Blocking the launches of U.S.–origin satellites by China—a sanction imposed in 1991 and briefly in 1993—threatened substantial financial losses to the Chinese organization that benefited from the sales of missile equipment to Pakistan. The missile-proliferation sanctions law (as interpreted until 1993) imposed such a sanction for a term of at least two years, unless the sanctions were waived. Under a "worse-off" criterion, the sanction need only be imposed on enough space launches to make the United States government confident that the target had lost more money than it had gained by the sanctionable exports. It would not be necessary to continue imposing the sanctions for an arbitrary number of years.

A "worse-off" criterion, if effectively administered, should meet two of the four goals of sanctions: to generate action against the offense and to deter such offenses. In the next section, we discuss ways of administering such sanctions to deal with the other two goals: constraint of the sanctionable activity and coercion to cease such activities.

(2) Automaticity

Judging from the historical record cited in this study, we would maintain that the determinations and waiver processes have been major points of ineffectiveness of nonproliferation sanctions.[1] Currently, a proliferator has good reason to believe that he will not be subject to sanctions—much less to effective sanctions.

It may be understandable that the Executive Branch has, in the words of President Clinton, tended to "fudge" the sanctions process when the sanctions were so draconian as to undercut major elements of U.S. foreign policy. The first recommendation, for a "worse-off" criterion that would result in appropriately scaled actions, should reduce the incentive to wink at sanctions.

Once sanctions are scaled appropriately, the authors recommend that their application be as automatic as the law can allow. The determinations process should incorporate the most "inflexible" requirements in current law, those for the use of chemical weapons. And there should be no waivers for any reason. Even friends of the United States, even nations and entities that agree to mend their ways, should understand that U.S. law automatically generates actions that will make them "worse off" if they contribute to proliferation.

It will always be possible for Congress to enact waivers as it did to ease the draconian sanctions that followed the Indian and Pakistani nuclear tests of 1998. But a sanctions law tailored to a "worse-off" criterion should be discriminating enough in its effects to not require such a congressional about-face.

Until a "worse-off" criterion can be incorporated into sanctions law and Executive Branch practice, the authors recommend that the Executive Branch be given the discretion to take actions "at least as effective as" those required by current sanctions law (with effectiveness evaluated with respect to the objectives of the law). This should increase the likelihood that sanctionable actions will carry consequences.

The automatic application of the "worse-off" criterion should operate in a straightforward manner when triggered by one-time sanctionable events for which the benefits to the actors can be compared

---

[1]The current Administration could be expected to disagree strenuously, arguing that the flexibility of the determinations and waiver processes has allowed productive negotiations. Chapter Three presents the record leading to the authors' conclusions.

to the costs imposed by the sanctions. But some sanctions legislation is aimed at continuing sanctionable activities, such as programs to develop weapons of mass destruction. For example, the Iran-Libya Sanctions Act prescribes continuing economic penalties in an attempt to constrain the programs and coerce their termination. The historical record shows that such sanctions—if drawn too broadly—lead to collateral damage to such parties as allies and civilians in the targeted nations. As a result, there are strong pressures to use the waiver process to mitigate the sanctions.

Even here, there is a better alternative than waivers: the certification process, which requires a finding by the Executive Branch that the sanctionable behavior has ceased. The historical record has shown that the Executive Branch is reluctant to provide such certifications without real changes in the behavior of the targeted entity.

Under the automaticity principle, the sanctions imposed by Congress on such continuing activities would go into effect on the timetable prescribed by Congress, with no way out except by Executive Branch certification. The decision on the appropriateness of the sanctions would be made in the process of enacting (or vetoing) the sanctions law. Because, once the law was passed, the imposition of the sanctions would be automatic, there would be a greater incentive for the law to prescribe appropriately scaled and targeted sanctions—or for the Executive Branch to attempt to defuse the legislative process by imposing sanctions on its own authority, as it has done in the case of the sanctions for missile-related transfers from Russia to Iran.

By combining the "worse-off" criterion and the automaticity principle, the sanctions process could perform well toward all the goals of sanctions: action, deterrence, and—for continuing sanctionable activities—constraint and coercion.

(3) Specialized Staff

The first two recommendations are feasible only if there is a dedicated staff capable of designing sanctions that make the targeted entity worse off. The preceding chapter describes the concept of such an Incentives and Sanctions Analysis Staff (ISAS) housed in the Executive Branch.

The ISAS staff must design and oversee the implementation of several processes, including multilateral support, time-phased measures and countermeasures with respect to the targeted entity, and a learning process for future rounds of sanctions and incentives. If the learning process succeeds, the staff will gradually improve their design and implementation of sanctions that are effective in making the targeted entity worse off but that are limited in scope and duration.

A major concern will be whether the staff is sufficiently independent of considerations that compete with the effective operation of sanctions. There is no perfect way to design such independence for an organization that must interact intimately with national security operations in the Executive Branch. However, Congress has developed management and reporting arrangements for the intelligence community and the Joint Chiefs of Staff to provide an extra degree of independence and congressional oversight. Such arrangements might serve as the starting points for a sufficiently independent ISAS.

Experience has shown that professional standards and multi-year assignments to a single security function will also contribute to the effectiveness of such a staff. The best career officials take professional pride in the quality of their work. If their staff assignments span a long enough period, they gain broader perspectives on national security issues than the view of the foreign policy pressures of the moment. Such a staff can greater improve the effectiveness of the sanctions process.

A LAST WORD

Nonproliferation is vital for international security. And sanctions can be an effective reinforcement for nonproliferation diplomacy. Even critics of sanctions often make an exception for well-designed nonproliferation sanctions. The next step should not be a retreat from sanctions. Rather, it should be the improvement and focusing of sanctions. The world needs effective sanctions because it needs alternatives to inaction or war.

Appendix

RELEVANT TEXTS OF U.S. NONPROLIFERATION SANCTIONS LAWS AND RELATED DOCUMENTS (September 1997; Section A-I Revised in April 1999)

CONTENTS

A-I. ABOUT THIS APPENDIX

A. Texts Selected for This Appendix

This Appendix presents, in convenient and compact form, the portions of all major U.S. nonproliferation sanctions laws (and some minor laws and related texts) that apply to foreign persons. The texts are generally current as of September 1997 and are often specifically stated to be current well into calendar year 1996. Several elements are left out:

- **Portions of the law applying to domestic persons.** The size of this Appendix would at least double if the laws applying to domestic persons were included. Not only do many sanctions laws have long sections prescribing sanctions against domestic persons, but entirely new legislation on export controls would come into play. This study and this Appendix are intended for readers interested in the international application of sanctions.
- **References.** Most references printed with the texts, such as historical notes, Executive Orders—especially those delegating authority—and case citations, have been deleted. For the purposes of this study, these would add "noise."
- **Portions of legislation not essential to sanctions.** These range from congressional findings to provisions regarding other aspects of U.S. nonproliferation and foreign policy—e.g., international organizations, terrorism, and human rights. Presidential reporting requirements were generally retained because they alert Congress to cases in which the imposition of sanctions might be appropriate.

Except for Article XII of the Chemical Weapons Convention, all texts have been derived directly from electronic sources in order to avoid transcription errors. Where deletions are not obvious, they are indicated by bracketed ellipses ("[....]").

B. Format of the Law

U.S. federal law is published in three basic forms: Public Laws, Statutes at Large, and the U.S. Code.

Public Laws are the versions of the laws passed by Congress and signed by the President. Nonproliferation officials are frequently most familiar with Public Laws because they are published first; initially, the officials must work with that format. But Public Laws have a major disadvantage: They accrue over the years. To understand missile-proliferation sanctions, it is necessary to have not only the National Defense Authorization Act for FY 1991 (the original legislation), but also the Helms Amendment, the Pressler Amendment, the "rebuttable presumption" amendment, and the texts (modified over many years) of the Arms Export Control Act (AECA) and the Export Administration Act (EAA) into which the missile sanctions texts are to be inserted as new or revised sections. The result is a thick sheaf of legal documents that is cumbersome and difficult to understand. And it is difficult to know whether an old Public Law has been superseded or modified by a later one.

Statutes at Large are unmodified Public Laws, codified by subject and published by the Archivist of the United States. They are the official texts for use in court; they prevail when there is a conflict with the U.S. Code (see below). Statutes at Large have the same liabilities as Public Laws, with one exception: Their codification makes it easier to find all Statutes relevant to a given subject.

The U.S. Code, compiled by the Law Revision Counsel of the House of Representatives, is different from the two previous formats. On a given subject, it is the net result of all previous legislation after adding and deleting text. For example, the U.S. Code Chapter on Arms Export Control has the sections enacted in the original missile sanctions legislation as amended over the intervening years. These are written smoothly, as if they were passed into law at one time. The U.S. Code Annotated adds Historical Notes to show when various amendments or modifications were passed, with their Public Law and Statutes at Large citations. But, unless one is interested in the evolution of the law, the basic texts are enough. The U.S. Code is by far the most compact and understandable format, and Congress has given many Titles of the U.S. Code a full legal status equivalent to that of the Statutes at Large.

For the purposes of this study, the U.S. Code has two significant problems. First, it takes time to compile. A revision of the U.S. Code can lag some two years behind the enactment of a Public Law.

Second, the Law Revision Counsel does not incorporate into the main text of the U.S. Code such legislation as the Counsel considers temporary in its effects. Such legislation appears as Notes to the U.S. Code, in the format of a Public Law. The net result is that, while the U.S. Code has decisive advantages for understandability, it is often necessary to wade through a succession of Notes, especially in a subject as ever-changing as nonproliferation. For example, the Nuclear Proliferation Prevention Act (NPPA) of 1994—the most important nuclear sanctions legislation in 16 years—was originally passed with a "sunset clause." As a result, it was not included in the main text of the U.S. Code but was printed as a set of amendments in a Historical and Statutory Note. In July 1996, the NPPA was made a permanent law, or—more precisely—its termination was repealed. But the relevant part of the U.S. Code had not been revised a year later. So the NPPA still appeared as a Note in 1997, with a later Public Law (that makes the NPPA permanent) hanging in temporary limbo because it was too recent even to appear as a Note.[1] Much country-specific sanctions legislation—such as that against Iran, Iraq, and Libya—also is consigned to Notes.

Because this Appendix seeks to make the sanctions texts compact and understandable, it uses the U.S. Code Annotated (USCA) as the basic text, with Notes and even separate Public Laws shown where there is no alternative. This approach has made possible an enormous compression of texts.

C. Finding the Law

As mentioned above, this Appendix derives its texts from electronic sources. Three basic electronic sources are available: Lexis/Nexis online, the West Publishing USCA CD-ROM, and the World Wide Web.

---

[1]To make matters even more complicated, some "permanent" portions of the NPPA were incorporated into the appropriate Titles of the U.S. Code. The relevant texts of these appear in this Appendix as "Nuclear nonproliferation controls" and "Enforcement of nuclear agreements." The next version of the U.S. Code after 1997 was to incorporate the remaining sanctions provisions of the NPPA as 22 USC 6301-6305.

Lexis/Nexis has the advantage of being a fairly complete and current database. But it is expensive ($200 per hour), difficult to browse, and somewhat awkwardly formatted. Beyond early use in the Office of the Secretary of Defense,[2] Lexis/Nexis was not used for this Appendix.

The West Publishing USCA CD-ROM cost $900 per year for a subscription in 1997; beyond that, it costs nothing (other than personnel time) to use, is easy to browse, and is well formatted. It can be searched by Boolean logic or by specific code citations. It suffers from time lags in its distribution, but users may do online queries to see whether items have been updated. This Appendix draws most of its texts from the November 1996 USCA CD-ROM, which has a legislation cutoff date of July 9, 1996.

To supply legislation passed after July 9, 1996, and to fill in other gaps that were discovered after the USCA CD-ROM search, this Appendix turned to the World Wide Web. There, legal databases are supplied on sites maintained by Cornell University, the Library of Congress ("Thomas"), and the Government Printing Office (GPO). All have serious gaps in coverage of older laws, and Thomas did not offer the U.S. Code in 1997. This Appendix supplements its USCA CD-ROM search with the GPO web site:

http://www.access.gpo.gov/su_docs/aces/aaces002.html

This site, known as GPO/Access, includes the U.S. Code and Public Laws from recent years. As used in this Appendix, the GPO/Access cutoff date for the U.S. Code is January 16, 1996, with a note in the citation on whether the document was affected by laws enacted through August 28, 1996. Laws enacted after that cutoff date but no later than the summer of 1997, if not already acquired on the USCA CD-ROM, were downloaded as Public Laws. The GPO/Access site is

---

[2]This Appendix started with laws found in the following OSD search of Lexis/Nexis:

Object: missile OR nuclear OR chemical OR biological OR weapon! OR material! OR device OR "by-product"OR delivery OR agent AND chemical w/100

Activity: transfer! OR sale OR sell OR buy OR purchase OR smugg! OR conspir!

Verb: sanction! OR penalt! OR prohibit!

best searched by key phrases in the title of a law or a U.S. Code section. The authors found that "proliferation" AND "sanctions" was a good initial search rule.

In February 1997, Cornell upgraded its U.S. Code site to make it the best place to search the Code by numerical section citation. But Cornell's site does not allow key-word searches; and the authors found its texts to be more awkwardly formatted than those of the GPO site. The Cornell site is

http://www4.law.cornell.edu/uscode

D. Recent Legislation

As is noted in the body of this report, the U.S. Code had not been updated by April 1999 to reflect laws enacted after January 1, 1998. Consequently, the important nonproliferation sanctions legislation of 1998 was not available in compact form at the time that this Appendix was last revised. This is especially unfortunate, because many of the 1998 provisions are amendments to sections of the previous sanctions laws.

To assist researchers willing to work with the Public Law versions of the 1998 nonproliferation sanctions legislation, Dianne E. Rennack of the Congressional Research Service has compiled citations for those Public Laws.[3] The citations relevant to this study are as follows:

- Public Law 105-194, Agricultural Export Relief Act of 1998

  Section 2 amends 102(b) of AECA to allow food, agricultural commodities, medicine and medical supplies to be exempted from application of sanctions under Section 102(b) of AECA through September 30, 1999.

---

[3]Personal communication from Dianne E. Rennack, Analyst in Foreign Policy Legislation, Foreign Affairs and National Defense Division, Congressional Research Service, "Nonproliferation sanctions in 105th Congress, 2nd session," Washington, D.C., January 26, 1999. Previously, Ms. Rennack published two exceedingly useful compilations of sanctions legislation, both available through the Congressional Research Service, Library of Congress, Washington, D.C.: (1) (with Robert D. Shuey) *Economic Sanctions to Achieve U.S. Foreign Policy Goals: Discussion and Guide to Current Law,* updated January 22, 1998; and (2) *Nuclear, Biological, Chemical, and Missile Proliferation Sanctions: Selected Current Law,* updated May 27, 1998.

- Public Law 105-277, Omnibus Consolidated and Emergency Supplemental Appropriations, 1999: Agriculture, Rural Development, Food and Drug Administration, and Related Agencies Appropriations Act, 1999:

  Title IX, India-Pakistan Relief Act of 1998. Authorizes the President to waive application of some sanctions under Sections 101 and 102 of AECA, Section 620E(e) of FAA 1961, and Section 2(b)(4) of Eximbank Act of 1945, with respect to India and Pakistan. Authority available for one year; ambiguous language leaves it unclear whether from enactment or first use.

- Public Law 105-277, Omnibus Consolidated and Emergency Supplemental Appropriations, 1999: Foreign Operations, Export Financing, and Related Programs Appropriations Act, 1999:

  Title I, restriction on ExIm funding for non–nuclear-weapons state (recurring language).

  Title II, Assistance for the New Independent States of the Former Soviet Union, subsection (c) withholds funds from Russia until the President determines and certifies certain Russia-Iran exchanges relating to nuclear and ballistic missile development.

  Title V, General Provisions:

  Section 506, prohibition on financing nuclear goods.

  Section 535, prohibition on assistance to countries not in compliance with UN Security Council resolutions against Iraq.

  Section 582, terms for providing funds to the Korean Peninsula Energy Development Organization (KEDO).

  Section 585, reporting requirement on Iraq's development of WMD.

- Public Law 105-277, Omnibus Consolidated and Emergency Supplemental Appropriations, 1999, Division I: Chemical Weapons Convention Implementation Act of 1998—especially Titles I and II.

In addition to these Public Laws, the sanctions documents of 1998 should be supplemented by the President's amendment of Executive

Order 12938, dated July 28, 1998. This is available as "Executive Order: Proliferation of Weapons of Mass Destruction," Washington, D.C.: The White House, Office of the Press Secretary, July 28, 1998. It can be found on the World Wide Web at

http://www.whitehouse.gov

A-II. NUCLEAR WEAPONS NONPROLIFERATION

A. (NNPA) Nuclear Nonproliferation Act

[Laws in effect as of January 16, 1996]

[Document not affected by Public Laws enacted between January 16, 1996, and August 28, 1996]

[CITE: 42USC2158]

TITLE 42—THE PUBLIC HEALTH AND WELFARE

CHAPTER 23—DEVELOPMENT AND CONTROL OF ATOMIC ENERGY

Division A—Atomic Energy

SUBCHAPTER X—INTERNATIONAL ACTIVITIES

Sec. 2158. Conduct resulting in termination of nuclear exports

No nuclear materials and equipment or sensitive nuclear technology shall be exported to—

(1) any non-nuclear-weapon state that is found by the President to have, at any time after March 10, 1978,

  (A) detonated a nuclear explosive device; or

  (B) terminated or abrogated IAEA safeguards; or

  (C) materially violated an IAEA safeguards agreement; or

  (D) engaged in activities involving source or special material and having direct significance for the manufacture or acquisition of nuclear explosive devices, and has failed to take steps which, in the President's judgment, represent sufficient progress toward terminating such activities; or

(2) any nation or group of nations that is found by the President to have, at any time after March 10, 1978,

(A) materially violated an agreement for cooperation with the United States, or, with respect to material or equipment not supplied under an agreement for cooperation, materially violated the terms under which such material or equipment was supplied or the terms of any commitments obtained with respect thereto pursuant to section 2153a(a) of this title; or

(B) assisted, encouraged, or induced any non-nuclear-weapon state to engage in activities involving source or special nuclear material and having direct significance for the manufacture or acquisition of nuclear explosive devices, and has failed to take steps which, in the President's judgment, represent sufficient progress toward terminating such assistance, encouragement, or inducement; or

(C) entered into an agreement after March 10, 1978, for the transfer of reprocessing equipment, materials, or technology to the sovereign control of a non-nuclear-weapon state except in connection with an international fuel cycle evaluation in which the United States is a participant or pursuant to a subsequent international agreement or understanding to which the United States subscribes;

unless the President determines that cessation of such exports would be seriously prejudicial to the achievement of United States non-proliferation objectives or otherwise jeopardize the common defense and security: Provided, That prior to the effective date of any such determination, the President's determination, together with a report containing the reasons for his determination, shall be submitted to the Congress and referred to the Committee on Foreign Affairs of the House of Representatives and the Committee on Foreign Relations of the Senate for a period of sixty days of continuous session (as defined in section 2159(g) of this title), but any such determination shall not become effective if during such sixty-day period the Congress adopts a concurrent resolution stating in substance that it does not favor the determination. Any such determination shall be considered pursuant to the procedures set forth in section 2159 of this title for the consideration of Presidential submissions.

B. Nuclear Nonproliferation Controls

[Laws in effect as of January 16, 1996]

[Document not affected by Public Laws enacted between

January 16, 1996, and August 28, 1996]

[CITE: 22USC2799aa]

TITLE 22—FOREIGN RELATIONS AND INTERCOURSE

CHAPTER 39—ARMS EXPORT CONTROL

SUBCHAPTER X—NUCLEAR NONPROLIFERATION CONTROLS

Sec. 2799aa. Nuclear enrichment transfers

(a) Prohibitions; safeguards and management

Except as provided in subsection (b) of this section, no funds made available to carry out the Foreign Assistance Act of 1961 [22 U.S.C. 2151 et seq.] or this chapter may be used for the purpose of providing economic assistance (including assistance under chapter 4 of part II of the Foreign Assistance Act of 1961 [22 U.S.C. 2346 et seq.]), providing military assistance or grant military education and training, providing assistance under chapter 6 of part II of that Act [22 U.S.C. 2348 et seq.], or extending military credits or making guarantees, to any country which the President determines delivers nuclear enrichment equipment, materials, or technology to any other country on or after August 4, 1977, or receives such equipment, materials, or technology from any other country on or after August 4, 1977, unless before such delivery—

(1) the supplying country and receiving country have reached agreement to place all such equipment, materials, or technology, upon delivery, under multilateral auspices and management when available; and

(2) the recipient country has entered into an agreement with the International Atomic Energy Agency to place all such equipment, materials, technology, and all nuclear fuel and facilities in such country under the safeguards system of such Agency.

(b) Certification by President of necessity of continued assistance; disapproval by Congress

(1) Notwithstanding subsection (a) of this section, the President may furnish assistance which would otherwise be prohibited under such subsection if he determines and certifies in writing to the Speaker of the House of Representatives and the Committee on Foreign Relations of the Senate that—

(A) the termination of such assistance would have a serious adverse effect on vital United States interests; and

(B) he has received reliable assurances that the country in question will not acquire or develop nuclear weapons or assist other nations in doing so.

Such certification shall set forth the reasons supporting such determination in each particular case.

(2)

(A) A certification under paragraph (1) of this subsection shall take effect on the date on which the certification is received by the Congress. However, if, within thirty calendar days after receiving this certification, the Congress enacts a joint resolution stating in substance that the Congress disapproves the furnishing of assistance pursuant to the certification, then upon the enactment of that resolution the certification shall cease to be effective and all deliveries of assistance furnished under the authority of that certification shall be suspended immediately.

(B) Any joint resolution under this paragraph shall be considered in the Senate in accordance with the provisions of section 601(b) of the International Security Assistance and Arms Export Control Act of 1976.

Sec. 2799aa-1. Nuclear reprocessing transfers, illegal exports for nuclear explosive devices, transfers of nuclear explosive devices, and nuclear detonations

(a) Prohibitions on assistance to countries involved in transfer of nuclear reprocessing equipment, materials, or technology; exceptions; procedures applicable

(1) Except as provided in paragraph (2) of this subsection, no funds made available to carry out the Foreign Assistance Act of 1961 [22 U.S.C. 2151 et seq.] or this chapter may be used for the purpose of providing economic assistance (including assistance under chapter 4 of part II of the Foreign Assistance Act of 1961 [22 U.S.C. 2346 et seq.]), providing military assistance or grant military education and training, providing assistance under chapter 6 of part II of that Act [22 U.S.C. 2348 et seq.], or extending military credits or making guarantees, to any country which the President determines—

(A) delivers nuclear reprocessing equipment, materials, or technology to any other country on or after August 4, 1977, or receives such equipment, materials, or technology from any other country on or after August 4, 1977 (except for the transfer of reprocessing technology associated with the investigation, under international evaluation programs in which the United States participates, of technologies which are alternatives to pure plutonium reprocessing), or

(B) is a non-nuclear-weapon state which, on or after August 8, 1985, exports illegally (or attempts to export illegally) from the United States any material, equipment, or technology which would contribute significantly to the ability of such country to manufacture a nuclear explosive device, if the President determines that the material, equipment, or technology was to be used by such country in the manufacture of a nuclear explosive device.

For purposes of clause (B), an export (or attempted export) by a person who is an agent of, or is otherwise acting on behalf of or in the interests of, a country shall be considered to be an export (or attempted export) by that country.

(2) Notwithstanding paragraph (1) of this subsection, the President in any fiscal year may furnish assistance which would otherwise be prohibited under that paragraph if he determines and certifies in writing during that fiscal year to the Speaker of the House of Representatives and the Committee on Foreign Relations of the Senate that the termination of such assistance would be seriously prejudicial to the achievement of United States nonproliferation objectives or otherwise jeopardize the common defense and security. The President shall transmit with such certification a statement setting forth the specific reasons therefor.

(3)

(A) A certification under paragraph (2) of this subsection shall take effect on the date on which the certification is received by the Congress. However, if, within 30 calendar days after receiving this certification, the Congress enacts a joint resolution stating in substance that the Congress disapproves the furnishing of assistance pursuant to the certification, then upon the enactment of that resolution the certification shall cease to be effective and all deliveries of assistance furnished under the authority of that certification shall be suspended immediately.

(B) Any joint resolution under this paragraph shall be considered in the Senate in accordance with the provisions of section 601(b) of the International Security Assistance and Arms Export Control Act of 1976.

(b) Prohibitions on assistance to countries involved in transfer or use of nuclear explosive devices; exceptions; procedures applicable

(1) Except as provided in paragraphs (4), (5), and (6), in the event that the President determines that any country, after the effective date of part B of the Nuclear Proliferation Prevention Act of 1994—

(A) transfers to a non-nuclear-weapon state a nuclear explosive device,

(B) is a non-nuclear-weapon state and either—

(i) receives a nuclear explosive device, or

(ii) detonates a nuclear explosive device,

(C) transfers to a non-nuclear-weapon state any design information or component which is determined by the President to be important to, and known by the transferring country to be intended by the recipient state for use in, the development or manufacture of any nuclear explosive device, or

(D) is a non-nuclear-weapon state and seeks and receives any design information or component which is determined by the President to be important to, and intended by the recipient state for use in, the development or manufacture of any nuclear explosive device,

then the President shall forthwith report in writing his determination to the Congress and shall forthwith impose the sanctions described in paragraph (2) against that country.

(2) The sanctions referred to in paragraph (1) are as follows:

(A) The United States Government shall terminate assistance to that country under the Foreign Assistance Act of 1961 [22 U.S.C. 2151 et seq.], except for humanitarian assistance or food or other agricultural commodities.

(B) The United States Government shall terminate—

(i) sales to that country under this chapter of any defense articles, defense services, or design and construction services, and

(ii) licenses for the export to that country of any item on the United States Munitions List.

(C) The United States Government shall terminate all foreign military financing for that country under this chapter.

(D) The United States Government shall deny to that country any credit, credit guarantees, or other financial assistance by any department, agency, or instrumentality of the United States Government, except that the sanction of this subparagraph shall not apply—

(i) to any transaction subject to the reporting requirements of title V of the National Security Act of 1947 [50 U.S.C. 413 et seq.] (relating to congressional oversight of intelligence activities), or

(ii) to humanitarian assistance.

(E) The United States Government shall oppose, in accordance with section 262d of this title, the extension of any loan or financial or technical assistance to that country by any international financial institution.

(F) The United States Government shall prohibit any United States bank from making any loan or providing any credit to the government of that country, except for loans or credits for the purpose of purchasing food or other agricultural commodities.

(G) The authorities of section 2405 of title 50, Appendix, shall be used to prohibit exports to that country of specific goods and technology (excluding food and other agricultural commodities), except that such prohibition shall not apply to any transaction subject to the reporting requirements of title V of the National Security Act of 1947 [50 U.S.C. 413 et seq.] (relating to congressional oversight of intelligence activities).

(3) As used in this subsection—

(A) the term "design information" means specific information that relates to the design of a nuclear explosive device and that is not available to the public; and

(B) the term "component" means a specific component of a nuclear explosive device.

(4)

(A) Notwithstanding paragraph (1) of this subsection, the President may, for a period of not more than 30 days of continuous session, delay the imposition of sanctions which would otherwise be required under paragraph (1)(A) or (1)(B) of this subsection if the President first transmits to the Speaker of the House of Representatives, and to the chairman of the Committee on Foreign Relations of the Senate, a certification that he has determined that an immediate imposition of sanctions on that country would be detrimental to the national security of the United States. Not more than one such certification may be transmitted for a country with respect to the same detonation, transfer, or receipt of a nuclear explosive device.

(B) If the President transmits a certification to the Congress under subparagraph (A), a joint resolution which would permit the President to exercise the waiver authority of paragraph (5) of this subsection shall, if introduced in either House within thirty days of continuous session after the Congress receives this certification, be considered in the Senate in accordance with subparagraph (C) of this paragraph.

(C) Any joint resolution under this paragraph shall be considered in the Senate in accordance with the provisions of section 601(b) of the International Security Assistance and Arms Export Control Act of 1976.

(D) For purposes of this paragraph, the term "joint resolution" means a joint resolution the matter after the resolving clause of which is as follows: "That the Congress having received on ____ a certification by the President under section 102(b)(4) of the Arms Export Control Act with respect to ____, the Congress hereby authorizes the President to exercise the waiver authority contained in section 102(b)(5) of that Act.", with the date of receipt of the certification inserted in the first blank and the name of the country inserted in the second blank.

(5) Notwithstanding paragraph (1) of this subsection, if the Congress enacts a joint resolution under paragraph (4) of this subsection, the President may waive any sanction which would otherwise be required under paragraph (1)(A) or (1)(B) if he determines and certifies in writing to the Speaker of the House of Representatives and the Committee on Foreign Relations of the Senate that the imposition of such sanction would be seriously prejudicial to the achievement of United States nonproliferation objectives or otherwise jeopardize the common defense and security. The President shall transmit with such certification a statement setting forth the specific reasons therefor.

(6)

(A) In the event the President is required to impose sanctions against a country under paragraph (1)(C) or (1)(D), the President shall forthwith so inform such country and shall impose the required sanctions beginning 30 days after submitting to the Congress the report required by paragraph (1) unless, and to the extent that, there is enacted during the 30-day period a law prohibiting the imposition of such sanctions.

(B) Notwithstanding any other provision of law, the sanctions which are required to be imposed against a country under paragraph (1)(C) or (1)(D) shall not apply if the President determines and certifies in writing to the Committee on Foreign Relations and the Committee on Governmental Affairs of the Senate and the Committee on Foreign Affairs of the House of Representatives that the application of such sanctions against such country would have a serious adverse effect on vital United States interests. The President shall transmit with such certification a statement setting forth the specific reasons therefor.

(7) For purposes of this subsection, continuity of session is broken only by an adjournment of Congress sine die and the days on which either House is not in session because of an adjournment of more than three days to a day certain are excluded in the computation of any period of time in which Congress is in continuous session.

(8) The President may not delegate or transfer his power, authority, or discretion to make or modify determinations under this subsection.

(c) "Non-nuclear-weapon state" defined

As used in this section, the term "non-nuclear-weapon state" means any country which is not a nuclear-weapon state, as defined in Article IX(3) of the Treaty on the Non-Proliferation of Nuclear Weapons.

C. Enforcement of Nuclear Agreements

UNITED STATES CODE ANNOTATED

TITLE 22. FOREIGN RELATIONS AND INTERCOURSE

CHAPTER 32—FOREIGN ASSISTANCE

SUBCHAPTER III—GENERAL AND ADMINISTRATIVE PROVISIONS

PART III—MISCELLANEOUS PROVISIONS

Current through P.L. 104-160, approved 7-9-96

§ 2429a-1. Annual report on nuclear transfer activities

Beginning with the fiscal year 1983 and for each fiscal year thereafter, the President shall prepare and transmit to the Congress, as part of the presentation materials for foreign assistance programs proposed for that fiscal year, a classified report describing the nuclear programs and related activities of any country for which a waiver of section 2799aa or 2799aa-1 of this title is in effect, including an assessment of—

(1) the extent and effectiveness of International Atomic Energy Agency safeguards at that country's nuclear facilities; and

(2) the capability, actions, and intentions of the government of that country with respect to the manufacture or acquisition of a nuclear explosive device.

§ 2429a-2. Enforcement of nonproliferation treaties

(a) Policy

It is the sense of the Congress that the President should instruct the United States Permanent Representative to the United Nations to enhance the role of that institution in the enforcement of nonproliferation treaties through the passage of a United Nations Security Council resolution which would state that, any non-nuclear weapon state that is found by the United Nations Security Council, in consultation with the International Atomic Energy Agency (IAEA), to have terminated, abrogated, or materially violated an IAEA full-scope safeguards agreement would be subjected to international economic sanctions, the scope of which to be determined by the United Nations Security Council.

(b) Prohibition

Notwithstanding any other provision of law, no United States assistance under the Foreign Assistance Act of 1961 [22 U.S.C.A. § 2151 et seq.] shall be provided to any non-nuclear weapon state that is found by the President to have terminated, abrogated, or materially violated an IAEA full-scope safeguard agreement or materially violated a bilateral United States nuclear cooperation agreement entered into after March 10, 1978.

(c) Waiver

The President may waive the application of subsection (b) of this section if—

(1) the President determines that the termination of such assistance would be seriously prejudicial to the achievement of United States nonproliferation objectives or otherwise jeopardize the common defense and security; and

(2) the President reports such determination to the Congress at least 15 days in advance of any resumption of assistance to that state.

[Laws in effect as of January 16, 1996]

[Document affected by Public Law 104-164 Section 141(a)]

[Document affected by Public Law 104-164 Section 142]

[Document affected by Public Law 104-164 Section 141(f)]

[CITE: 22USC2753]

TITLE 22—FOREIGN RELATIONS AND INTERCOURSE

CHAPTER 39—ARMS EXPORT CONTROL

SUBCHAPTER I—FOREIGN AND NATIONAL SECURITY POLICY OBJECTIVES AND RESTRAINTS

Sec. 2753. Eligibility for defense services or defense articles [....]

(f) Sales and leases to countries in breach of nuclear nonproliferation agreements and treaties

No sales or leases shall be made to any country that the President has determined is in material breach of its binding commitments to the United States under international treaties or agreements concerning the nonproliferation of nuclear explosive devices (as defined in section 830(4) of the Nuclear Proliferation Prevention Act of 1994) and unsafeguarded special nuclear material (as defined in section 830(8) of that Act).

D. (NPPA) Nuclear Proliferation Prevention Act

UNITED STATES CODE ANNOTATED

TITLE 22. FOREIGN RELATIONS AND INTERCOURSE

CHAPTER 47—NUCLEAR NON-PROLIFERATION

Current through P.L. 104-160, approved 7-9-96

§ 3201. Congressional declaration of policy [....]

HISTORICAL AND STATUTORY NOTES [....]

Nuclear Proliferation Prevention
Pub.L. 103-236, Title VIII, Apr. 30, 1994, 108 Stat. 507, provided that:

"Sec. 801. Short title.

"This title [enacting sections 2799a to 2799a-2 of this title, amending sections 262d, 2295a, 2295b, 2375, 2429a-1, 2593a, 2708, 2753, 2780, and 3281 of this title, section 635 of Title 12, Banks and Banking, and section 2160c of Title 42, The Public Health and Welfare, repealing section 2429 and 2429a of this title, and enacting this provision] may be cited as the 'Nuclear Proliferation Prevention Act of 1994'.

"PART A—REPORTING ON NUCLEAR EXPORTS

"Sec. 811. Reports to Congress [Amended section 3281 of this title].

"PART B—SANCTIONS FOR NUCLEAR PROLIFERATION

"Sec. 821. Imposition of Procurement Sanction on Persons Engaging in Export Activities that Contribute to Proliferation.

"(a) Determination by the President.—

"(1) In general.—Except as provided in subsection (b)(2), the President shall impose the sanction described in subsection (c) if the President determines in writing that, on or after the effective date of this part [see section 831 of Pub. L. 103-236, set out in this note], a foreign person or a United States person has materially and with requisite knowledge contributed, through the export from the United States or any other country of any goods or technology (as defined in section 830(2)), to the efforts by any individual, group, or non-nuclear-weapon state to acquire unsafeguarded special nuclear material or to use, develop, produce, stockpile, or otherwise acquire any nuclear explosive device.

"(2) Persons against which the sanction is to be imposed.—The sanction shall be imposed pursuant to paragraph (1) on—

"(A) the foreign person or United States person with respect to which the President makes the determination described in that paragraph;

"(B) any successor entity to that foreign person or United States person;

"(C) any foreign person or United States person that is a parent or subsidiary of that person if that parent or subsidiary materially and with requisite knowledge assisted in the activities which were the basis of that determination; and

"(D) any foreign person or United States person that is an affiliate of that person if that affiliate materially and with requisite knowledge assisted in the activities which were the basis of that determination and if that affiliate is controlled in fact by that person.

"(3) Other sanctions available.—The sanction which is required to be imposed for activities described in this subsection is in addition to any other sanction which may be imposed for the same activities under any other provision of law.

"(4) Definition.—For purposes of this subsection, the term 'requisite knowledge' means situations in which a person 'knows', as 'knowing' is defined in section 104 of the Foreign Corrupt Practices Act of 1977 (15 U.S.C. 78dd-2).

"(b) Consultation with and actions by foreign government of jurisdiction.—

"(1) Consultations.—If the President makes a determination described in subsection (a)(1) with respect to a foreign person, the Congress urges the President to initiate consultations immediately with the government with primary jurisdiction over that foreign person with respect to the imposition of the sanction pursuant to this section.

"(2) Actions by government of jurisdiction.—In order to pursue such consultations with that government, the President may delay imposition of the sanction pursuant to this section for up to 90 days. Following these consultations, the President shall impose the sanction unless the President determines and certifies in writing to the Congress that that [sic] government has taken specific and effective actions, including appropriate penalties, to terminate the involvement of the foreign person in the activities described in subsection (a)(1). The President may delay the imposition of the sanction for up to an additional 90 days if the President determines and certifies in writing to the Congress that that government is in the process of taking the actions described in the preceding sentence.

"(3) Report to Congress.—Not later than 90 days after making a determination under subsection (a)(1), the President shall submit to the Committee on Foreign Relations and the Committee on Governmental Affairs of the Senate and the Committee on Foreign Affairs of the House of Representatives a report on the status of consultations with the appropriate government under this subsection, and the basis for any determination under paragraph (2) of this subsection that such government has taken specific corrective actions.

"(c) Sanction.—

"(1) Description of sanction.—The sanction to be imposed pursuant to subsection (a)(1) is, except as provided in paragraph (2) of this subsection, that the United States Government shall not procure, or enter into any contract for the procurement of, any goods or services from any person described in subsection (a)(2).

"(2) Exceptions.—The President shall not be required to apply or maintain the sanction under this section—

"(A) in the case of procurement of defense articles or defense services—

"(i) under existing contracts or subcontracts, including the exercise of options for production quantities to satisfy requirements essential to the national security of the United States;

"(ii) if the President determines in writing that the person or other entity to which the sanction would otherwise be applied is a sole source supplier of the defense articles or services, that the defense articles or services are essential, and that alternative sources are not readily or reasonably available; or

"(iii) if the President determines in writing that such articles or services are essential to the national security under defense coproduction agreements;

"(B) to products or services provided under contracts entered into before the date on which the President publishes his intention to impose the sanction;

"(C) to—

"(i) spare parts which are essential to United States products or production;

"(ii) component parts, but not finished products, essential to United States products or production; or

"(iii) routine servicing and maintenance of products, to the extent that alternative sources are not readily or reasonably available;

"(D) to information and technology essential to United States products or production; or

"(E) to medical or other humanitarian items.

"(d) Advisory opinions.—Upon the request of any person, the Secretary of State may, in consultation with the Secretary of Defense, issue in writing an advisory opinion to that person as to whether a proposed activity by that person would subject that person to the sanction under this section. Any person who relies in good faith on such an advisory opinion which states that the proposed activity would not subject a person to such sanction, and any person who thereafter engages in such activity, may not be made subject to such sanction on account of such activity.

"(e) Termination of the sanction.—The sanction imposed pursuant to this section shall apply for a period of at least 12 months following the imposition of the sanction and shall cease to apply thereafter only if the President determines and certifies in writing to the Congress that—

"(1) reliable information indicates that the foreign person or United States person with respect to which the determination was made under subsection (a)(1) has ceased to aid or abet any individual, group, or non-nuclear-weapon state in its efforts to acquire unsafeguarded special nuclear material or any nuclear explosive device, as described in that subsection; and

"(2) the President has received reliable assurances from the foreign person or United States person, as the case may be, that such person will not, in the future, aid or abet any individual, group, or non-nuclear-weapon state in its efforts to acquire unsafeguarded special nuclear material or any nuclear explosive device, as described in subsection (a)(1).

"(f) Waiver.—

"(1) Criterion for waiver.—The President may waive the application of the sanction imposed on any person pursuant to this section, after the end of the 12-month period beginning on the date on which that sanction was imposed on that person, if the President determines and certifies in writing to the Congress that the continued imposition of the sanction would have a serious adverse effect on vital United States interests.

"(2) Notification of and report to Congress.—If the President decides to exercise the waiver authority provided in paragraph (1), the President shall so notify the Congress not less than 20 days before the waiver takes effect. Such notification shall include a report fully articulating the rationale and circumstances which led the President to exercise the waiver authority.

"Sec. 822. Eligibility for assistance.

"(a) Amendments to the Arms Export Control Act [Amended sections 2753 and 2780 of this title].

"(b) Foreign Assistance Act of 1961.—

"(1) Presidential Determination 82-7.—Notwithstanding any other provision of law, Presidential Determination No. 82-7 of February 10, 1982, made pursuant to section 670(a)(2) of the Foreign Assistance Act of 1961 [section 2429a(a)(2) of this title], shall have no force or effect with respect to any grounds for the prohibition of assistance under section 102(a)(1) of the Arms Export Control Act [section 2799aa-1(a)(1) of this title] arising on or after the effective date of this part [see section 831 of Pub.L. 103-236 set out in this note].

"(2) Amendment [Amended section 2375(d) of this title].

"Sec. 823. Role of international financial institutions.

"(a) In general.—The Secretary of the Treasury shall instruct the United States executive director to each of the international financial institutions described in section 701(a) of the International Financial Institutions Act (22 U.S.C. 262d(a)) to use the voice and vote of the United States to oppose any use of the institution's funds to promote the acquisition of unsafeguarded special nuclear material or the development, stockpiling, or use of any nuclear explosive device by any non-nuclear-weapon state.

"(b) Duties of United States Executive Directors [Amended section 262d of this title].

"Sec. 824. Prohibition on assisting nuclear proliferation through the provision of financing.

"(a) Prohibited activity defined.—For purposes of this section, the term 'prohibited activity' means the act of knowingly, materially, and directly contributing or attempting to contribute, through the provision of financing, to—

"(1) the acquisition of unsafeguarded special nuclear material; or

"(2) the use, development, production, stockpiling, or other acquisition of any nuclear explosive device,

by any individual, group, or non-nuclear-weapon state.

"(b) Prohibition.—To the extent that the United States has jurisdiction to prohibit such activity by such person, no United States person and no foreign person may engage in any prohibited activity.

"(c) Presidential determination and order with respect to United States and foreign persons.—If the President determines, in writing after opportunity for a hearing on the record, that a United States person or a foreign person has engaged in a prohibited activity (without regard to whether subsection (b) applies), the President shall, by order, impose the sanctions described in subsection (d) on such person.

"(d) Sanctions.—The following sanctions shall be imposed pursuant to any order issued under subsection (c) with respect to any United States person or any foreign person:

"(1) Ban on dealings in government finance.—

"(A) Designation as primary dealer.—Neither the Board of Governors of the Federal Reserve System nor the Federal Reserve Bank of New York may designate, or permit the continuation of any prior designation of, the person as a primary dealer in United States Government debt instruments.

"(B) Service as depository.—The person may not serve as a depository for United States Government funds.

"(2) Restrictions on operations.—The person may not, directly or indirectly—

"(A) commence any line of business in the United States in which the person was not engaged as of the date of the order; or

"(B) conduct business from any location in the United States at which the person did not conduct business as of the date of the order.

"(e) Judicial review.—Any determination of the President under subsection (c) shall be subject to judicial review in accordance with chapter 7 of part I of title 5, United States Code [5 U.S.C.A. § 701 et seq.].

"(f) Consultation with and actions by foreign government of jurisdiction.—

"(1) Consultations.—If the President makes a determination under subsection (c) with respect to a foreign person, the Congress urges the President to initiate consultations immediately with any appropriate foreign government with respect to the imposition of any sanction pursuant to this section.

"(2) Actions by government of jurisdiction.—

"(A) Suspension of period for imposing sanctions.—In order to pursue consultations described in paragraph (1) with any government referred to in such paragraph, the President may delay, for up to 90 days, the effective date of an order under subsection (c) imposing any sanction.

"(B) Coordination with activities of foreign government.—Following consultations described in paragraph (1), the order issued by the President under subsection (c) imposing any sanction on a foreign person shall take effect unless the President determines, and certifies in writing to the Congress, that the government referred to in paragraph (1) has taken specific and effective actions, including the imposition of appropriate penalties, to terminate the involvement of the foreign person in any prohibited activity.

"(C) Extension of period.—After the end of the period described in subparagraph (A), the President may delay, for up to an additional 90 days, the effective date of an order issued under subsection (b) imposing any sanction on a foreign person if the President determines, and certifies in writing to the Congress, that the appropriate foreign government is in the process of taking actions described in subparagraph (B).

"(3) Report to Congress.—Before the end of the 90-day period beginning on the date on which an order is issued under subsection (c), the President shall submit to the Congress a report on—

"(A) the status of consultations under this subsection with the government referred to in paragraph (1); and

"(B) the basis for any determination under paragraph (2) that such government has taken specific corrective actions.

"(g) Termination of the sanctions.—Any sanction imposed on any person pursuant to an order issued under subsection (c) shall—

"(1) remain in effect for a period of not less than 12 months; and

"(2) cease to apply after the end of such 12-month period only if the President determines, and certifies in writing to the Congress, that—

"(A) the person has ceased to engage in any prohibited activity; and

"(B) the President has received reliable assurances from such person that the person will not, in the future, engage in any prohibited activity.

"(h) Waiver.—The President may waive the continued application of any sanction imposed on any person pursuant to an order issued under subsection (c) if the President determines, and certifies in writing to the Congress, that the continued imposition of the sanction would have a serious adverse effect on the safety and soundness of the domestic or international financial system or on domestic or international payments systems.

"(i) Enforcement action.—The Attorney General may bring an action in an appropriate district court of the United States for injunctive and other appropriate relief with respect to—

"(1) any violation of subsection (b); or

"(2) any order issued pursuant to subsection (c).

"(j) Knowingly defined.—

"(1) In general.—For purposes of this section, the term 'knowingly' means the state of mind of a person with respect to conduct, a circumstance, or a result in which—

"(A) such person is aware that such person is engaging in such conduct, that such circumstance exists, or that such result is substantially certain to occur; or

"(B) such person has a firm belief that such circumstance exists or that such result is substantially certain to occur.

"(2) Knowledge of the existence of a particular circumstance.—If knowledge of the existence of a particular circumstance is required for an offense, such knowledge is established if a person is aware of a high probability of the existence of such circumstance, unless the person actually believes that such circumstance does not exist.

"(k) Scope of application.—This section shall apply with respect to prohibited activities which occur on or after the date this part takes effect [see section 831 of Pub.L. 103-236 set out in this note].

"Sec. 825. Export-Import Bank [Amended section 635(b)(4) of Title 12, Banks and Banking].

"Sec. 826. Amendment to the Arms Export Control Act.

"(a) In general [Enacted sections 2799aa, 2799aa-1, and 2799aa-2 of this title].

"(b) Repeals.—Sections 669 and 670 of the Foreign Assistance Act of 1961 [sections 2429 and 2429a of this title] are hereby repealed.

"(c) References in law.—Any reference in law as of the date of enactment of this Act [Apr. 30, 1994] to section 669 or 670 of the Foreign Assistance Act of 1961 [sections 2429 or 2429a of this title] shall, after such date, be deemed to be a reference to section 101 or 102, as the case may be, of the Arms Export Control Act [sections 2799aa or 2799aa-1 of this title].

"Sec. 827. Reward [Amended section 2708 of this title].

"Sec. 828. Reports.

"(a) Content of ACDA annual report [Amended section 2593a of this title].

"(b) Reporting on demarches.—

(1) It is the sense of the Congress that the Department of State should, in the course of implementing its reporting responsibilities under section 602(c) of the Nuclear Non-Proliferation Act of 1978 [section 3282(c) of this title], include a summary of demarches that the United States has issued or received from foreign governments with respect to activities which are of significance from the proliferation standpoint.

"(2) For purposes of this section, the term 'demarche' means any official communication by one government to another, by written or oral means, intended by the originating government to express—

"(A) a concern over a past, present, or possible future action or activity of the recipient government, or of a person within the jurisdiction of that government, contributing to the global spread of unsafeguarded special nuclear material or of nuclear explosive devices;

"(B) a request for the recipient government to counter such action or activity; or

"(C) both the concern and request described in subparagraphs (A) and (B).

"Sec. 829. Technical correction [Amended section 2160c of Title 42].

"Sec. 830. Definitions.

"For purposes of this part—

"(1) the term 'foreign person' means—

"(A) an individual who is not a citizen of the United States or an alien admitted for permanent residence to the United States; or

"(B) a corporation, partnership, or other nongovernment entity which is created or organized under the laws of a foreign country or which has its principal place of business outside the United States;

"(2) the term 'goods or technology' means—

"(A) nuclear materials and equipment and sensitive nuclear technology (as such terms are defined in section 4 of the Nuclear Non-Proliferation Act of 1978 [section 3203(c) of this title]), all export items designated by the President pursuant to section 309(c) of the Nuclear Non-Proliferation Act of 1978 [section 2139a(c) of Title 42, The Public Health and Welfare], and all technical assistance requiring authorization under section 57 b. of the Atomic Energy Act of 1954 [section 2077(b) of Title 42], and

"(B) in the case of exports from a country other than the United States, any goods or technology that, if exported from the United States, would be goods or technology described in subparagraph (A);

"(3) the term 'IAEA safeguards' means the safeguards set forth in an agreement between a country and the International Atomic Energy Agency, as authorized by Article III(A)(5) of the Statute of the International Atomic Energy Agency;

"(4) the term 'nuclear explosive device' means any device, whether assembled or disassembled, that is designed to produce an instantaneous release of an amount of nuclear energy from special nuclear material that is greater than the amount of energy that would be released from the detonation of one pound of trinitrotoluene (TNT);

"(5) the term 'non-nuclear-weapon state' means any country which is not a nuclear-weapon state, as defined by Article IX(3) of the Treaty on the Non-Proliferation of Nuclear Weapons, signed at Washington, London, and Moscow on July 1, 1968;

"(6) the term 'special nuclear material' has the meaning given that term in section 11 aa. of the Atomic Energy Act of 1954 (42 U.S.C. 2014aa) [42 U.S.C.A. § 2014(aa)];

"(7) the term 'United States person' means—

"(A) an individual who is a citizen of the United States or an alien admitted for permanent residence to the United States; or

"(B) a corporation, partnership, or other nongovernment entity which is not a foreign person; and

"(8) the term 'unsafeguarded special nuclear material' means special nuclear material which is held in violation of IAEA safeguards or not subject to IAEA safeguards (excluding any quantity of material that could, if it were exported from the United States, be exported under a general license issued by the Nuclear Regulatory Commission).

"Sec. 831. Effective date.

"The provisions of this part, and the amendments made by this part [enacting sections 2799aa, 2799aa-1, and 2799aa-2 of this title, amending sections 262d, 2295a, 2295b, 2375, 2429a-1, 2593a, 2708, 2753, and 2780 of this title, section 635 of Title 12, Banks and Banking, and section 2160c of Title 42, and repealing sections 2429 and 2429a of this title], shall take effect 60 days after the date of the enactment of this Act [Apr. 30, 1974].

"PART C—INTERNATIONAL ATOMIC ENERGY AGENCY [....]

"PART D—TERMINATION

"Sec. 851. Termination upon enactment of next Foreign Relations Act.

"On the date of enactment of the first Foreign Relations Authorization Act that is enacted after the enactment of this Act [Apr. 30, 1994], the provisions of parts A and B of this title [enacting sections 2799a to 2799a-2 of this title, amending sections 262d, 2295a, 2295b, 2375, 2429a-1, 2593a, 2708, 2753, 2780, and 3281 of this title, section 635 of Title 12, Banks and Banking, and section 2160c of Title 42, The Public Health and Welfare, and repealing sections 2429 and 2429a of this title] shall cease to be effective, the amendments made by those parts shall be repealed, and any provision of law repealed by those parts shall be reenacted."

§ 3202. Congressional statement of purpose [....]

Public Law 104-164

104th Congress

An Act

To amend the Foreign Assistance Act of 1961 and the Arms Export Control Act to make improvements to certain defense and security assistance provisions under those Acts, to authorize the transfer of naval vessels to certain foreign countries, and for other purposes. <<NOTE: July 21, 1996 - [H.R. 3121]>>

Be it enacted by the Senate and House of Representatives of the United States of America in Congress assembled,

SEC. 157. REPEAL OF TERMINATION OF PROVISIONS OF THE NUCLEAR PROLIFERATION PREVENTION ACT OF 1994; PRESIDENTIAL DETERMINATIONS.

(a) Repeal.—Part D of the Nuclear Proliferation Prevention Act of 1994 (part D of title VIII of the Foreign Relations Authorization Act, Fiscal Years 1994 and 1995; Public Law 103-236; 108 Stat. 525) <<NOTE: 22 USC 3201 note.>> is hereby repealed.

(b) Judicial Review.—Section 824 of the Nuclear Proliferation Prevention Act of 1994 (22 U.S.C. 3201 note) is amended—

(1) in subsection (c), by striking "in writing after opportunity for a hearing on the record";

(2) by striking subsection (e); and

(3) by redesignating subsections (f) through (k) as subsections (e) through (j), respectively.

E. Eximbank Act

UNITED STATES CODE ANNOTATED

TITLE 12. BANKS AND BANKING

CHAPTER 6A—EXPORT-IMPORT BANK OF THE UNITED STATES

SUBCHAPTER I—GENERAL PROVISIONS

Current through P.L. 104-181, approved 8-6-96

§ 635. Powers and functions of Bank

(a) General banking business; use of mails; publication of documents, reports, contracts, etc.; use of assets and allocated or borrowed money; payment of dividends; medium-term financing; dissemination of information; enhancement of medium-term program [....]

(b) Guarantees, insurance, and extension of credit functions; competitive with Government-supported rates and terms and conditions of foreign exporting countries; survey and report; interest rates; private capital encouragement; national interest determinations; delivery of United States services in international commerce; small business concern encouragement; coverage of losses by Foreign Credit Insurance Association; loans to Union of Soviet Socialist Republics for fossil fuel research, etc.; nuclear safeguards violations resulting in limitations on exports and credits; defense article credit sales to less developed countries; amount outstanding; supplementation of Commodity Credit Corporation programs; limitations on authority of Bank; prohibitions relating to Angola

(1)

(A) It is the policy of the United States [....]

(B) It is further the policy of the United States [....] Only in cases where the President determines that such action would be in the national interest where such action would clearly and importantly advance United States policy in such areas as international terrorism, nuclear proliferation, environmental protection and human rights, should the Export-Import Bank deny applications for credit for nonfinancial or noncommercial considerations. [....]

(2) Prohibition on aid to Marxist-Leninist countries [....]

(3) Except as provided by the fourth sentence of this paragraph, no loan or financial guarantee or general guarantee or insurance facility or combination thereof (i) in an amount which equals or exceeds $100,000,000, or (ii) for the export of technology, fuel, equipment, materials, or goods or services to be used in the construction, alteration, operation, or maintenance of nuclear power, enrichment, reprocessing, research, or heavy water production facilities, shall be finally approved by the Board of Directors of the Bank, unless in each case the Bank has submitted to the Congress with respect to such loan, financial guarantee, or combination thereof, a detailed statement describing and explaining the

transaction, at least 25 days of continuous session of the Congress prior to the date of final approval. For the purpose of the preceding sentence, continuity of a session of the Congress shall be considered as broken only by an adjournment of the Congress sine die, and the days on which either House is not in session because of an adjournment of more than 3 days to a day certain shall be excluded in the computation of the 25 day period referred to in such sentence. Such statement shall contain—

(A) in the case of a loan or financial guarantee—

(i) a brief description of the purposes of the transaction;

(ii) the identity of the party or parties requesting the loan or financial guarantee;

(iii) the nature of the goods or services to be exported and the use for which the goods or services are to be exported; and

(iv) in the case of a general guarantee or insurance facility—

(I) a description of the nature and purpose of the facility;

(II) the total amount of guarantees or insurance; and

(III) the reasons for the facility and its methods of operation; and

(B) a full explanation of the reasons for Bank financing of the transaction, the amount of the loan to be provided by the Bank, the approximate rate and repayment terms at which such loan will be made available and the approximate amount of the financial guarantee.

If the Bank submits a statement to the Congress under this paragraph and either House of Congress is in an adjournment for a period which continues for at least ten days after the date of submission of the statement, then any such loan or guarantee or combination thereof may, subject to the second sentence of this paragraph, be finally approved by the Board of Directors upon the termination of the twenty-five-day period referred to in the first sentence of this paragraph or upon the termination of a thirty-five-calendar-day period (which commences upon the date of submission of the statement), whichever occurs sooner.

(4) The Secretary of State shall report to the appropriate committees of Congress and to the Board of Directors of the Export-Import Bank if the Secretary determines that any country that has agreed to International Atomic Energy Agency nuclear safeguards materially violates, abrogates, or terminates, after October 26, 1977, such safeguards or that any country that has entered into an agreement for cooperation concerning the civil use of nuclear energy with the United States materially violates, abrogates, or terminates, after October 26, 1977, any guarantee or other undertaking to the United States made in such agreement or that any country that is not a nuclear-weapons state (as defined in article IX(3) of the Treaty on the Non-Proliferation of Nuclear Weapons) detonates, after October 26, 1977, a nuclear explosive device (as defined in section 830(4) of the Nuclear Proliferation Prevention Act of 1994), or that any country has willfully aided or abetted any non-nuclear-weapon state (as defined in section 830(5) of that Act) to acquire any such nuclear explosive device or to acquire unsafeguarded special nuclear material (as defined in section 830(8) of that Act).... The Secretary shall specify which country or countries the Secretary has determined to have so acted, and the Board shall not give approval to guarantee, insure, or extend credit, or participate in the extension of credit in support of United States exports to such country unless the President determines that it is in the national interest for the Bank to guarantee, insure, or

extend credit, or participate in the extension of credit in support of United States exports to such country and such determination has been reported to the Congress not less than twenty-five days of continuous session of the Congress prior to the date of such approval. For the purpose of the preceding sentence, continuity of a session of the Congress shall be considered as broken only by an adjournment of the Congress sine die, and the days on which either House is not in session because of an adjournment of more than three days to a day certain shall be excluded in the computation of the twenty-five day period referred to in such sentence.

(5) The Bank shall not guarantee, insure, or extend credit, or participate in the extension of credit in connection with (A) the purchase of any product, technical data, or other information by a national or agency of any nation which engages in armed conflict, declared or otherwise, with the Armed Forces of the United States, (B) the purchase by any nation (or national or agency thereof) of any product, technical data, or other information which is to be used principally by or in any such nation described in clause (A), or (C) the purchase of any liquid metal fast breeder nuclear reactor or any nuclear fuel reprocessing facility. The Bank shall not guarantee, insure, or extend credit, or participate in the extension of credit in connection with the purchase of any product, technical data, or other information by a national or agency of any nation if the President determines that any such transaction would be contrary to the national interest.

NATIONAL DEFENSE AUTHORIZATION ACT FOR FISCAL YEAR 1997

[[Page 110 STAT. 2422]]

Public Law 104-201

104th Congress

SEC. 1303. STRENGTHENING CERTAIN SANCTIONS AGAINST NUCLEAR PROLIFERATION ACTIVITIES.

(a) Sanctions.—Section 2(b)(4) of the Export-Import Bank Act of 1945 (12 U.S.C. 635(b)(4)) is amended to read as follows:

"(4)

(A) <<NOTE: Reports.>> If the Secretary of State determines that—

"(i) any country that has agreed to International Atomic Energy Agency nuclear safeguards materially violates, abrogates, or terminates, after October 26, 1977, such safeguards;

"(ii) any country that has entered into an agreement for cooperation concerning the civil use of nuclear energy with the United States materially violates, abrogates, or terminates, after October 26, 1977, any guarantee or other undertaking to the United States made in such agreement;

"(iii) any country that is not a nuclear-weapon state detonates, after October 26, 1977, a nuclear explosive device;

"(iv) any country willfully aids or abets, after June 29, 1994, any non-nuclear-weapon state to acquire any such nuclear explosive device or to acquire unsafeguarded special nuclear material; or

"(v) any person knowingly aids or abets, after the date of enactment of the National Defense Authorization Act for Fiscal Year 1997, any non-nuclear-weapon state to acquire any such nuclear explosive device or to acquire unsafeguarded special nuclear material, then the Secretary of State shall submit a report to the appropriate committees of the Congress and to the Board of Directors of the Bank stating such determination and identifying each country or person the Secretary determines has so acted.

"(B)

(i) If the Secretary of State makes a determination under subparagraph (A)(v) with respect to a foreign person, the Congress urges the Secretary to initiate consultations immediately with the government with primary jurisdiction over that person with respect to the imposition of the prohibition contained in subparagraph (C).

"(ii) In order that consultations with that government may be pursued, the Board of Directors of the Bank shall delay imposition of the prohibition contained in subparagraph (C) for up to 90 days if the Secretary of State requests the Board to make such delay. Following these consultations, the prohibition contained in subparagraph (C) shall apply immediately unless the Secretary determines and certifies to the Congress that that government has taken specific and effective actions, including appropriate penalties, to terminate the involvement of the foreign person in the activities described in subparagraph (A)(v). The Board of Directors of the Bank shall delay the imposition of the prohibition contained in subparagraph (C) for up to an additional 90 days if the Secretary requests the Board to make such additional delay and if the Secretary determines and certifies to the Congress that that government is in the process of taking the actions described in the preceding sentence.

"(iii) <<NOTE: Reports.>> Not later than 90 days after making a determination under subparagraph (A)(v), the Secretary of State shall submit to the appropriate committees of the Congress a report on the status of consultations with the appropriate government under this subparagraph, and the basis or any determination under clause (ii) that such government has taken specific corrective actions.

"(C) The Board of Directors of the Bank shall not give approval to guarantee, insure, or extend credit, or participate in the extension of credit in support of United States exports to any country, or to or by any person, identified in the report described in subparagraph (A).

"(D) The prohibition in subparagraph (C) shall not apply to approvals to guarantee, insure, or extend credit, or participate in the extension of credit in support of United States exports to a country with respect to which a determination is made under clause (i), (ii), (iii), or (iv) of subparagraph (A) regarding any specific event described in such clause if the President determines and certifies in writing to the Congress not less than 45 days prior to the date of the first approval following the determination that it is in the national interest for the Bank to give such approvals.

"(E) The prohibition in subparagraph (C) shall not apply to approvals to guarantee, insure, or extend credit, or participate in the extension of credit in support of United States exports to or by a person with respect to whom a determination is made under clause (v) of subparagraph (A) regarding any specific event described in such clause if—

"(i) the Secretary of State determines and certifies to the Congress that the appropriate government has taken the corrective actions described in subparagraph (B)(ii); or

"(ii) the President determines and certifies in writing to the Congress not less than 45 days prior to the date of the first approval following the determination that—

"(I) reliable information indicates that—

"(aa) such person has ceased to aid or abet any non-nuclear-weapon state to acquire any nuclear explosive device or to acquire unsafeguarded special nuclear material; and

"(bb) steps have been taken to ensure that the activities described in item (aa) will not resume; or

"(II) the prohibition would have a serious adverse effect on vital United States interests.

"(F) For purposes of this paragraph:

"(i) The term 'country' has the meaning given to 'foreign state' in section 1603(a) of title 28, United States Code.

"(ii) The term 'knowingly' is used within the meaning of the term 'knowing' in section 104(h)(3) of the Foreign Corrupt Practices Act (15 U.S.C. 78dd-2(h)(3)).

"(iii) The term 'person' means a natural person as well as a corporation, business association, partnership, society, trust, any other nongovernmental entity, organization, or group, and any governmental entity operating as a business enterprise, and any successor of any such entity.

"(iv) The term 'nuclear-weapon state' has the meaning given the term in Article IX(3) of the Treaty on the Non-Proliferation of Nuclear Weapons, signed at Washington, London, and Moscow on July 1, 1968.

"(v) The term 'non-nuclear-weapon state' has the meaning given the term in section 830(5) of the Nuclear Proliferation Prevention Act of 1994 (Public Law 103-236; 108 Stat. 521).

"(vi) The term 'nuclear explosive device' has the meaning given the term in section 830(4) of the Nuclear Proliferation Prevention Act of 1994 (Public Law 103-236; 108 Stat. 521).

"(vii) The term 'unsafeguarded special nuclear material' has the meaning given the term in section 830(8) of the Nuclear Proliferation Prevention Act of 1994."

(b) Recommendations To Make Nonproliferation Laws More Effective.—

Not <<NOTE: President.>> later than 180 days after the date of the enactment of this Act, the President shall submit to the Congress his recommendations on ways to make the laws of the United States more effective in controlling and preventing the proliferation of weapons of mass destruction and missiles.

The report shall identify all sources of Government funds used for such nonproliferation activities.

F. China Certification Requirements

1. 1985

S.J.R.238 As finally approved by the House and Senate (Enrolled)

Ninety-ninth Congress of the United States of America

AT THE FIRST SESSION

Begun and held at the City of Washington on Thursday, the third day of January, one thousand nine hundred and eighty-five

Joint Resolution

Relating to the approval and implementation of the proposed agreement for nuclear cooperation between the United States and the People's Republic of China.

===============================

Resolved by the Senate and House of Representatives of the United States of America in Congress assembled, That

(a)

(1) the Congress does favor the Agreement for Cooperation Between the Government of the United States of America and the Government of the People's Republic of China Concerning Peaceful Uses of Nuclear Energy, done on July 23, 1985 (hereafter in this joint resolution referred to as the "Agreement").

(2) Notwithstanding section 123 of the Atomic Energy Act of 1954, the Agreement becomes effective in accordance with the provisions of this joint resolution and other applicable provisions of law.

(b) Notwithstanding any other provision of law or any international agreement, no license may be issued for export to the People's Republic of China of any nuclear material, facilities, or components subject to the Agreement, and no approval for the transfer or retransfer to the People's Republic of China of any nuclear material, facilities, or components subject to the Agreement shall be given—

(1) until the expiration of a period of thirty days of continuous session of Congress after the President has certified to the Congress that—

(A) the reciprocal arrangements made pursuant to Article 8 of the Agreement have been designed to be effective in ensuring that any nuclear material, facilities, or components provided under the Agreement shall be utilized solely for intended peaceful purposes as set forth in the Agreement;

(B) the Government of the People's Republic of China has provided additional information concerning its nuclear nonproliferation policies and that, based on this and all other information available to the United States Government, the People's Republic of China is not in violation of paragraph (2) of section 129 of the Atomic Energy Act of 1954; and

(C) the obligation to consider favorably a request to carry out activities described in Article 5(2) of the Agreement shall not prejudice the decision of the

United States to approve or disapprove such a request; and

(2) until the President has submitted to the Speaker of the House of Representatives and the chairman of the Committee on Foreign Relations of the Senate a report detailing the history and current developments in the nonproliferation policies and practices of the People's Republic of China.

The report described in paragraph (2) shall be submitted in unclassified form with a classified addendum.

(c) Each proposed export pursuant to the Agreement shall be subject to United States laws and regulations in effect at the time of each such export.

(d) Nothing in the Agreement or this joint resolution may be construed as providing a precedent or other basis for the negotiation or renegotiation of any other agreement for nuclear cooperation.

(e) For purposes of subsection (b)—

(1) the continuity of a session of Congress is broken only by adjournment of the Congress sine die at the end of a Congress; and

(2) the days on which either House is not in session because of an adjournment of more than three days to a day certain are excluded in the computation of the period indicated.

2. 1990

UNITED STATES CODE ANNOTATED

TITLE 22. FOREIGN RELATIONS AND INTERCOURSE

CHAPTER 32—FOREIGN ASSISTANCE

SUBCHAPTER I—INTERNATIONAL DEVELOPMENT

PART I—DECLARATION OF POLICY; DEVELOPMENT ASSISTANCE AUTHORIZATIONS

Current through P.L. 104-160, approved 7-9-96

§ 2151. Congressional findings and declaration of policy [....]

HISTORICAL AND STATUTORY NOTES

Suspension of Certain Programs and Activities Relating to the People's Republic of China

Pub.L. 101-246, Title IX, § 902, Feb. 16, 1990, 104 Stat. 83, as amended by Pub.L. 102-549, Title II, § 202(e), Oct. 28, 1992, 106 Stat. 3658, provided that:

"(a) Suspensions.—

"(1) Overseas private investment corporation.—The Overseas Private Investment Corporation shall continue to suspend the issuance of any new insurance, reinsurance, guarantees, financing, or other financial support with respect to the People's Republic of China, unless the President makes a report under subsection (b)(1) or (2) of this section.

"(2) Trade and Development Agency.—The President shall suspend the obligation of funds under the Foreign Assistance Act of 1961 [this chapter] for any new activities of the Trade and Development Agency with respect to the People's Republic of China, unless the President makes a report under subsection (b)(1) or (2) of this section.

"(3) Munitions export licenses.—

(A) The issuance of licenses under section 38 of the Arms Export Control Act [section 2778 of this title] for the export to the People's Republic of China of any defense article on the United States Munitions List, including helicopters and helicopter parts, shall continue to be suspended, subject to subparagraph (B), unless the President makes a report under subsection (b)(1) or (2) of this section.

"(B) The suspension set forth in subparagraph (A) shall not apply to systems and components designed specifically for inclusion in civil products and controlled as defense articles only for purposes of export to a controlled country, unless the President determines that the intended recipient of such items is the military or security forces of the People's Republic of China.

"(4) Crime control and detection instruments and equipment.—The issuance of any license under section 6(k) of the Export Administration Act of 1979 [section 2405(k) of the Appendix to Title 50, War and National Defense] for the export to the People's Republic of China of any crime control or detection instruments or equipment shall be suspended, unless the President makes a report under subsection (b)(1) or (2) of this section.

"(5) Export of satellites for launch by the People's Republic of China.—Exports of any satellite of United States origin that is intended for launch from a launch vehicle owned by the People's Republic of China shall remain suspended, unless the President makes a report under subsection (b)(1) or (2) of this section.

"(6) Nuclear cooperation with the People's Republic of China.—

(A) Any—

"(i) application for a license under the Export Administration Act of 1979 [section 2401 et seq. of the Appendix to Title 50] for the export to the People's Republic of China for use in a nuclear production or utilization facility of any goods or technology which, as determined under section 309(c) of the Nuclear Non-Proliferation Act of 1978 [section 2139a(c) of Title 42, The Public Health and Welfare], could be of significance for nuclear explosive purposes, or which, in the judgment of the President, is likely to be diverted for use in such a facility, for any nuclear explosive device, or for research on or development of any nuclear explosive device, shall be suspended,

"(ii) application for a license for the export to the People's Republic of China of any nuclear material, facilities, or components subject to the Agreement shall be suspended,

"(iii) approval for the transfer or retransfer to the People's Republic of China of any nuclear material, facilities, or components subject to the Agreement shall not be given, and

"(iv) specific authorization for assistance in any activities with respect to the People's Republic of China relating to the use of nuclear energy under section 57b.(2) of the Atomic Energy Act of 1954 [section 2077(b)(2) of Title 42] shall not be given,

until the conditions specified in subparagraph (B) are met.

"(B) Subparagraph (A) applies until—

"(i) the President certifies to the Congress that the People's Republic of China has provided clear and unequivocal assurances to the United States that it is not assisting and will not assist any nonnuclear-weapon state, either directly or indirectly, in acquiring nuclear explosive devices or the materials and components for such devices;

"(ii) the President makes the certifications and submits the report required by Public Law 99-183 [Pub.L. 99-183, Dec. 16, 1985, 99 Stat. 1174]; and

"(iii) the President makes a report under subsection (b)(1) or (2) of this section.

"(C) For purposes of this paragraph, the term 'Agreement' means the Agreement for Cooperation Between the Government of the United States of America and the Government of the People's Republic of China Concerning Peaceful Uses of Nuclear Energy (done on July 23, 1985).

"(7) Liberalization of export controls.—

(A) The President shall negotiate with the governments participating in the group known as the Coordinating Committee (COCOM) to suspend, on a multilateral basis, any liberalization by the Coordinating Committee of controls on exports of goods and technology to the People's Republic of China under section 5 of the Export Administration Act of 1979 [section 2404 of the Appendix to Title 50], including—

"(i) the implementation of bulk licenses for exports to the People's Republic of China; and

"(ii) the raising of the performance levels of goods or technology below which no authority or permission to export to the People's Republic of China would be required.

"(B) The President shall oppose any liberalization by the Coordinating Committee of controls which is described in subparagraph (A)(ii), until the end of the 6-month period beginning on the date of enactment of this Act [Feb. 16, 1990] or until the President makes a report under subsection (b)(1) or (2) of this section, whichever occurs first.

"(b) Termination of suspensions.—A report referred to in subsection (a) is a report by the President to the Congress either—

"(1) that the Government of the People's Republic of China has made progress on a program of political reform throughout the country, including Tibet, which includes—

"(A) lifting of martial law;

"(B) halting of executions and other reprisals against individuals for the nonviolent expression of their political beliefs;

"(C) release of political prisoners;

"(D) increased respect for internationally recognized human rights, including freedom of expression, the press, assembly, and association; and

"(E) permitting a freer flow of information, including an end to the jamming of Voice of America and greater access for foreign journalists; or

"(2) that it is in the national interest of the United States to terminate a suspension under subsection (a)(1), (2), (3), (4), or (5), to terminate a suspension or disapproval under subsection (a)(6), or to terminate the opposition required by subsection (a)(7), as the case may be.

"(c) Reporting Requirement.—Sixty days after the date of enactment of this Act [Feb. 16, 1990], the President shall submit to the Congress a report on—

"(1) any steps taken by the Government of China to achieve the objectives described in subsection (b)(1);

"(2) the effect of multilateral sanctions on political and economic developments in China and on China's international economic relations;

"(3) the impact of the President's actions described in section 901(a)(9) [section 901(a)(9) of Pub.L. 101-246] and of the suspensions under subsection (a) of this section on—

"(A) political and economic developments in China;

"(B) the standard of living of the Chinese people;

"(C) relations between the United States and China; and

"(D) the actions taken by China to promote a settlement in Cambodia which will ensure Cambodian independence, facilitate an act of self-determination by the Cambodian people, and prevent the Khmer Rouge from returning to exclusive power;

"(4) the status of programs and activities suspended under subsection (a); and

"(5) the additional measures taken by the President under section 901(c) [section 901(c) of Pub.L. 101-246] if repression in China deepens."

G. Pakistan Provisions

UNITED STATES CODE ANNOTATED

TITLE 22. FOREIGN RELATIONS AND INTERCOURSE

CHAPTER 32—FOREIGN ASSISTANCE

SUBCHAPTER III—GENERAL AND ADMINISTRATIVE PROVISIONS

PART I—GENERAL PROVISIONS

Current through P.L. 104-160, approved 7-9-96

§ 2375. Assistance to Pakistan

(a) Congressional policy, findings, and goals

The Congress recognizes that Soviet forces occupying Afghanistan pose a security threat to Pakistan. The Congress also recognizes that an independent and democratic Pakistan with continued friendly ties with the United States is in the interest of both nations. The Congress finds that United States assistance will help Pakistan maintain its independence. Assistance to Pakistan is intended to benefit the people of Pakistan by helping them meet the burdens imposed by the presence of Soviet forces in Afghanistan and by promoting economic development. In authorizing assistance to Pakistan, it is the intent of Congress to promote the expeditious restoration of full civil liberties and representative government in Pakistan. The Congress further recognizes that it is in the mutual interest of Pakistan and the United States to avoid the profoundly destabilizing effects of the proliferation of nuclear explosive devices or the capacity to manufacture or otherwise acquire nuclear devices.

(b) Reaffirmation of 1959 bilateral agreement

The United States reaffirms the commitment made in its 1959 bilateral agreement with Pakistan relating to aggression from a Communist or Communist-dominated state.

(c) Availability; defensive aspects of assistance

Security assistance for Pakistan shall be made available in order to assist Pakistan in dealing with the threat to its security posed by the Soviet presence in Afghanistan. The United States will take appropriate steps to ensure that defense articles provided by the United States to Pakistan are used for defensive purposes.

(d) Waiver of limitations respecting nuclear transfers

The President may waive the prohibitions of section 2799aa of this title with respect to any grounds for the prohibition of assistance under that section arising before the effective date of part B of the Nuclear Proliferation Prevention Act of 1994 to provide assistance to Pakistan if he determines that to do so is in the national interest of the United States.

(e) Nuclear non-proliferation conditions on military assistance; exception

(1) No military assistance shall be furnished to Pakistan and no military equipment or technology shall be sold or transferred to Pakistan, pursuant to the authorities contained in this chapter or any other Act, unless the President shall have certified in writing to the Speaker of the House of Representatives and the chairman of the Committee on Foreign Relations of the Senate, during the fiscal year in which military assistance is to be furnished or military equipment or technology is to be sold or transferred, that Pakistan does not possess a nuclear explosive device and that the proposed United States military assistance program will reduce significantly the risk that Pakistan will possess a nuclear explosive device.

(2) The prohibitions in this section do not apply to any assistance or transfer provided for the purposes of:

(A) International narcotics control (including part VIII of subchapter I of this chapter) or any provision of law available for providing assistance for counternarcotics purposes.

(B) Facilitating military-to-military contact, training (including part V of subchapter II of this chapter) and humanitarian and civic assistance projects.

(C) Peacekeeping and other multilateral operations (including part VI of subchapter II of this chapter relating to peacekeeping) or any provision of law available for providing assistance for peacekeeping purposes, except that lethal military equipment provided under this subparagraph shall be provided on a lease or loan basis only and shall be returned upon completion of the operation for which it was provided.

(D) Antiterrorism assistance (including part VIII of subchapter II of this chapter relating to antiterrorism assistance) or any provision of law available for antiterrorism assistance purposes.

(3) The restrictions of this subsection shall continue to apply to contracts for the delivery of F-16 aircraft to Pakistan.

(4) Notwithstanding the restrictions contained in this subsection, military equipment, technology, or defense services, other than F-16 aircraft, may be transferred to Pakistan pursuant to contracts or cases entered into before October 1, 1990.

(f) Storage costs

The President may release the Government of Pakistan of its contractual obligation to pay the United States Government for the storage costs of items purchased prior to October 1, 1990, but not delivered by the United States Government pursuant to subsection (e) of this section and may reimburse the Government of Pakistan for any such amount paid, on such terms and conditions as the President may prescribe: Provided, That such payments have no budgetary impact.

(g) Inapplicability of restrictions to previously owned items

Subsection (e) of this section does not apply to broken, worn or unupgraded items or their equivalent which Pakistan paid for and took possession of prior to October 1, 1990 and which the Government of Pakistan sent to the United States for repair or upgrade. Such equipment or its equivalent may be returned to the Government of Pakistan: Provided, That the President determines and so certifies to the appropriate congressional committees that such equipment or equivalent neither constitutes nor has received any significant qualitative upgrade since being transferred to the United States and that its total value does not exceed $25,000,000.

(h) Ballistic missile sanctions not affected

Nothing contained herein shall affect sanctions for transfers of missile equipment or technology required under section 2410b of the Appendix to Title 50 or section 2797b of this title.

REPEAL OF 1994 AMENDMENT

<Pub.L. 103-236, Title VIII, § 851, Apr. 30, 1994, 108 Stat. 525, provided that the amendment of this section by section 822(b)(2) of Pub.L. 103-236 shall cease to be effective on the date of enactment of the first Foreign Relations Authorization Act enacted after April 30, 1994, and that on the date of enactment of such Foreign Relations Authorization Act the amendment of this section by section 822(b)(2) of Pub.L. 103-236 shall be repealed. >

DETERMINATION OF PRESIDENT NO. 90-15

< Mar. 28, 1990, 55 F.R. 17417 >

SECURITY ASSISTANCE FOR PAKISTAN

By the authority vested in me as President by the Constitution and laws of the United States of America, including section 620E(d) of the Foreign Assistance Act of 1961, as amended ("the Act") (22 U.S.C. 2375(d)) [subsec. (d) of this section], I hereby determine, pursuant to section 620E(d) of the Act, that provision of assistance to Pakistan under the Act through April 1, 1991 [subsec. (d) of this section], is in the national interest of the United States, and therefore waive the prohibitions of section 669 of the Act (22 U.S.C. 2429) [section 2429 of this title] with respect to that period.

You are authorized and directed to transmit this determination, together with the statement setting forth specific reasons therefor, to the Congress immediately.

This determination shall be published in the Federal Register.

GEORGE BUSH

DETERMINATION OF PRESIDENT NO. 90-1

< Oct. 5, 1989, 54 F.R. 43797 >

SECURITY ASSISTANCE FOR PAKISTAN

Pursuant to Section 620E(e) of the Foreign Assistance Act of 1961, as amended, 22 U.S.C. 2375(e) [subsec. (e) of this section], I hereby certify that Pakistan does not possess a nuclear explosive device and that the proposed United States assistance program will reduce significantly the risk that Pakistan will possess a nuclear explosive device.

You are authorized and directed to publish this determination and certification in the Federal Register.

GEORGE BUSH

Prior determinations and certifications were contained in the following:

Determination of the President of the United States, No. 89-7, Nov. 18, 1988, 53 F.R. 49111.

Determination of the President of the United States, No. 88-5, Jan. 15, 1988, 53 F.R. 3325.

Determination of the President of the United States, No. 88-4, Dec. 17, 1987, 53 F.R. 773.

Determination of the President of the United States, No. 87-3, Oct. 27, 1986, 51 F.R. 40301.

Determination of the President of the United States, No. 86-03, Nov. 25, 1985, 50 F.R. 50273.

Determination of the President of the United States, No. 82-7, Feb. 10, 1982, 47 F.R. 9803.

A-III. Missile Nonproliferation

A. (AECA) Missile Technology Controls Provisions of the Arms Export Control Act

UNITED STATES CODE ANNOTATED

TITLE 22. FOREIGN RELATIONS AND INTERCOURSE

CHAPTER 39—ARMS EXPORT CONTROL

SUBCHAPTER VII—CONTROL OF MISSILES AND MISSILE EQUIPMENT OR TECHNOLOGY

Current through P.L. 104-160, approved 7-9-96

§ 2797. Licensing [....]

§ 2797a. Denial of the transfer of missile equipment or technology by United States persons [....]

§ 2797b. Transfers of missile equipment or technology by foreign persons

(a) Sanctions

(1) Subject to subsections (c) through (g) of this section, if the President determines that a foreign person, after Nov. 5, 1990, knowingly—

(A) exports, transfers, or otherwise engages in the trade of any MTCR equipment or technology that contributes to the acquisition, design, development, or production of missiles in a country that is not an MTCR adherent and would be, if it were United States-origin equipment or technology, subject to the jurisdiction of the United States under this chapter.

(B) conspires to or attempts to engage in such export, transfer, or trade, or

(C) facilitates such export, transfer, or trade by any other person,

or if the President has made a determination with respect to a foreign person under section 2410b(b)(1) of Appendix to Title 50, then the President shall impose on that foreign person the applicable sanctions under paragraph (2).

(2) The sanctions which apply to a foreign person under paragraph (1) are the following:

(A) If the item involved in the export, transfer, or trade is within category II of the MTCR Annex, then the President shall deny, for a period of 2 years—

(i) United States Government contracts relating to missile equipment or technology; and

(ii) licenses for the transfer to such foreign person of missile equipment or technology controlled under this chapter.

(B) If the item involved in the export, transfer, or trade is within category I of the MTCR Annex, then the President shall deny, for a period of not less than 2 years—

(i) all United States Government contracts with such foreign person; and

(ii) licenses for the transfer to such foreign person of all items on the United States Munitions List.

(C) If, in addition to actions taken under subparagraphs (A) and (B), the President determines that the export, transfer, or trade has substantially contributed to the design, development, or production of missiles in a country that is not an MTCR adherent, then the President shall prohibit, for a period of not less than 2 years, the importation into the United States of products produced by that foreign person.

(b) In applicability with respect to MTCR adherents

Subsection (a) of this section does not apply with respect to—

(1) any export, transfer, or trading activity that is authorized by the laws of an MTCR adherent, if such authorization is not obtained by misrepresentation or fraud; or

(2) any export, transfer, or trade of an item to an end user in a country that is an MTCR adherent.

(c) Effect of enforcement actions by MTCR adherents

Sanctions set forth in subsection (a) of this section may not be imposed under this section on a person with respect to acts described in such subsection or, if such sanctions are in effect against a person on account of such acts, such sanctions shall be terminated, if an MTCR adherent is taking judicial or other enforcement action against that person with respect to such acts, or that person has been found by the government of an MTCR adherent to be innocent of wrongdoing with respect to such acts.

(d) Advisory opinions

The Secretary of State, in consultation with the Secretary of Defense, the Secretary of Commerce, and the Director of the United States Arms Control and Disarmament Agency, may, upon the request of any person, issue an advisory opinion to that person as to whether a proposed activity by that person would subject that person to sanctions under this section. Any person who relies in good faith on such an advisory opinion which states that the proposed activity would not subject a person to such sanctions, and any person who thereafter engages in such activity, may not be made subject to such sanctions on account of such activity.

(e) Waiver and report to Congress

(1) In any case other than one in which an advisory opinion has been issued under subsection (d) of this section stating that a proposed activity would not subject a person to sanctions under this section, the President may waive the application of subsection (a) of this section to a foreign person if the President determines that such

waiver is essential to the national security of the United States.

(2) In the event that the President decides to apply the waiver described in paragraph (1), the President shall so notify the Committee on Armed Services and the Committee on Foreign Relations of the Senate and the Committee on National Security and the Committee on International Relations of the House of Representatives not less than 45 working days before issuing the waiver. Such notification shall include a report fully articulating the rationale and circumstances which led the President to apply the waiver.

(f) Presumption

In determining whether to apply sanctions under subsection (a) of this section to a foreign person involved in the export, transfer, or trade of an item on the MTCR Annex, it should be a rebuttable presumption that such item is designed for use in a missile listed in the MTCR Annex if the President determines that the final destination of the item is a country the government of which the Secretary of State has determined, for purposes of section 2405(j)(1)(A) of the Appendix to Title 50, has repeatedly provided support for acts of international terrorism.

(g) Additional waiver

The President may waive the imposition of sanctions under paragraph (1) on a person with respect to a product or service if the President certifies to the Congress that—

(1) the product or service is essential to the national security of the United States; and

(2) such person is a sole source supplier of the product or service, the product or service is not available from any alternative reliable supplier, and the need for the product or service cannot be met in a timely manner by improved manufacturing processes or technological developments.

(h) Exceptions

The President shall not apply the sanction under this section prohibiting the importation of the products of a foreign person—

(1) in the case of procurement of defense articles or defense services—

(A) under existing contracts or subcontracts, including the exercise of options for production quantities to satisfy requirements essential to the national security of the United States;

(B) if the President determines that the person to which the sanctions would be applied is a sole source supplier of the defense articles and services, that the defense articles or services are essential to the national security of the United States, and that alternative sources are not readily or reasonably available; or

(C) if the President determines that such articles or services are essential to the national security of the United States under defense coproduction agreements or NATO Programs of Cooperation;

(2) to products or services provided under contracts entered into before the date on which the President publishes his intention to impose the sanctions; or

(3) to—

(A) spare parts,

(B) component parts, but not finished products, essential to United States products or production,

(C) routine services and maintenance of products, to the extent that alternative sources are not readily or reasonably available, or

(D) information and technology essential to United States products or production.

§ 2797b-1. Notification of admittance of MTCR adherents

Following any action by the United States that results in a country becoming a MTCR adherent, the President shall transmit promptly to the Congress a report which describes the rationale for such action, together with an assessment of that country's nonproliferation policies, practices, and commitments. Such report shall also include the text of any agreements or understandings between the United States and such country regarding the terms and conditions of the country's adherence to the MTCR.

§ 2797c. Definitions

For purposes of this chapter—

(1) the term "missile" means a category I system as defined in the MTCR Annex, and any other unmanned delivery system of similar capability, as well as the specially designed production facilities for these systems;

(2) the term "Missile Technology Control Regime" or "MTCR" means the policy statement, between the United States, the United Kingdom, the Federal Republic of Germany, France, Italy, Canada, and Japan, announced on April 16, 1987, to restrict sensitive missile-relevant transfers based on the MTCR Annex, and any amendments thereto;

(3) the term "MTCR adherent" means a country that participates in the MTCR or that, pursuant to an international understanding to which the United States is a party, controls MTCR equipment or technology in accordance with the criteria and standards set forth in the MTCR;

(4) the term "MTCR Annex" means the Guidelines and Equipment and Technology Annex of the MTCR, and any amendments thereto;

(5) the terms "missile equipment or technology" and "MTCR equipment or technology" means those items listed in category I or category II of the MTCR Annex;

(6) the term "United States person" has the meaning given that term in section 2415(2) of Appendix to Title 50;

(7) the term "foreign person" means any person other than a United States person;

(8)

(A) the term "person" means a natural person as well as a corporation, business association, partnership, society, trust, any other nongovernmental entity, organization, or group, and any governmental entity operating as a business enterprise, and any successor of any such entity; and

(B) in the case of countries with non-market economies (excluding former members of the Warsaw Pact), the term "person" means—

(i) all activities of that government relating to the development or production of any missile equipment or technology; and

(ii) all activities of that government affecting the development or production of electronics, space systems or equipment, and military aircraft; and

(9) the term "otherwise engaged in the trade of" means, with respect to a particular export or transfer, to be a freight forwarder or designated exporting agent, or a consignee or end user of the item to be exported or transferred.

B. (EAA) Missile Technology Controls Provisions of the Export Administration Act

TITLE 50, APPENDIX—WAR AND NATIONAL DEFENSE

EXPORT REGULATION

Sec. 2410b. Missile proliferation control violations

(a) Violations by United States persons [....]

(b) Transfers of missile equipment or technology by foreign persons

(1) Sanctions

(A) Subject to paragraphs (3) through (7), if the President determines that a foreign person, after the date of the enactment of this section [Nov. 5, 1990], knowingly—

(i) exports, transfers, or otherwise engages in the trade of any MTCR equipment or technology that contributes to the design, development, or production of missiles in a country that is not an MTCR adherent and would be, if it were United States-origin equipment or technology, subject to the jurisdiction of the United States under this Act [sections 2401 to 2420 of this Appendix],

(ii) conspires to or attempts to engage in such export, transfer, or trade, or

(iii) facilitates such export, transfer, or trade by any other person,

or if the President has made a determination with respect to a foreign person under section 73(a) of the Arms Export Control Act [22 U.S.C. 2797b(a)], then the President shall impose on that foreign person the applicable sanctions under subparagraph (B).

(B) The sanctions which apply to a foreign person under subparagraph (A) are the following:

(i) If the item involved in the export, transfer, or trade is within category II of the MTCR Annex, then the President shall deny, for a period of 2 years, licenses for the transfer to such foreign person of missile equipment or technology the export of which is controlled under this Act [sections 2401 to 2420 of this Appendix].

(ii) If the item involved in the export, transfer, or trade is within category I of the MTCR Annex, then the President shall deny, for a period of not less than 2 years, licenses for the transfer to such foreign person of items the export of which is controlled under this Act [sections 2401 to 2420 of this Appendix].

(iii) If, in addition to actions taken under clauses (i) and (ii), the President determines that the export, transfer, or trade has substantially contributed to the design, development, or production of missiles in a country that is not an MTCR adherent, then the President shall prohibit, for a period of not less than 2 years, the importation into the United States of products produced by that foreign person.

(2) Inapplicability with respect to MTCR adherents

Paragraph (1) does not apply with respect to—

(A) any export, transfer, or trading activity that is authorized by the laws of an MTCR adherent, if such authorization is not obtained by misrepresentation or fraud; or

(B) any export, transfer, or trade of an item to an end user in a country that is an MTCR adherent.

(3) Effect of enforcement actions by MTCR adherents

Sanctions set forth in paragraph (1) may not be imposed under this subsection on a person with respect to acts described in such paragraph or, if such sanctions are in effect against a person on account of such acts, such sanctions shall be terminated, if an MTCR adherent is taking judicial or other enforcement action against that person with respect to such acts, or that person has been found by the government of an MTCR adherent to be innocent of wrongdoing with respect to such acts.

(4) Advisory opinions

The Secretary, in consultation with the Secretary of State and the Secretary of Defense, may, upon the request of any person, issue an advisory opinion to that person as to whether a proposed activity by that person would subject that person to sanctions under this subsection. Any person who relies in good faith on such an advisory opinion which states that the proposed activity would not subject a person to such sanctions, and any person who thereafter engages in such activity, may not be made subject to such sanctions on account of such activity.

(5) Waiver and report to Congress

(A) In any case other than one in which an advisory opinion has been issued under paragraph (4) stating that a proposed activity would not subject a person to sanctions under this subsection, the President may waive the application of paragraph (1) to a foreign person if the President determines that such waiver is essential to the national security of the United States.

(B) In the event that the President decides to apply the waiver described in subparagraph (A), the President shall so notify the Congress not less than 20 working days before issuing the waiver. Such notification shall include a report fully articulating the rationale and circumstances which led the President to apply the waiver.

(6) Additional waiver

The President may waive the imposition of sanctions under paragraph (1) on a person with respect to a product or service if the President certifies to the Congress that—

(A) the product or service is essential to the national security of the United States; and

(B) such person is a sole source supplier of the product or service, the product or service is not available from any alternative reliable supplier, and the need for the product or service cannot be met in a timely manner by improved manufacturing processes or technological developments.

(7) Exceptions

The President shall not apply the sanction under this subsection prohibiting the importation of the products of a foreign person—

(A) in the case of procurement of defense articles or defense services—

(i) under existing contracts or subcontracts, including the exercise of options for production quantities to satisfy requirements essential to the national security of the United States;

(ii) if the President determines that the person to which the sanctions would be applied is a sole source supplier of the defense articles and services, that the defense articles or services are essential to the national security of the United States, and that alternative sources are not readily or reasonably available; or

(iii) if the President determines that such articles or services are essential to the national security of the United States under defense coproduction agreements or NATO Programs of Cooperation;

(B) to products or services provided under contracts entered into before the date on which the President publishes his intention to impose the sanctions; or

(C) to—

(i) spare parts,

(ii) component parts, but not finished products, essential to United States products or production,

(iii) routine services and maintenance of products, to the extent that alternative sources are not readily or reasonably available, or

(iv) information and technology essential to United States products or production.

(c) Definitions

For purposes of this section and subsections (k) and (l) of section 6 [section 2405(k) and (l) of this Appendix]—

(1) the term "missile" means a category I system as defined in the MTCR Annex, and any other unmanned delivery system of similar capability, as well as the specially designed production facilities for these systems;

(2) the term "Missile Technology Control Regime" or "MTCR" means the policy statement, between the United States, the United Kingdom, the Federal Republic of Germany, France, Italy, Canada, and Japan, announced on April 16, 1987, to restrict sensitive missile-relevant transfers based on the MTCR Annex, and any amendments thereto;

(3) the term "MTCR adherent" means a country that participates in the MTCR or that, pursuant to an international understanding to which the United States is a party, controls MTCR equipment or technology in accordance with the criteria and standards set forth in the MTCR;

(4) the term "MTCR Annex" means the Guidelines and Equipment and Technology Annex of the MTCR, and any amendments thereto;

(5) the terms "missile equipment or technology" and "MTCR equipment or technology" mean those items listed in category I or category II of the MTCR Annex;

(6) the term "foreign person" means any person other than a United States person;

(7)

(A) the term "person" means a natural person as well as a corporation, business association, partnership, society, trust, any other nongovernmental entity, organization, or group, and any governmental entity operating as a business enterprise, and any successor of any such entity; and

(B) in the case of countries where it may be impossible to identify a specific governmental entity referred to in subparagraph (A), the term "person" means—

(i) all activities of that government relating to the development or production of any missile equipment or technology; and

(ii) all activities of that government affecting the development or production of aircraft, electronics, and space systems or equipment; and

(8) the term "otherwise engaged in the trade of" means, with respect to a particular export or transfer, to be a freight forwarder or designated exporting agent, or a consignee or end user of the item to be exported or transferred.

A-IV. CHEMICAL AND BIOLOGICAL WEAPONS NONPROLIFERATION

A. (AECA) Chemical and Biological Weapons Transfer Provisions of the Arms Export Control Act

[Laws in effect as of January 16, 1996]

[Document not affected by Public Laws enacted between

January 16, 1996, and August 28, 1996]

[CITE: 22USC2798]

TITLE 22—FOREIGN RELATIONS AND INTERCOURSE

CHAPTER 39—ARMS EXPORT CONTROL

SUBCHAPTER VIII—CHEMICAL OR BIOLOGICAL WEAPONS PROLIFERATION

Sec. 2798. Sanctions against certain foreign persons

(a) Imposition of sanctions

(1) Determination by the President

Except as provided in subsection (b)(2) of this section, the President shall impose both of the sanctions described in subsection (c) of this section if the President determines that a foreign person, on or after October 28, 1991, has knowingly and materially contributed—

(A) through the export from the United States of any goods or technology that are subject to the jurisdiction of the United States,

(B) through the export from any other country of any goods or technology that would be, if they were

United States goods or technology, subject to the jurisdiction of the United States, or

(C) through any other transaction not subject to sanctions pursuant to the Export Administration Act of 1979 [50 App. U.S.C. 2401 et seq.],

to the efforts by any foreign country, project, or entity described in paragraph (2) to use, develop, produce, stockpile, or otherwise acquire chemical or biological weapons.

(2) Countries, projects, or entities receiving assistance

Paragraph (1) applies in the case of—

(A) any foreign country that the President determines has, at any time after January 1, 1980—

(i) used chemical or biological weapons in violation of international law;

(ii) used lethal chemical or biological weapons against its own nationals; or

(iii) made substantial preparations to engage in the activities described in clause (i) or (ii);

(B) any foreign country whose government is determined for purposes of section 6(j) of the Export Administration Act of 1979 [50 App. U.S.C. 2405(j)] to be a government that has repeatedly provided support for acts of international terrorism; or

(C) any other foreign country, project, or entity designated by the President for purposes of this section.

(3) Persons against whom sanctions are to be imposed

Sanctions shall be imposed pursuant to paragraph (1) on—

(A) the foreign person with respect to which the President makes the determination described in that paragraph;

(B) any successor entity to that foreign person;

(C) any foreign person that is a parent or subsidiary of that foreign person if that parent or subsidiary knowingly assisted in the activities which were the basis of that determination; and

(D) any foreign person that is an affiliate of that foreign person if that affiliate knowingly assisted in the activities which were the basis of that determination and if that affiliate is controlled in fact by that foreign person.

(b) Consultations with and actions by foreign government of jurisdiction

(1) Consultations

If the President makes the determinations described in subsection (a)(1) of this section with respect to a foreign person, the Congress urges the President to initiate consultations immediately with the government with primary jurisdiction over that foreign person with respect to the imposition of sanctions pursuant to this section.

(2) Actions by government of jurisdiction

In order to pursue such consultations with that government, the President may delay imposition of sanctions pursuant to this section for a period of up to 90 days. Following these consultations, the President shall impose sanctions unless the President determines and certifies to the Congress that that government has taken specific and effective actions, including appropriate penalties, to terminate the involvement of the foreign person in the activities described in subsection (a)(1) of this section. The President may delay imposition of sanctions for an additional period of up to 90 days if the President determines and certifies to the Congress that that government is in the process of taking the actions described in the preceding sentence.

(3) Report to Congress

The President shall report to the Congress, not later than 90 days after making a determination under subsection (a)(1) of this section, on the status of consultations with the appropriate government under this subsection, and the basis for any determination under paragraph (2) of this subsection that such government has taken specific corrective actions.

(c) Sanctions

(1) Description of sanctions

The sanctions to be imposed pursuant to subsection (a)(1) of this section are, except as provided in paragraph (2) of this subsection, the following:

(A) Procurement sanction

The United States Government shall not procure, or enter into any contract for the procurement of, any goods or services from any person described in subsection (a)(3) of this section.

(B) Import sanctions

The importation into the United States of products produced by any person described in subsection (a)(3) of this section shall be prohibited.

(2) Exceptions

The President shall not be required to apply or maintain sanctions under this section—

(A) in the case of procurement of defense articles or defense services—

(i) under existing contracts or subcontracts, including the exercise of options for production quantities to satisfy United States operational military requirements;

(ii) if the President determines that the person or other entity to which the sanctions would otherwise be applied is a sole source supplier of the defense articles or services, that the defense articles or services are essential, and that alternative sources are not readily or reasonably available; or

(iii) if the President determines that such articles or services are essential to the national security under defense coproduction agreements;

(B) to products or services provided under contracts entered into before the date on which the President publishes his intention to impose sanctions;

(C) to—

(i) spare parts,

(ii) component parts, but not finished products, essential to United States products or production, or

(iii) routine servicing and maintenance of products, to the extent that alternative sources are not readily or reasonably available;

(D) to information and technology essential to United States products or production; or

(E) to medical or other humanitarian items.

(d) Termination of sanctions

The sanctions imposed pursuant to this section shall apply for a period of at least 12 months following the imposition of sanctions and shall cease to apply thereafter only if the President determines and certifies to the Congress that reliable information indicates that the foreign person with respect to which the determination was made under subsection (a)(1) of this section has ceased to aid or abet any foreign government, project, or entity in its efforts to acquire chemical or biological weapons capability as described in that subsection.

(e) Waiver

(1) Criterion for waiver

The President may waive the application of any sanction imposed on any person pursuant to this section, after the end of the 12-month period beginning on the date on which that sanction was imposed on that person, if the President determines and certifies to the Congress that such waiver is important to the national security interests of the United States.

(2) Notification of and report to Congress

If the President decides to exercise the waiver authority provided in paragraph (1), the President shall so notify the Congress not less than 20 days before the waiver takes effect. Such notification shall include a report fully articulating the rationale and circumstances which led the President to exercise the waiver authority.

(f) "Foreign person" defined

For the purposes of this section, the term "foreign person" means—

(1) an individual who is not a citizen of the United States or an alien admitted for permanent residence to the United States; or

(2) a corporation, partnership, or other entity which is created or organized under the laws of a foreign country or which has its principal place of business outside the United States.

B. (EAA) Chemical and Biological Weapons Transfer Provisions of the Export Administration Act

[Laws in effect as of January 16, 1996]

[Document not affected by Public Laws enacted between

January 16, 1996, and August 28, 1996]

[CITE: 50USC—App. 2410c]

TITLE 50, APPENDIX—WAR AND NATIONAL DEFENSE
EXPORT REGULATION

Sec. 2410c. Chemical and biological weapons proliferation sanctions

(a) Imposition of sanctions

(1) Determination by the President

Except as provided in subsection (b)(2), the President shall impose both of the sanctions described in subsection (c) if the President determines that a foreign person, on or after October 28, 1991, has knowingly and materially contributed—

(A) through the export from the United States of any goods or technology that are subject to the jurisdiction of the United States under this Act [sections 2401 to 2420 of this Appendix], or

(B) through the export from any other country of any goods or technology that would be, if they were United States goods or technology, subject to the jurisdiction of the United States under this Act [sections 2401 to 2420 of this Appendix],

to the efforts by any foreign country, project, or entity described in paragraph (2) to use, develop, produce, stockpile, or otherwise acquire chemical or biological weapons.

(2) Countries, projects, or entities receiving assistance

Paragraph (1) applies in the case of—

(A) any foreign country that the President determines has, at any time after January 1, 1980—

(i) used chemical or biological weapons in violation of international law;

(ii) used lethal chemical or biological weapons against its own nationals; or

(iii) made substantial preparations to engage in the activities described in clause (i) or (ii);

(B) any foreign country whose government is determined for purposes of section 6(j) of this Act [section 2405(j) of this Appendix] to be a government that has repeatedly provided support for acts of international terrorism; or

(C) any other foreign country, project, or entity designated by the President for purposes of this section.

(3) Persons against which sanctions are to be imposed

Sanctions shall be imposed pursuant to paragraph (1) on—

(A) the foreign person with respect to which the President makes the determination described in that paragraph;

(B) any successor entity to that foreign person;

(C) any foreign person that is a parent or subsidiary of that foreign person if that parent or subsidiary knowingly assisted in the activities which were the basis of that determination; and

(D) any foreign person that is an affiliate of that foreign person if that affiliate knowingly assisted in the activities which were the basis of that determination and if that affiliate is controlled in fact by that foreign person.

(b) Consultations with and actions by foreign government of jurisdiction

(1) Consultations

If the President makes the determinations described in subsection (a)(1) with respect to a foreign person, the Congress urges the President to initiate consultations immediately with the government with primary jurisdiction over that foreign person with respect to the imposition of sanctions pursuant to this section.

(2) Actions by government of jurisdiction

In order to pursue such consultations with that government, the President may delay imposition of sanctions pursuant to this section for a period of up to 90 days. Following these consultations, the President shall impose sanctions unless the President determines and certifies to the Congress that that government has taken specific and effective actions, including appropriate penalties, to terminate the involvement of the foreign person in the activities described in subsection (a)(1). The President may delay imposition of sanctions for an additional period of up to 90 days if the President determines and certifies to the Congress that that government is in the process of taking the actions described in the preceding sentence.

(3) Report to Congress

The President shall report to the Congress, not later than 90 days after making a determination under subsection (a)(1), on the status of consultations with the appropriate government under this subsection, and the basis for any determination under paragraph (2) of this subsection that such government has taken specific corrective actions.

(c) Sanctions

(1) Description of sanctions

The sanctions to be imposed pursuant to subsection (a)(1) are, except as provided in paragraph (2) of this subsection, the following:

(A) Procurement sanction

The United States Government shall not procure, or enter into any contract for the procurement of, any goods or services from any person described in subsection (a)(3).

(B) Import sanctions

The importation into the United States of products produced by any person described in subsection (a)(3) shall be prohibited.

(2) Exceptions

The President shall not be required to apply or maintain sanctions under this section—

(A) in the case of procurement of defense articles or defense services—

(i) under existing contracts or subcontracts, including the exercise of options for production quantities to satisfy United States operational military requirements;

(ii) if the President determines that the person or other entity to which the sanctions would otherwise be applied is a sole source supplier of the defense articles or services, that the defense articles or services are essential, and that alternative sources are not readily or reasonably available; or

(iii) if the President determines that such articles or services are essential to the national security under defense coproduction agreements;

(B) to products or services provided under contracts entered into before the date on which the President publishes his intention to impose sanctions;

(C) to—

(i) spare parts,

(ii) component parts, but not finished products, essential to United States products or production, or

(iii) routine servicing and maintenance of products, to the extent that alternative sources are not readily or reasonably available;

(D) to information and technology essential to United States products or production; or

(E) to medical or other humanitarian items.

(d) Termination of sanctions

The sanctions imposed pursuant to this section shall apply for a period of at least 12 months following the imposition of sanctions and shall cease to apply thereafter only if the President determines and certifies to the Congress that reliable information indicates that the foreign person with respect to which the determination was made under subsection (a)(1) has ceased to aid or abet any foreign government, project, or entity in its efforts to acquire chemical or biological weapons capability as described in that subsection.

(e) Waiver

(1) Criterion for waiver

The President may waive the application of any sanction imposed on any person pursuant to this section, after the end of the 12-month period beginning on the date on which that sanction was imposed on that person, if the President determines and certifies to the Congress that such waiver is important to the national security interests of the United States.

(2) Notification of and report to Congress

If the President decides to exercise the waiver authority provided in paragraph (1), the President shall so notify the Congress not less than 20 days before the waiver takes effect. Such notification shall include a report fully articulating the rationale and circumstances which led the President to exercise the waiver authority.

(f) Definition of foreign person

For the purposes of this section, the term "foreign person" means—

(1) an individual who is not a citizen of the United States or an alien admitted for permanent residence to the United States; or

(2) a corporation, partnership, or other entity which is created or organized under the laws of a foreign country or which has its principal place of business outside the United States.

C. Use of Chemical and Biological Weapons, Provisions of the Chemical and Biological Weapons Control and Warfare Elimination Act

UNITED STATES CODE ANNOTATED

TITLE 22. FOREIGN RELATIONS AND INTERCOURSE

CHAPTER 65—CONTROL AND ELIMINATION OF CHEMICAL AND BIOLOGICAL WEAPONS

Current through P.L. 104-160, approved 7-9-96

§ 5601. Purposes

The purposes of this chapter are—

(1) to mandate United States sanctions, and to encourage international sanctions, against countries that use chemical or biological weapons in violation of international law or use lethal chemical or biological weapons against their own nationals, and to impose sanctions against companies that aid in the proliferation of chemical and biological weapons;

(2) to support multilaterally coordinated efforts to control the proliferation of chemical and biological weapons;

(3) to urge continued close cooperation with the Australia Group and cooperation with other supplier nations to devise ever more effective controls on the transfer of materials, equipment, and technology applicable to chemical or biological weapons production; and

(4) to require Presidential reports on efforts that threaten United States interests or regional stability by Iran, Iraq, Syria, Libya, and others to acquire the materials and technology to develop, produce, stockpile, deliver, transfer, or use chemical or biological weapons. [....]

Sec. 5604. Determinations regarding use of chemical or biological weapons

(a) Determination by President

(1) When determination required; nature of determination

Whenever persuasive information becomes available to the executive branch indicating the substantial possibility that, on or after October 28, 1991, the government of a foreign country has made substantial preparation to use or has used chemical or biological weapons, the President shall, within 60 days after the receipt of such information by the executive branch, determine whether that government, on or after October 28, 1991, has used chemical or biological weapons in violation of international law or has used lethal chemical or biological weapons against its own nationals. Section 5605 of this title applies if the President determines that that government has so used chemical or biological weapons.

(2) Matters to be considered

In making the determination under paragraph (1), the President shall consider the following:

(A) All physical and circumstantial evidence available bearing on the possible use of such weapons.

(B) All information provided by alleged victims, witnesses, and independent observers.

(C) The extent of the availability of the weapons in question to the purported user.

(D) All official and unofficial statements bearing on the possible use of such weapons.

(E) Whether, and to what extent, the government in question is willing to honor a request from the Secretary General of the United Nations to grant timely access to a United Nations fact-finding team to investigate the possibility of chemical or biological weapons use or to grant such access to other legitimate outside parties.

(3) Determination to be reported to Congress

Upon making a determination under paragraph (1), the President shall promptly report that determination to the Congress. If the determination is that a foreign government had used chemical or biological weapons as described in that paragraph, the report shall specify the sanctions to be imposed pursuant to section 5605 of this title.

(b) Congressional requests; report

(1) Request

The Chairman of the Committee on Foreign Relations of the Senate (upon consultation with the ranking minority member of such committee) or the Chairman of the Committee on Foreign Affairs of the House of Representatives (upon consultation with the ranking minority member of such committee) may at any time request the President to consider whether a particular foreign government, on or after December 4, 1991, has used chemical or biological weapons in violation of international law or has used lethal chemical or biological weapons against its own nationals.

(2) Report to Congress

Not later than 60 days after receiving such a request, the President shall provide to the Chairman of the Committee on Foreign Relations of the Senate and the Chairman of the Committee on Foreign Affairs of the House of Representatives a written report on the information held by the executive branch which is pertinent to the issue of whether the specified government, on or after December 4, 1991, has used chemical or biological weapons in violation of international law or has used lethal chemical or biological weapons against its own nationals. This report shall contain an analysis of each of the items enumerated in subsection (a)(2) of this section.

Sec. 5605. Sanctions against use of chemical or biological weapons

(a) Initial sanctions

If, at any time, the President makes a determination pursuant to section 5604(a)(1) of this title with respect to the government of a foreign country, the President shall forthwith impose the following sanctions:

(1) Foreign assistance

The United States Government shall terminate assistance to that country under the Foreign Assistance Act of 1961 [22 U.S.C. 2151 et seq.], except for urgent humanitarian assistance and food or other agricultural commodities or products.

(2) Arms sales

The United States Government shall terminate—

(A) sales to that country under the Arms Export Control Act [22 U.S.C. 2751 et seq.] of any defense articles, defense services, or design and construction services, and

(B) licenses for the export to that country of any item on the United States Munitions List.

(3) Arms sales financing

The United States Government shall terminate all foreign military financing for that country under the Arms Export Control Act.

(4) Denial of United States Government credit or other financial assistance

The United States Government shall deny to that country any credit, credit guarantees, or other financial assistance by any department, agency, or instrumentality of the United States Government, including the Export-Import Bank of the United States.

(5) Exports of national security-sensitive goods and technology

The authorities of section 2405 of title 50, Appendix, shall be used to prohibit the export to that country of any goods or technology on that part of the control list established under section 2404(c)(1) of title 50, Appendix.

(b) Additional sanctions if certain conditions not met

(1) Presidential determination

Unless, within 3 months after making a determination pursuant to section 5604(a)(1) of this title with respect to a foreign government, the President determines and certifies in writing to the Congress that—

(A) that government is no longer using chemical or biological weapons in violation of international law or using lethal chemical or biological weapons against its own nationals,

(B) that government has provided reliable assurances that it will not in the future engage in any such activities, and

(C) that government is willing to allow on-site inspections by United Nations observers or other internationally recognized, impartial observers, or other reliable means exist, to ensure that that government is not using chemical or biological weapons in violation of international law and is not using lethal chemical or biological weapons against its own nationals,

then the President, after consultation with the Congress, shall impose on that country the sanctions set forth in at least 3 of subparagraphs (A) through (F) of paragraph (2).

(2) Sanctions

The sanctions referred to in paragraph (1) are the following:

(A) Multilateral development bank assistance

The United States Government shall oppose, in accordance with section 262d of this title, the extension of any loan or financial or technical assistance to that country by international financial institutions.

(B) Bank loans

The United States Government shall prohibit any United States bank from making any loan or providing any credit to the government of that country, except for loans or credits for the purpose of purchasing food or other agricultural commodities or products.

(C) Further export restrictions

The authorities of section 2405 of title 50, Appendix, shall be used to prohibit exports to that country of all other goods and technology (excluding food and other agricultural commodities and products).

(D) Import restrictions

Restrictions shall be imposed on the importation into the United States of articles (which may include petroleum or any petroleum product) that are the growth, product, or manufacture of that country.

(E) Diplomatic relations

The President shall use his constitutional authorities to downgrade or suspend diplomatic relations between the United States and the government of that country.

(F) Presidential action regarding aviation

(i)

(I) The President is authorized to notify the government of a country with respect to which the President has made a determination pursuant to section 5604(a)(1) of this title of his intention to suspend the authority of foreign air carriers owned or controlled by the government of that country to engage in foreign air transportation to or from the United States.

(II) Within 10 days after the date of notification of a government under subclause (I), the Secretary of Transportation shall take all steps necessary to suspend at the earliest possible date the authority of any foreign air carrier owned or controlled, directly or indirectly, by that government to engage in foreign air transportation to or from the United States, notwithstanding any agreement relating to air services.

(ii)

(I) The President may direct the Secretary of State to terminate any air service agreement between the United States and a country with respect to which the President has made a determination pursuant to section 5604(a)(1) of this title, in accordance with the provisions of that agreement.

(II) Upon termination of an agreement under this clause, the Secretary of Transportation shall take such steps as may be necessary to revoke at the earliest possible date the right of any foreign air carrier owned, or controlled, directly or indirectly, by the government of that country to engage in foreign air transportation to or from the United States.

(iii) The Secretary of Transportation may provide for such exceptions from clauses (i) and (ii) as the Secretary considers necessary to provide for emergencies in which the safety of an aircraft or its crew or passengers is threatened.

(iv) For purposes of this subparagraph, the terms "air transportation", "air carrier", "foreign air carrier", and "foreign air transportation" have the meanings such terms have under section 40102(a) of title 49.

(c) Removal of sanctions

The President shall remove the sanctions imposed with respect to a country pursuant to this section if the President determines and so certifies to the Congress, after the end of the 12-month period beginning on the date on which sanctions were initially imposed on that country pursuant to subsection (a) of this section, that—

(1) the government of that country has provided reliable assurances that it will not use chemical or biological weapons in violation of international law and will not use lethal chemical or biological weapons against its own nationals;

(2) that government is not making preparations to use chemical or biological weapons in violation of international law or to use lethal chemical or biological weapons against its own nationals;

(3) that government is willing to allow on-site inspections by United Nations observers or other internationally recognized, impartial observers to verify that it is not making preparations to use chemical or biological weapons in violation of international law or to use lethal chemical or biological weapons against its own nationals, or other reliable means exist to verify that it is not making such preparations; and

(4) that government is making restitution to those affected by any use of chemical or biological weapons in violation of

international law or by any use of lethal chemical or biological weapons against its own nationals.

(d) Waiver

(1) Criteria for waiver

The President may waive the application of any sanction imposed with respect to a country pursuant to this section—

(A) if—

(i) in the case of any sanction other than a sanction specified in subsection (b)(2)(D) of this section (relating to import restrictions) or (b)(2)(E) of this section (relating to the downgrading or suspension of diplomatic relations), the President determines and certifies to the Congress that such waiver is essential to the national security interests of the United States, and if the President notifies the Committee on Foreign Relations of the Senate and the Committee on Foreign Affairs of the House of Representatives of his determination and certification at least 15 days before the waiver takes effect, in accordance with the procedures applicable to reprogramming notifications under section 634A of the Foreign Assistance Act of 1961 [22 U.S.C. 2394-1], or

(ii) in the case of any sanction specified in subsection (b)(2)(D) of this section (relating to import restrictions), the President determines and certifies to the Congress that such waiver is essential to the national security interest of the United States, and if the President notifies the Committee on Finance of the Senate and the Committee on Ways and Means of the House of Representatives of his determination and certification at least 15 days before the waiver takes effect; or

(B) if the President determines and certifies to the Congress that there has been a fundamental change in the leadership and policies of the government of that country, and if the President notifies the Congress at least 20 days before the waiver takes effect.

(2) Report

In the event that the President decides to exercise the waiver authority provided in paragraph (1) with respect to a country, the President's notification to the Congress under such paragraph shall include a report fully articulating the rationale and circumstances which led the President to exercise that waiver authority, including a description of the steps which the government of that country has taken to satisfy the conditions set forth in paragraphs (1) through (4) of subsection (c) of this section.

(e) Contract sanctity

(1) Sanctions not applied to existing contracts

(A) A sanction described in paragraph (4) or (5) of subsection (a) of this section or in any of subparagraphs (A) through (D) of subsection (b)(2) of this section shall not apply to any activity pursuant to any contract or international agreement entered into before the date of the presidential determination under section 5604(a)(1) of this title unless the President determines, on a case-by-case basis, that to apply such sanction to that activity would prevent the performance of a contract or agreement that would have the effect of assisting a country in using chemical or biological weapons in violation of international law or in using lethal chemical or biological weapons against its own nationals.

(B) The same restrictions of subsection (p) of section 2405 of title 50, Appendix, as that subsection is so redesignated by section 304(b) of this title, which are applicable to exports prohibited under section 2405 of title 50, Appendix, shall apply to exports prohibited under subsection (a)(5) or (b)(2)(C) of this section. For purposes of this subparagraph, any contract or agreement the performance of which (as determined by the President) would have the effect of assisting a foreign government in using chemical or biological weapons in violation of international law or in using lethal chemical or biological weapons against its own nationals shall be treated as constituting a breach of the peace that poses a serious and direct threat to the strategic interest of the United States, within the meaning of subparagraph (A) of section 2405(p) of title 50, Appendix.

(2) Sanctions applied to existing contracts

The sanctions described in paragraphs (1), (2), and (3) of subsection (a) of this section shall apply to contracts, agreements, and licenses without regard to the date the contract or agreement was entered into or the license was issued (as the case may be), except that such sanctions shall not apply to any contract or agreement entered into or license issued before the date of the presidential determination under section 5604(a)(1) of this title if the President determines that the application of such sanction would be detrimental to the national security interests of the United States.

Sec. 5606. Presidential reporting requirements

(a) Reports to Congress

Not later than 90 days after December 4, 1991, and every 12 months thereafter, the President shall transmit to the Congress a report which shall include—

(1) a description of the actions taken to carry out this chapter, including the amendments made by this chapter;

(2) a description of the current efforts of foreign countries and subnational groups to acquire equipment, materials, or technology to develop, produce, or use chemical or biological weapons, together with an assessment of the current and likely future capabilities of such countries and groups to develop, produce, stockpile, deliver, transfer, or use such weapons;

(3) a description of—

(A) the use of chemical weapons by foreign countries in violation of international law,

(B) the use of chemical weapons by subnational groups,

(C) substantial preparations by foreign countries and subnational groups to do so, and

(D) the development, production, stockpiling, or use of biological weapons by foreign countries and subnational groups; and

(4) a description of the extent to which foreign persons or governments have knowingly and materially assisted third countries or subnational groups to acquire equipment, material, or technology intended to develop, produce, or use chemical or biological weapons.

(b) Protection of classified information

To the extent practicable, reports submitted under subsection (a) of this section or any other provision of this chapter should be based on unclassified information. Portions of such reports may be classified.

D. (CWC) Chemical Weapons Convention, Article XII

CONVENTION ON THE PROHIBITION OF THE DEVELOPMENT, PRODUCTION, STOCKPILING AND USE OF CHEMICAL WEAPONS AND ON THEIR DESTRUCTION

Ratified by the United States, April 1997

ARTICLE XII

MEASURES TO REDRESS A SITUATION AND TO ENSURE COMPLIANCE INCLUDING SANCTIONS

1. The Conference shall take the necessary measures, as set forth in paragraphs 2, 3, and 4, to ensure compliance with this Convention and to redress and remedy any situation which contravenes the provisions of this Convention. In considering action pursuant to this paragraph, the Conference shall take into account all information and recommendations on the issues submitted by the Executive Council.

2. In cases where a State Party has been requested by the Executive Council to take measures to redress a situation raising problems with regard to its compliance, and where the State Party fails to fulfill the request within the specified time, the Conference may, *inter alia,* upon the recommendation of the Executive Council, restrict or suspend the State Party's rights and privileges under this Convention until it undertakes the necessary action to conform with its obligations under this Convention.

3. In cases where serious damage to the object and purpose of this Convention may result from activities prohibited under this Convention, in particular by Article I, the Conference may recommend collective measures to States Parties in conformity with international law.

4. The Conference shall, in cases of particular gravity, bring the issue, including relevant information and conclusions, to the attention of the United Nations General Assembly and the United Nations Security Council.

E. Russia Certification Requirements

NATIONAL DEFENSE AUTHORIZATION ACT FOR FISCAL YEAR 1996

[[Page 110 STAT. 186]]

Public Law 104-106

104th Congress

SEC. 1208. <<NOTE: President.>> LIMITATION RELATING TO OFFENSIVE BIOLOGICAL WARFARE PROGRAM OF RUSSIA.

(a) Limitation.—Of the amount appropriated pursuant to the authorization of appropriations in section 301 for Cooperative Threat Reduction programs that is available for the purpose stated in section 1202(a)(6), $60,000,000 may not be obligated or expended until the President submits to Congress either a certification as provided in subsection (b) or a certification as provided in subsection (c).

(b) Certification With Respect to Offensive Biological Warfare Program of Russia.—A certification under this subsection is a certification by the President of each of the following:

(1) That Russia is in compliance with its obligations under the Biological Weapons Convention.

(2) That Russia has agreed with the United States and the United Kingdom on a common set of procedures to govern visits by officials of the United States and United Kingdom to military biological facilities of Russia, as called for under the Joint Statement on Biological

Weapons issued by officials of the United States, the United Kingdom, and Russia on September 14, 1992.

(3) That visits by officials of the United States and United Kingdom to the four declared military biological facilities of Russia have occurred.

(c) Alternative Certification.—A certification under this subsection is a certification by the President that the President is unable to make a certification under subsection (b).

(d) Use of Funds Upon Alternative Certification.—If the President makes a certification under subsection (c), the $60,000,000 specified in subsection (a)—

(1) shall not be available for the purpose stated in section 1202(a)(6); and

(2) shall be available for activities in Ukraine, Kazakhstan, and Belarus—

(A) for the elimination of strategic offensive weapons (in addition to the amount specified in section 1202(a)(1)); and

(B) for nuclear infrastructure elimination (in addition to the amount specified in section 1202(a)(4)).

SEC. 1209. LIMITATION ON USE OF FUNDS FOR CHEMICAL WEAPONS DESTRUCTION FACILITY.

(a) Limitation.—Of the amount appropriated pursuant to the authorization of appropriations in section 301 for Cooperative Threat Reduction programs that is available for planning and design of a chemical weapons destruction facility, not more than one-half of such amount may be obligated or expended until the President certifies to Congress the following:

(1) That the United States and Russia have completed a joint laboratory study to determine the feasibility of an appropriate technology for destruction of chemical weapons of Russia.

(2) That Russia is making reasonable progress, with the assistance of the United States (if necessary), toward the completion of a comprehensive implementation plan for managing and funding the dismantlement and destruction of Russia's chemical weapons stockpile.

(3) That the United States and Russia have made substantial progress toward resolution, to the satisfaction of the United States, of outstanding compliance issues under the 1989 Wyoming Memorandum of Understanding and the 1990 Bilateral Destruction Agreement.

(b) Definitions.—In this section:

(1) The term "1989 Wyoming Memorandum of Understanding" means the Memorandum of Understanding between the Government of the United States of America and the Government of the Union of Soviet Socialist Republics Regarding a Bilateral Verification Experiment and Data Exchange Related to Prohibition on Chemical Weapons, signed at Jackson Hole, Wyoming, on September 23, 1989.

(2) The term "1990 Bilateral Destruction Agreement" means the Agreement between the United States of America and the Union of Soviet Socialist Republics on destruction and nonproduction of chemical weapons and on measures to facilitate the multilateral convention on banning chemical weapons signed on June 1, 1990.

A-V. COMBINED WEAPONS NONPROLIFERATION

A. (IEEPA) International Emergency Economic Powers Act

UNITED STATES CODE ANNOTATED

TITLE 50. WAR AND NATIONAL DEFENSE

CHAPTER 35—INTERNATIONAL EMERGENCY ECONOMIC POWERS

Current through P.L. 104-181, approved 8-6-96

§ 1701. Unusual and extraordinary threat; declaration of national emergency; exercise of Presidential authorities

(a) Any authority granted to the President by section 1702 of this title may be exercised to deal with any unusual and extraordinary threat, which has its source in whole or substantial part outside the United States, to the national security, foreign policy, or economy of the United States, if the President declares a national emergency with respect to such threat.

(b) The authorities granted to the President by section 1702 of this title may only be exercised to deal with an unusual and extraordinary threat with respect to which a national emergency has been declared for purposes of this chapter and may not be exercised for any other purpose. Any exercise of such authorities to deal with any new threat shall be based on a new declaration of national emergency which must be with respect to such threat.

§ 1702. Presidential authorities

(a)

(1) At the times and to the extent specified in section 1701 of this title, the President may, under such regulations as he may prescribe, by means of instructions, licenses, or otherwise—

(A) investigate, regulate, or prohibit—

(i) any transactions in foreign exchange,

(ii) transfers of credit or payments between, by, through, or to any banking institution, to the extent that such transfers or payments involve any interest of any foreign country or a national thereof,

(iii) the importing or exporting of currency or securities; and

(B) investigate, regulate, direct and compel, nullify, void, prevent or prohibit, any acquisition, holding, withholding, use, transfer, withdrawal, transportation, importation or exportation of, or dealing in, or exercising any right, power, or privilege with respect to, or transactions involving, any property in which any foreign country or a national thereof has any interest;

by any person, or with respect to any property, subject to the jurisdiction of the United States.

(2) In exercising the authorities granted by paragraph (1), the President may require any person to keep a full record of, and to furnish under oath, in the form of reports or otherwise, complete information relative to any act or transaction referred to in paragraph (1) either before, during, or after the completion thereof, or relative to any interest in foreign property, or relative to any property in which any foreign country or any national thereof has or has had any interest, or as may be otherwise necessary to enforce the provisions of such paragraph. In any case in which a report by a person could be required under this

paragraph, the President may require the production of any books of account, records, contracts, letters, memoranda, or other papers, in the custody or control of such person.

(3) Compliance with any regulation, instruction, or direction issued under this chapter shall to the extent thereof be a full acquittance and discharge for all purposes of the obligation of the person making the same. No person shall be held liable in any court for or with respect to anything done or omitted in good faith in connection with the administration of, or pursuant to and in reliance on, this chapter, or any regulation, instruction, or direction issued under this chapter.

(b) The authority granted to the President by this section does not include the authority to regulate or prohibit, directly or indirectly—

(1) any postal, telegraphic, telephonic, or other personal communication, which does not involve a transfer of anything of value;

(2) donations, by persons subject to the jurisdiction of the United States, of articles, such as food, clothing, and medicine, intended to be used to relieve human suffering, except to the extent that the President determines that such donations (A) would seriously impair his ability to deal with any national emergency declared under section 1701 of this title, (B) are in response to coercion against the proposed recipient or donor, or (C) would endanger Armed Forces of the United States which are engaged in hostilities or are in a situation where imminent involvement in hostilities is clearly indicated by the circumstances; or

(3) the importation from any country, or the exportation to any country, whether commercial or otherwise, regardless of format or medium of transmission, of any information or informational materials, including but not limited to, publications, films, posters, phonograph records, photographs, microfilms, microfiche, tapes, compact disks, CD ROMs, artworks, and news wire feeds. The

exports exempted from regulation or prohibition by this paragraph do not include those which are otherwise controlled for export under section 2404 of the Appendix to this title, or under section 2405 of the Appendix to this title to the extent that such controls promote the nonproliferation or antiterrorism policies of the United States, or with respect to which acts are prohibited by chapter 37 of Title 18;

(4) any transactions ordinarily incident to travel to or from any country, including importation of accompanied baggage for personal use, maintenance within any country including payment of living expenses and acquisition of goods or services for personal use, and arrangement or facilitation of such travel including nonscheduled air, sea, or land voyages.

B. Iraq Note to IEEPA § 1701

Economic Sanctions Against the Republic of Iraq

Pub.L. 101-510, Div. A, Title XIV, § 1458, Nov. 5, 1990, 104 Stat. 1697, provided that:

"If the President considers that the taking of such action would promote the effectiveness of the economic sanctions of the United Nations and the United States imposed with respect to Iraq, and is consistent with the national interest, the President may prohibit, for such a period of time as he considers appropriate, the importation into the United States of any or all products of any foreign country that has not—

"(1) prohibited—

"(A) the importation of products of Iraq into its customs territory, and

"(B) the export of its products to Iraq; or

"(2) given assurances satisfactory to the President that such import and export sanctions will be promptly implemented."

Pub.L. 101-513, Title V, §§ 586 to 586J, Nov. 5, 1990, 104 Stat. 2047, provided that:

"Sec. 586. Short title.

"Sections 586 through 586J of this Act [this note] may be cited as the 'Iraq Sanctions Act of 1990'. [....]

"Sec. 586A. Declarations regarding Iraq's invasion of Kuwait. [....]

"Sec. 586B. Consultations with Congress. [....]

"Sec. 586C. Trade embargo against Iraq.

"(a) Continuation of embargo.—Except as otherwise provided in this section, the President shall continue to impose the trade embargo and other economic sanctions with respect to Iraq and Kuwait that the United States is imposing, in response to Iraq's invasion of Kuwait, pursuant to Executive Orders Numbered 12724 and 12725 (August 9, 1990) and, to the extent they are still in effect, Executive Orders Numbered 12722 and 12723 (August 2, 1990). Notwithstanding any other provision of law, no funds, credits, guarantees, or insurance appropriated or otherwise made available by this or any other Act for fiscal year 1991or any fiscal year thereafter shall be used to support or administer any financial or commercial operation of any United States Government department, agency, or other entity, or of any person subject to the jurisdiction of the United States, for the benefit of the Government of Iraq, its agencies or instrumentalities, or any person working on behalf of the

Government of Iraq, contrary to the trade embargo and other economic sanctions imposed in accordance with this section.

"(b) Humanitarian assistance.—To the extent that transactions involving foodstuffs or payments for foodstuffs are exempted 'in humanitarian circumstances' from the prohibitions established by the United States pursuant to United Nations Security Council Resolution 661 (1990), those exemptions shall be limited to foodstuffs that are to be provided consistent with United Nations Security Council Resolution 666 (1990) and other relevant Security Council resolutions.

"(c) Notice to Congress of exceptions to and termination of sanctions.—

"(1) Notice of regulations.—Any regulations issued after the date of enactment of this Act [Nov. 5, 1990] with respect to the economic sanctions imposed with respect to Iraq and Kuwait by the United States under Executive Orders Numbered 12722 and 12723 (August 2, 1990) and Executive Orders Numbered 12724 and 12725 (August 9, 1990) shall be submitted to the Congress before those regulations take effect.

"(2) Notice of termination of sanctions.—The President shall notify the Congress at least 15 days before the termination, in whole or in part, of any sanction imposed with respect to Iraq or Kuwait pursuant to those Executive orders.

"(d) Relation to other laws.—

"(1) Sanctions legislation.—The sanctions that are described in subsection (a) are in addition to, and not in lieu of the sanctions provided for in section 586G of this Act or any other provision of law.

"(2) National emergencies and United Nations legislation.—Nothing in this section supersedes any provision of the National Emergencies Act [section 1601 et seq. of this title] or any authority of the President under the International Emergency Economic Powers Act [this chapter] or section 5(a) of the United Nations Participation Act of 1945 [section 287c(a) of Title 22].

"Sec. 586D. Compliance with United Nations sanctions against Iraq.

"(a) Denial of assistance.—None of the funds appropriated or otherwise made available pursuant to this Act [this note] to carry out the Foreign Assistance Act of 1961 [section 2151 et seq. of Title 22] (including title IV of chapter 2 of part I [section 2191 et seq. of Title 22], relating to the Overseas Private Investment Corporation) or the Arms Export Control Act [section 2751 et seq. of Title 22] may be used to provide assistance to any country that is not in compliance with the United Nations Security Council sanctions against Iraq unless the President determines and so certifies to the Congress that—

"(1) such assistance is in the national interest of the United States;

"(2) such assistance will directly benefit the needy people in that country; or

"(3) the assistance to be provided will be humanitarian assistance for foreign nationals who have fled Iraq and Kuwait.

"(b) Import sanctions.—If the President considers that the taking of such action would promote the effectiveness of the economic sanctions of the United Nations and the United States imposed with respect to Iraq, and is consistent with the national interest, the President may prohibit, for such a period of time as he considers appropriate, the importation into the United States of any or all products of any foreign country that has not prohibited—

"(1) the importation of products of Iraq into its customs territory, and

"(2) the export of its products to Iraq.

"Sec. 586E. Penalties for violations of embargo. [....]

"Sec. 586F. Declarations regarding Iraq's long-standing violations of international law.

"(a) Iraq's violations of international law.—The Congress determines that—

[....]

"(6) Iraq has blatantly violated international law by initiating use of chemical weapons in the Iran-Iraq war;

"(7) Iraq has also violated international law by using chemical weapons against its own Kurdish citizens, resulting in tens of thousands of deaths and more than 65,000 refugees;

"(8) Iraq continues to expand its chemical weapons capability, and President Saddam Hussein has threatened to use chemical weapons against other nations;

"(9) persuasive evidence exists that Iraq is developing biological weapons in violation of international law;

"(10) there are strong indications that Iraq has taken steps to produce nuclear weapons and has attempted to smuggle from the United States, in violation of United States law, components for triggering devices used in nuclear warheads whose manufacture would contravene the Treaty on the Non-Proliferation of Nuclear Weapons, to which Iraq is a party; and

"(11) Iraqi President Saddam Hussein has threatened to use terrorism against other nations in violation of international law and has increased Iraq's support for the Palestine Liberation Organization and other Palestinian groups that have conducted terrorist acts.

"(b) Human rights violations. [....]

"(c) Support for international terrorism. [....]

"(2) The provisions of law referred to in paragraph (1) are—

"(A) section 40 of the Arms Export Control Act [section 2780 of Title 22];

"(B) section 620A of the Foreign Assistance Act of 1961 [section 2371 of Title 22];

"(C) sections 555 and 556 of this Act [not classified to the Code] (and the corresponding sections of predecessor foreign operations appropriations Acts); and

"(D) section 555 of the International Security and Development Cooperation Act of 1985 [not classified to the Code].

"(d) Multilateral cooperation.—The Congress calls on the President to seek multilateral cooperation—

"(1) to deny dangerous technologies to Iraq;

"(2) to induce Iraq to respect internationally recognized human rights; and

"(3) to induce Iraq to allow appropriate international humanitarian and human rights organizations to have access to Iraq and Kuwait, including the areas in northern Iraq traditionally inhabited by Kurds.

"Sec. 586G. Sanctions against Iraq.

"(a) Imposition.—Except as provided in section 586H, the following sanctions shall apply with respect to Iraq:

"(1) FMS sales.—The United States Government shall not enter into any sale with Iraq under the Arms Export Control Act [section 2751 et seq. of Title 22].

"(2) Commercial arms sales.—Licenses shall not be issued for the export to Iraq of any item on the United States Munitions List.

"(3) Exports of certain goods and technology.—The authorities of section 6 of the Export Administration Act of 1979 (50 U.S.C. App. 2405) [section 2405 of the Appendix to this title] shall be used to prohibit the export to Iraq of any goods or technology listed pursuant to that section or section 5(c)(1) of that Act (50 U.S.C. App. 2404(c)(1)) [section 2404(c)(1) of the Appendix to this title] on the control list provided for in section 4(b) of that Act (50

U.S.C. App. 2403(b)) [section 2403(b) of the Appendix to this title].

"(4) Nuclear equipment, materials, and technology.—

"(A) NRC licenses.—The Nuclear Regulatory Commission shall not issue any license or other authorization under the Atomic Energy Act of 1954 (42 U.S.C. 2011 and following) [section 2011 et seq. of Title 42] for the export to Iraq of any source or special nuclear material, any production or utilization facility, any sensitive nuclear technology, any component, item, or substance determined to have significance for nuclear explosive purposes pursuant to section 109b. of the Atomic Energy Act of 1954 (42 U.S.C. 2139(b)) [section 2139(b) of Title 42], or any other material or technology requiring such a license or authorization.

"(B) Distribution of nuclear materials.—The authority of the Atomic Energy Act of 1954 [section 2011 et seq. of Title 42] shall not be used to distribute any special nuclear material, source material, or byproduct material to Iraq.

"(C) DOE authorizations.—The Secretary of Energy shall not provide a specific authorization under section 57(b)(2) of the Atomic Energy Act of 1954 (42 U.S.C. 2077(b)(2)) [section 2077(b)(2) of Title 42] for any activity that would constitute directly or indirectly engaging in Iraq in activities that require a specific authorization under that section.

"(5) Assistance from international financial institutions.—The United States shall oppose any loan or financial or technical assistance to Iraq by international financial institutions in accordance with section 701 of the International Financial Institutions Act (22 U.S.C. 262d) [section 262d of Title 22].

"(6) Assistance through the Export-Import Bank.—Credits and credit guarantees through the Export-Import Bank of the United States shall be denied to Iraq.

"(7) Assistance through the Commodity Credit Corporation.—Credit, credit guarantees, and other assistance through the Commodity Credit Corporation shall be denied to Iraq.

"(8) Foreign assistance.—All forms of assistance under the Foreign Assistance Act of 1961 (22 U.S.C. 2151 and following) [section 2751 et seq. of Title 22] other than emergency assistance for medical supplies and other forms of emergency humanitarian assistance, and under the Arms Export Control Act (22 U.S.C. 2751 and following) [section 2751 et seq. of Title 22] shall be denied to Iraq.

"(b) Contract sanctity.—For purposes of the export controls imposed pursuant to subsection (a)(3), the date described in subsection (m)(1) of section 6 of the Export Administration Act of 1979 (50 U.S.C. App. 2405) [section 2405 of the Appendix to this title] shall be deemed to be August 1, 1990.

"Sec. 586H. Waiver authority.

"(a) In general.—The President may waive the requirements of any paragraph of section 586G(a) if the President makes a certification under subsection (b) or subsection (c).

"(b) Certification of fundamental changes in Iraqi policies and actions.—The authority of subsection (a) may be exercised 60 days after the President certifies to the Congress that—

"(1) the Government of Iraq—

"(A) has demonstrated, through a pattern of conduct, substantial improvement in its respect for internationally recognized human rights;

"(B) is not acquiring, developing, or manufacturing (i) ballistic missiles, (ii) chemical, biological, or nuclear weapons, or (iii) components for such weapons; has forsworn the first use of such weapons; and is taking substantial and verifiable steps to destroy or otherwise dispose of any such missiles and weapons it possesses; and

"(C) does not provide support for international terrorism;

"(2) the Government of Iraq is in substantial compliance with its obligations under international law, including—

"(A) the Charter of the United Nations;

"(B) the International Covenant on Civil and Political Rights (done at New York, December 16, 1966) and the International Covenant on Economic, Social, and Cultural Rights (done at New York, December 16, 1966);

"(C) the Convention on the Prevention and Punishment of the Crime of Genocide (done at Paris, December 9, 1948);

"(D) the Protocol for the Prohibition of the Use in War of Asphyxiating, Poisonous or Other Gases, and of Bacteriological Methods of Warfare (done at Geneva, June 17, 1925);

"(E) the Treaty on the Non-Proliferation of Nuclear Weapons (done at Washington, London, and Moscow, July 1, 1968); and

"(F) the Convention on the Prohibition of the Development, Production and Stockpiling of Bacteriological (Biological) and Toxin Weapons and on Their Destruction (done at Washington, London, and Moscow, April 10, 1972); and

"(3) the President has determined that it is essential to the national interests of the United States to exercise the authority of subsection (a).

"(c) Certification of fundamental changes in Iraqi leadership and policies.—The authority of subsection (a) may be exercised 30 days after the President certifies to the Congress that—

"(1) there has been a fundamental change in the leadership of the Government of Iraq; and

"(2) the new Government of Iraq has provided reliable and credible assurance that—

"(A) it respects internationally recognized human rights and it will demonstrate such respect through its conduct;

"(B) it is not acquiring, developing, or manufacturing and it will not acquire, develop, or manufacture (i) ballistic missiles, (ii) chemical, biological, or nuclear weapons, or (iii) components for such weapons; has forsworn the first use of such weapons; and is taking substantial and verifiable steps to destroy or otherwise dispose of any such missiles and weapons it possesses;

"(C) it is not and will not provide support for international terrorism; and

"(D) it is and will continue to be in substantial compliance with its obligations under international law, including all the treaties specified in subparagraphs (A) through (F) of subsection (b)(2).

"(d) Information to be included in certifications.—Any certification under subsection (b) or (c) shall include the justification for each determination required by that subsection. The certification shall also specify which paragraphs of section 586G(a) the President will waive pursuant to that certification.

"Sec. 586I. Denial of licenses for certain exports to countries assisting Iraq's rocket or chemical, biological, or nuclear weapons capability.

"(a) Restriction on export licenses.—None of the funds appropriated by this or any other Act may be used to approve the licensing for export of any supercomputer to any country whose government the President determines is assisting, or whose government officials the President determines are assisting, Iraq to improve its rocket technology or chemical, biological, or nuclear weapons capability.

"(b) Negotiations.—The President is directed to begin immediate negotiations with those governments with which the United States has bilateral supercomputer agreements, including the Government of the United Kingdom and the Government of Japan, on conditions restricting the transfer to Iraq of supercomputer or associated technology.

"Sec. 586J. Reports to Congress.

"(a) Study and report on the international export to Iraq of nuclear, biological, chemical, and ballistic missile technology.—

(1) The President shall conduct a study on the sale, export, and third party transfer or development of nuclear, biological, chemical, and ballistic missile technology to or with Iraq including—

"(A) an identification of specific countries, as well as companies and individuals, both foreign and domestic, engaged in such sale or export of, nuclear, biological, chemical, and ballistic missile technology;

"(B) a detailed description and analysis of the international supply, information, support, and coproduction network, individual, corporate, and state, responsible for Iraq's current capability in the area of nuclear, biological, chemical, and ballistic missile technology; and

"(C) a recommendation of standards and procedures against which to measure and verify a decision of the Government of Iraq to terminate the development, production, coproduction, and deployment of nuclear, biological, chemical, and offensive ballistic missile technology as well as the destruction of all existing facilities associated with such technologies.

"(2) The President shall include in the study required by paragraph (1) specific recommendations on new mechanisms, to include, but not be limited to, legal, political, economic and regulatory, whereby the United States might contribute, in conjunction with its friends, allies, and the international community, to the management, control, or elimination of the threat of nuclear, biological, chemical, and ballistic missile proliferation.

"(3) Not later than March 30, 1991, the President shall submit to the Committee on Appropriations and the Committee on Foreign Relations of the Senate and the Committee on Appropriations and the Committee on Foreign Affairs of the House of Representatives, a report, in both classified and unclassified form, setting forth the findings of the study required by paragraph (1) of this subsection.

"(b) Study and report on Iraq's offensive military capability.—

(1) The President shall conduct a study on Iraq's offensive military capability and its effect on the Middle East balance of power including an assessment of Iraq's power projection capability, the prospects for another sustained conflict with Iran, joint Iraqi-Jordanian military cooperation, the threat Iraq's arms transfer activities pose to United States allies in the Middle East, and the extension of Iraq's political-military influence into Africa and Latin America.

"(2) Not later than March 30, 1991, the President shall submit to the Committee on Appropriations and the Committee on Foreign Relations of the Senate and the Committee on Appropriations and the Committee on Foreign Affairs of the House of Representatives, a report, in both classified and unclassified form, setting forth the findings of the study required by paragraph (1).

"(c) Report on sanctions taken by other nations against Iraq.—

(1) The President shall prepare a report on the steps taken by other nations, both before and after the August 2, 1990, invasion of Kuwait, to curtail the export of goods, services, and technologies to Iraq which might contribute to, or enhance, Iraq's nuclear, biological, chemical, and ballistic missile capability.

"(2) The President shall provide a complete accounting of international compliance with each of the sanctions resolutions adopted by the United Nations Security Council against Iraq since August 2, 1990, and shall list, by name, each country which to his knowledge, has provided any assistance to Iraq and the amount and type of that assistance in violation of each United Nations resolution.

"(3) The President shall make every effort to encourage other nations, in whatever forum or context, to adopt sanctions toward Iraq similar to those contained in this section.

"(4) Not later than every 6 months after the date of enactment of this Act, the President shall submit to the Committee on Appropriations and the Committee on Foreign Relations of the Senate and the Committee on Appropriations and the Committee on Foreign Affairs of the House of Representatives, a report in both classified and unclassified form, setting forth the findings of the study required by paragraph (1) of this subsection."

C. Iran and Libya Sanctions Act Note to IEEPA § 1701

Public Law 104-172

104th Congress

An Act

To impose sanctions on persons making certain investments directly and significantly contributing to the enhancement of the ability of Iran or Libya to develop its petroleum resources, and on persons exporting certain items that enhance Libya's weapons or aviation capabilities or enhance Libya's ability to develop its petroleum resources, and for other purposes. <<NOTE: Aug. 5, 1996 - [H.R. 3107]>>

Be it enacted by the Senate and House of Representatives of the United States of America in Congress <<NOTE: Iran and Libya Sanctions Act of 1996. 50 USC 1701 note.>> assembled,

SECTION 1. SHORT TITLE.

This Act may be cited as the "Iran and Libya Sanctions Act of 1996".

SEC. 2. FINDINGS.

The Congress makes the following findings:

(1) The efforts of the Government of Iran to acquire weapons of mass destruction and the means to deliver them and its support of acts of international terrorism endanger the national security and foreign policy interests of the United States and those countries with which the United States shares common strategic and foreign policy objectives.

(2) The objective of preventing the proliferation of weapons of mass destruction and acts of international terrorism

through existing multilateral and bilateral initiatives requires additional efforts to deny Iran the financial means to sustain its nuclear, chemical, biological, and missile weapons programs.

(3) The Government of Iran uses its diplomatic facilities and quasi-governmental institutions outside of Iran to promote acts of international terrorism and assist its nuclear, chemical, biological, and missile weapons programs.

(4) The failure of the Government of Libya to comply with Resolutions 731, 748, and 883 of the Security Council of the United Nations, its support of international terrorism, and its efforts to acquire weapons of mass destruction constitute a threat to international peace and security that endangers the national security and foreign policy interests of the United States and those countries with which it shares common strategic and foreign policy objectives.

SEC. 3. DECLARATION OF POLICY.

(a) Policy With Respect to Iran.—The Congress declares that it is the policy of the United States to deny Iran the ability to support acts of international terrorism and to fund the development and acquisition of weapons of mass destruction and the means to deliver them by limiting the development of Iran's ability to explore for, extract, refine, or transport by pipeline petroleum resources of Iran.

(b) Policy With Respect to Libya.—The Congress further declares that it is the policy of the United States to seek full compliance by Libya with its obligations under Resolutions 731, 748, and 883 of the Security Council of the United Nations, including ending all support for acts of international terrorism and efforts to develop or acquire weapons of mass destruction.

SEC. 4. MULTILATERAL REGIME.

(a) Multilateral Negotiations.—In order to further the objectives of section 3, the Congress urges the President to commence immediately diplomatic efforts, both in appropriate international fora such as the United Nations, and bilaterally with allies of the United States, to establish a multilateral sanctions regime against Iran, including provisions limiting the development of petroleum resources, that will inhibit Iran's efforts to carry out activities described in section 2.

(b) Reports to Congress.—The President shall report to the appropriate congressional committees, not later than 1 year after the date of the enactment of this Act, and periodically thereafter, on the extent that diplomatic efforts described in subsection (a) have been successful. Each report shall include—

(1) the countries that have agreed to undertake measures to further the objectives of section 3 with respect to Iran, and a description of those measures; and

(2) the countries that have not agreed to measures described in paragraph (1), and, with respect to those countries, other measures (in addition to that provided in subsection (d)) the President recommends that the United States take to further the objectives of section 3 with respect to Iran.

(c) Waiver.—The President may waive the application of section 5(a) with respect to nationals of a country if—

(1) that country has agreed to undertake substantial measures, including economic sanctions, that will inhibit Iran's efforts to carry out activities described in section 2 and information required by subsection (b)(1) has been included in a report submitted under subsection (b); and

(2) the <<NOTE: Notification.>> President, at least 30 days before the waiver takes effect, notifies the appropriate congressional committees of his intention to exercise the waiver.

(d) Enhanced Sanction.—

(1) Sanction.—With respect to nationals of countries except those with respect to which the President has exercised the waiver authority of subsection (c), at any time after the first report is required to be submitted under subsection (b), section 5(a) shall be applied by substituting "$20,000,000" for "$40,000,000" each place it appears, and by substituting "$5,000,000" for "$10,000,000".

(2) Report to Congress.—The President shall report to the appropriate congressional committees any country with respect to which paragraph (1) applies.

(e) Interim Report on Multilateral Sanctions; Monitoring.—The President, not later than 90 days after the date of the enactment of this Act, shall report to the appropriate congressional committees on—

(1) whether the member states of the European Union, the Republic of Korea, Australia, Israel, or Japan have legislative or administrative standards providing for the imposition of trade sanctions on persons or their affiliates doing business or having investments in Iran or Libya;

(2) the extent and duration of each instance of the application of such sanctions; and

(3) the disposition of any decision with respect to such sanctions by the World Trade Organization or its predecessor organization.

SEC. 5. IMPOSITION OF SANCTIONS.

(a) Sanctions With Respect to Iran.—Except as provided in subsection (f), the President shall impose 2 or more of the sanctions described in paragraphs (1) through (6) of section 6 if the President determines that a person has, with actual knowledge, on or after the date of the enactment of this Act, made an investment of $40,000,000 or more (or any combination of investments of at least $10,000,000 each, which in the aggregate equals or exceeds $40,000,000 in any 12-month period), that directly and significantly contributed to the enhancement of Iran's ability to develop petroleum resources of Iran.

(b) Mandatory Sanctions With Respect to Libya.—

(1) Violations of prohibited transactions.—Except as provided in subsection (f), the President shall impose 2 or more of the sanctions described in paragraphs (1) through (6) of section 6 if the President determines that a person has, with actual knowledge, on or after the date of the enactment of this Act, exported, transferred, or otherwise provided to Libya any goods, services, technology, or other items the provision of which is prohibited under paragraph 4(b) or 5 of Resolution 748 of the Security Council of the United Nations, adopted March 31, 1992, or under paragraph 5 or 6 of Resolution 883 of the Security Council of the United Nations, adopted November 11, 1993, if the provision of such items significantly and materially—

(A) contributed to Libya's ability to acquire chemical, biological, or nuclear weapons or destabilizing numbers and types of advanced conventional weapons or enhanced Libya's military or paramilitary capabilities;

(B) contributed to Libya's ability to develop its petroleum resources; or

(C) contributed to Libya's ability to maintain its aviation capabilities.

(2) Investments that contribute to the development of petroleum resources.—Except as provided in subsection (f), the President shall impose 2 or more of the sanctions described in paragraphs (1) through (6) of section 6 if the President determines that a person has, with actual knowledge, on or after the date of the enactment of this Act, made an investment of $40,000,000 or more (or any combination of investments of at east $10,000,000 each, which in the aggregate equals or exceeds $40,000,000 in any 12-month period), that directly and significantly

contributed to the enhancement of Libya's ability to develop its petroleum resources.

(c) Persons Against Which the Sanctions Are to Be Imposed.—The sanctions described in subsections (a) and (b) shall be imposed on—

(1) any person the President determines has carried out the activities described in subsection (a) or (b); and

(2) any person the President determines—

(A) is a successor entity to the person referred to in paragraph (1);

(B) is a parent or subsidiary of the person referred to in paragraph (1) if that parent or subsidiary, with actual knowledge, engaged in the activities referred to in paragraph (1); or

(C) is an affiliate of the person referred to in paragraph (1) if that affiliate, with actual knowledge, engaged in the activities referred to in paragraph (1) and if that affiliate is controlled in fact by the person referred to in paragraph (1).

For purposes of this Act, any person or entity described in this subsection shall be referred to as a "sanctioned person".

(d) Publication in Federal Register.—The President shall cause to be published in the Federal Register a current list of persons and entities on whom sanctions have been imposed under this Act. The removal of persons or entities from, and the addition of persons and entities to, the list, shall also be so published.

(e) Publication of Projects.—The President shall cause to be published in the Federal Register a list of all significant projects which have been publicly tendered in the oil and gas sector in Iran.

(f) Exceptions.—The President shall not be required to apply or maintain the sanctions under subsection (a) or (b)—

(1) in the case of procurement of defense articles or defense services—

(A) under existing contracts or subcontracts, including the exercise of options for production quantities to satisfy requirements essential to the national security of the United States;

(B) if the President determines in writing that the person to which the sanctions would otherwise be applied is a sole source supplier of the defense articles or services, that the defense articles or services are essential, and that alternative sources are not readily or reasonably available; or

(C) if the President determines in writing that such articles or services are essential to the national security under defense coproduction agreements;

(2) in the case of procurement, to eligible products, as defined in section 308(4) of the Trade Agreements Act of 1979 (19 U.S.C. 2518(4)), of any foreign country or instrumentality designated under section 301(b)(1) of that Act (19 U.S.C. 2511(b)(1));

(3) to products, technology, or services provided under contracts entered into before the date on which the President publishes in the Federal Register the name of the person on whom the sanctions are to be imposed;

(4) to—

(A) spare parts which are essential to United States products or production;

(B) component parts, but not finished products, essential to United States products or production; or

(C) routine servicing and maintenance of products, to the extent that alternative sources are not readily or reasonably available;

[Authors' note: Item (5) is missing from the original text.]

(6) to information and technology essential to United States products or production; or

(7) to medicines, medical supplies, or other humanitarian items.

SEC. 6. DESCRIPTION OF SANCTIONS.

The sanctions to be imposed on a sanctioned person under section 5 are as follows:

(1) Export-import bank assistance for exports to sanctioned persons.—The President may direct the Export-Import Bank of the United States not to give approval to the issuance of any guarantee, insurance, extension of credit, or participation in the extension of credit in connection with the export of any goods or services to any sanctioned person.

(2) Export sanction.—The President may order the United States Government not to issue any specific license and not to grant any other specific permission or authority to export any goods or technology to a sanctioned person under—

(i) the Export Administration Act of 1979;

(ii) the Arms Export Control Act;

(iii) the Atomic Energy Act of 1954; or

(iv) any other statute that requires the prior review and approval of the United States Government as a condition for the export or reexport of goods or services.

(3) Loans from United States financial institutions.—The United States Government may prohibit any United States financial institution from making loans or providing credits to any sanctioned person totaling more than $10,000,000 in any 12-month period unless such person is engaged in activities to relieve human suffering and the loans or credits are provided for such activities.

(4) Prohibitions on financial institutions.—The following prohibitions may be imposed against a sanctioned person that is a financial institution:

(A) Prohibition on designation as primary dealer.—Neither the Board of Governors of the Federal Reserve System nor the Federal Reserve Bank of New York may designate, or permit the continuation of any prior designation of, such financial institution as a primary dealer in United States Government debt instruments.

(B) Prohibition on service as a repository of government funds.—Such financial institution may not serve as agent of the United States Government or serve as repository for United States Government funds.

The imposition of either sanction under subparagraph (A) or (B) shall be treated as 1 sanction for purposes of section 5, and the imposition of both such sanctions shall be treated as 2 sanctions for purposes of section 5.

(5) Procurement sanction.—The United States Government may not procure, or enter into any contract for the procurement of, any goods or services from a sanctioned person.

(6) Additional sanctions.—The President may impose sanctions, as appropriate, to restrict imports with respect to a sanctioned person, in accordance with the International Emergency Economic Powers Act (50 U.S.C. 1701 and following).

SEC. 7. ADVISORY OPINIONS.

The Secretary of State may, upon the request of any person, issue an advisory opinion to that person as to whether a proposed activity by that person would subject that person to sanctions under this Act. Any person who relies in good faith on such an advisory opinion which states that the proposed activity would not subject a person to such sanctions, and any person who thereafter engages in such activity, will not be made subject to such sanctions on account of such activity.

SEC. 8. TERMINATION OF SANCTIONS.

(a) Iran.—The requirement under section 5(a) to impose sanctions shall no longer have force or effect with respect to Iran if the President determines and certifies to the appropriate congressional committees that Iran—

(1) has ceased its efforts to design, develop, manufacture, or acquire—

(A) a nuclear explosive device or related materials and technology;

(B) chemical and biological weapons; and

(C) ballistic missiles and ballistic missile launch technology; and

(2) has been removed from the list of countries the governments of which have been determined, for purposes of section 6(j) of the Export Administration Act of 1979, to have repeatedly provided support for acts of international terrorism.

(b) Libya.—The requirement under section 5(b) to impose sanctions shall no longer have force or effect with respect to Libya if the President determines and certifies to the appropriate congressional committees that Libya has fulfilled the requirements of United Nations Security Council Resolution 731, adopted January 21, 1992, United Nations Security Council Resolution 748, adopted March 31, 1992, and United Nations Security Council Resolution 883, adopted November 11, 1993.

SEC. 9. DURATION OF SANCTIONS; PRESIDENTIAL WAIVER.

(a) Delay of Sanctions.—

(1) Consultations.—If the President makes a determination described in section 5(a) or 5(b) with respect to a foreign person, the Congress urges the President to initiate consultations immediately with the government with primary jurisdiction over that foreign person with respect to the imposition of sanctions under this Act.

(2) Actions by government of jurisdiction.—In order to pursue consultations under paragraph (1) with the government concerned, the President may delay imposition of sanctions under this Act for up to 90 days. Following such consultations, the President shall immediately impose sanctions unless the President determines and certifies to the Congress that the government has taken specific and effective actions, including, as appropriate, the imposition of appropriate penalties, to terminate the involvement of the foreign person in the activities that resulted in the determination by the President under section 5(a) or 5(b) concerning such person.

(3) Additional delay in imposition of sanctions.—The President may delay the imposition of sanctions for up to an additional 90 days if the President determines and certifies to the Congress that the government with primary jurisdiction over the person concerned is in the process of taking the actions described in paragraph (2).

(4) Report to Congress.—Not later than 90 days after making a determination under section 5(a) or 5(b), the President shall submit to the appropriate congressional committees a report on the status of consultations with the appropriate foreign government under this subsection, and the basis for any determination under paragraph (3).

(b) Duration of Sanctions.—A sanction imposed under section 5 shall remain in effect—

(1) for a period of not less than 2 years from the date on which it is imposed; or

(2) until such time as the President determines and certifies to the Congress that the person whose activities were the basis for imposing the sanction is no longer engaging in such activities and that the President has received reliable assurances that such person will not knowingly engage in such activities in the future, except that such sanction shall remain in effect for a period of at least 1 year.

(c) Presidential Waiver.—

(1) Authority.—The President may waive the requirement in section 5 to impose a sanction or sanctions on a person described in section 5(c), and may waive the continued imposition of a sanction or sanctions under subsection (b) of this section, 30 days or more after the President determines and so reports to the appropriate congressional committees that it is important to the national interest of the United States to exercise such waiver authority.

(2) Contents of report.—Any report under paragraph (1) shall provide a specific and detailed rationale for the determination under paragraph (1), including—

(A) a description of the conduct that resulted in the determination under section 5(a) or (b), as the case may be;

(B) in the case of a foreign person, an explanation of the efforts to secure the cooperation of the government with primary jurisdiction over the sanctioned person to terminate or, as appropriate, penalize the activities that resulted in the determination under section 5(a) or (b), as the case may be;

(C) an estimate as to the significance—

(i) of the provision of the items described in section 5(a) to Iran's ability to develop its petroleum resources, or

(ii) of the provision of the items described in section 5(b)(1) to the abilities of Libya described in subparagraph (A), (B), or (C) of section 5(b)(1), or of the investment described in section 5(b)(2) on Libya's ability to develop its petroleum resources,

as the case may be; and

(D) a statement as to the response of the United States in the event that the person concerned engages in other activities that would be subject to section 5(a) or (b).

(3) Effect of report on waiver.—If the President makes a report under paragraph (1) with respect to a waiver of sanctions on a person described in section 5(c), sanctions need not be imposed under section 5(a) or (b) on that person during the 30-day period referred to in paragraph (1).

SEC. 10. REPORTS REQUIRED.

(a) Report on Certain International Initiatives.—Not later than 6 months after the date of the enactment of this Act, and every 6 months thereafter, the President shall transmit a report to the appropriate congressional committees describing—

(1) the efforts of the President to mount a multilateral campaign to persuade all countries to pressure Iran to cease its nuclear, chemical, biological, and missile weapons programs and its support of acts of international terrorism;

(2) the efforts of the President to persuade other governments to ask Iran to reduce the presence of Iranian diplomats and representatives of other government and military or quasi-governmental institutions of Iran and to withdraw

any such diplomats or representatives who participated in the takeover of the United States embassy in Tehran on November 4, 1979, or the subsequent holding of United States hostages for 444 days;

(3) the extent to which the International Atomic Energy Agency has established regular inspections of all nuclear facilities in Iran, including those presently under construction; and

(4) Iran's use of Iranian diplomats and representatives of other government and military or quasi-governmental institutions of Iran to promote acts of international terrorism or to develop or sustain Iran's nuclear, chemical, biological, and missile weapons programs.

(b) Other Reports.—The President shall ensure the continued transmittal to the Congress of reports describing—

(1) the nuclear and other military capabilities of Iran, as required by section 601(a) of the Nuclear Non-Proliferation Act of 1978 and section 1607 of the National Defense Authorization Act for Fiscal Year 1993; and

(2) the support provided by Iran for acts of international terrorism, as part of the Department of State's annual report on international terrorism.

SEC. 11. DETERMINATIONS NOT REVIEWABLE.

A determination to impose sanctions under this Act shall not be reviewable in any court.

SEC. 12. EXCLUSION OF CERTAIN ACTIVITIES.

Nothing in this Act shall apply to any activities subject to the reporting requirements of title V of the National Security Act of 1947.

SEC. 13. EFFECTIVE DATE; SUNSET.

(a) Effective Date.—This Act shall take effect on the date of the enactment of this Act.

(b) Sunset.—This Act shall cease to be effective on the date that is 5 years after the date of the enactment of this Act.

SEC. 14. DEFINITIONS.

As used in this Act:

(1) Act of international terrorism.—The term "act of international terrorism" means an act—

(A) which is violent or dangerous to human life and that is a violation of the criminal laws of the United States or of any State or that would be a criminal violation if committed within the jurisdiction of the United States or any State; and

(B) which appears to be intended—

(i) to intimidate or coerce a civilian population;

(ii) to influence the policy of a government by intimidation or coercion; or

(iii) to affect the conduct of a government by assassination or kidnapping.

(2) Appropriate congressional committees.—The term "appropriate congressional committees" means the Committee on Finance, the Committee on Banking, Housing, and Urban Affairs, and the Committee on Foreign Relations of the Senate and the Committee on Ways and Means, the Committee on Banking and Financial Services, and the Committee on International Relations of the House of Representatives.

(3) Component part.—The term "component part" has the meaning given that term in section 11A(e)(1) of the Export Administration Act of 1979 (50 U.S.C. App. 2410a(e)(1)).

(4) Develop and development.—To "develop", or the "development" of, petroleum resources means the exploration for, or the extraction, refining, or transportation by pipeline of, petroleum resources.

(5) Financial institution.—The term "financial institution" includes—

  (A) a depository institution (as defined in section 3(c)(1) of the Federal Deposit Insurance Act), including a branch or agency of a foreign bank (as defined in section 1(b)(7) of the International Banking Act of 1978);

  (B) a credit union;

  (C) a securities firm, including a broker or dealer;

  (D) an insurance company, including an agency or underwriter; and

  (E) any other company that provides financial services.

(6) Finished product.—The term "finished product" has the meaning given that term in section 11A(e)(2) of the Export Administration Act of 1979 (50 U.S.C. App. 2410a(e)(2)).

(7) Foreign person.—The term "foreign person" means—

  (A) an individual who is not a United States person or an alien lawfully admitted for permanent residence into the United States; or

  (B) a corporation, partnership, or other nongovernmental entity which is not a United States person.

(8) Goods and technology.—The terms "goods" and "technology" have the meanings given those terms in section 16 of the Export Administration Act of 1979 (50 U.S.C. App. 2415).

(9) Investment.—The term "investment" means any of the following activities if such activity is undertaken pursuant to an agreement, or pursuant to the exercise of rights under such an agreement, that is entered into with the

Government of Iran or a nongovernmental entity in Iran, or with the Government of Libya or a nongovernmental entity in Libya, on or after the date of the enactment of this Act:

(A) The entry into a contract that includes responsibility for the development of petroleum resources located in Iran or Libya (as the case may be), or the entry into a contract providing for the general supervision and guarantee of another person's performance of such a contract.

(B) The purchase of a share of ownership, including an equity interest, in that development.

(C) The entry into a contract providing for the participation in royalties, earnings, or profits in that development, without regard to the form of the participation.

The term "investment" does not include the entry into, performance, or financing of a contract to sell or purchase goods, services, or technology.

(10) Iran.—The term "Iran" includes any agency or instrumentality of Iran.

(11) Iranian diplomats and representatives of other government and military or quasi-governmental institutions of Iran.—The term "Iranian diplomats and representatives of other government and military or quasi-governmental institutions of Iran" includes employees, representatives, or affiliates of Iran's—

(A) Foreign Ministry;

(B) Ministry of Intelligence and Security;

(C) Revolutionary Guard Corps;

(D) Crusade for Reconstruction;

(E) Qods (Jerusalem) Forces;

(F) Interior Ministry;

(G) Foundation for the Oppressed and Disabled;

(H) Prophet's Foundation;

(I) June 5th Foundation;

(J) Martyr's Foundation;

(K) Islamic Propagation Organization; and

(L) Ministry of Islamic Guidance.

(12) Libya.—The term "Libya" includes any agency or instrumentality of Libya.

(13) Nuclear explosive device.—The term "nuclear explosive device" means any device, whether assembled or disassembled, that is designed to produce an instantaneous release of an amount of nuclear energy from special nuclear material (as defined in section 11(aa) of the Atomic Energy Act of 1954) that is greater than the amount of energy that would be released from the detonation of one pound of trinitrotoluene (TNT).

(14) Person.—The term "person" means—

(A) a natural person;

(B) a corporation, business association, partnership, society, trust, any other nongovernmental entity, organization, or group, and any governmental entity operating as a business enterprise; and

(C) any successor to any entity described in subparagraph (B).

(15) Petroleum resources.—The term "petroleum resources" includes petroleum and natural gas resources.

(16) United States or State.—The term "United States" or "State" means the several States, the District of Columbia, the Commonwealth of Puerto Rico, the Commonwealth of the Northern Mariana Islands, American Samoa, Guam, the United States Virgin Islands, and any other territory or possession of the United States.

(17) United States person.—The term "United States person" means—

(A) a natural person who is a citizen of the United States or who owes permanent allegiance to the United States; and

(B) a corporation or other legal entity which is organized under the laws of the United States, any State or territory thereof, or the District of Columbia, if natural persons described in subparagraph (A) own, directly or indirectly, more than 50 percent of the outstanding capital stock or other beneficial interest in such legal entity.

Approved August 5, 1996.

D. Iran-Iraq Arms Non-Proliferation Act Note to IEEPA § 1701

Iran-Iraq Arms Non-Proliferation Act of 1992

Pub.L. 102-484, Div. A, Title XVI, Oct. 23, 1992, 106 Stat. 2571, as amended Pub.L. 104-106, Div. A, Title XIV, § 1408(a) to (c), Feb. 10, 1996, 110 Stat. 494, provided that:

"Sec. 1601. Short title

This title [enacting this note] may be cited as the 'Iran-Iraq Arms Non-Proliferation Act of 1992'.

"Sec. 1602. United States Policy

"(a) In general.—It shall be the policy of the United States to oppose, and urgently to seek the agreement of other nations also to oppose, any transfer to Iran or Iraq of any goods or technology, including dual-use goods or technology, wherever that transfer could materially contribute to either country's acquiring chemical, biological, nuclear, or destabilizing numbers and types of advanced conventional weapons.

"(b) Sanctions.—

(1) In the furtherance of this policy, the President shall apply sanctions and controls with respect to Iran, Iraq, and those nations and persons who assist them in acquiring weapons of mass destruction in accordance with the Foreign Assistance Act of 1961 [section 2151 et seq. of Title 22, Foreign Relations and Intercourse], the Nuclear Non-Proliferation Act of 1978 [section 3201 et seq. of Title 22], the Chemical and Biological Weapons Control and Warfare Elimination Act of 1991 [section 5601 et seq. of Title 22], chapter 7 of the Arms Export Control Act [section 2797 et seq. of Title 22], and other relevant statutes, regarding the non-proliferation of weapons of mass destruction and the means of their delivery.

"(2) The President should also urgently seek the agreement of other nations to adopt and institute, at the earliest practicable date, sanctions and controls comparable to those the United States is obligated to apply under this subsection.

"(c) Public identification.—The Congress calls on the President to identify publicly (in the report required by section 1607) any country or person that transfers goods or technology to Iran or Iraq contrary to the policy set forth in subsection (a).

"Sec. 1603. Application to Iran of certain Iraq sanctions

"The sanctions against Iraq specified in paragraphs (1) through (4) of section 586G(a) of the Iraq Sanctions Act of 1990 (as contained in Public Law 101-513) [set out as a note under this section], including denial of export licenses for United States persons and prohibitions on United States Government sales, shall be applied to the same extent and in the same manner with respect to Iran.

"Sec. 1604. Sanctions against certain persons

"(a) Prohibition.—If any person transfers or retransfers goods or technology so as to contribute knowingly and materially to the efforts by Iran or Iraq (or any agency or instrumentality of either such country) to acquire chemical, biological, or nuclear weapons or to acquire destabilizing numbers and types of advanced conventional weapons, then the sanctions described in subsection (b) shall be imposed.

"(b) Mandatory sanctions.—The sanctions to be imposed pursuant to subsection (a) are as follows:

"(1) Procurement sanction.—For a period of two years, the United States Government shall not procure, or enter into any contract for the procurement of, any goods or services from the sanctioned person.

"(2) Export sanction.—For a period of two years, the United States Government shall not issue any license for any export by or to the sanctioned person.

"Sec. 1605. Sanctions against certain foreign countries

"(a) Prohibition.—If the President determines that the government of any foreign country transfers or retransfers goods or technology so as to contribute knowingly and materially to the efforts by Iran or Iraq (or any agency or instrumentality of either such country) to acquire chemical, biological, or nuclear weapons or to acquire destabilizing numbers and types of advanced conventional weapons, then—

"(1) the sanctions described in subsection (b) shall be imposed on such country; and

"(2) in addition, the President may apply, in the discretion of the President, the sanction described in subsection (c).

"(b) Mandatory sanctions.—Except as provided in paragraph (2), the sanctions to be imposed pursuant to subsection (a)(1) are as follows:

"(1) Suspension of United States assistance.—The United States Government shall suspend, for a period of one year, United States assistance to the sanctioned country.

"(2) Multilateral development bank assistance.—The Secretary of the Treasury shall instruct the United States Executive Director to each appropriate international financial institution to oppose, and vote against, for a period of one year, the extension by such institution of any loan or financial or technical assistance to the sanctioned country.

"(3) Suspension of codevelopment or coproduction agreements.—The United States shall suspend, for a period of one year, compliance with its obligations under any memorandum of understanding with the sanctioned country for the codevelopment or coproduction of any item on the United States Munitions List (established under section 38 of the Arms Export Control Act [section 2778 of Title 22]), including any obligation for implementation of the memorandum of understanding through the sale to the sanctioned country of technical data or assistance or the licensing for export to the sanctioned country of any component part.

"(4) Suspension of military and dual-use technical exchange agreements.—The United States shall suspend, for a period of one year, compliance with its obligations under any technical exchange agreement involving military and dual-use technology between the United States and the sanctioned country that does not directly contribute to the security of the United States, and no military or dual-use technology may be exported from the United States to the sanctioned country pursuant to that agreement during that period.

"(5) United States Munitions List.—No item on the United States Munitions List (established pursuant to section 38 of the Arms Export Control Act section 2778 of Title 22]) may be exported to the sanctioned country for a period of one year.

"(c) Discretionary sanction.—The sanction referred to in subsection (a)(2) is as follows:

"(1) Use of authorities of International Emergency Economic Powers Act.—Except as provided in paragraph (2), the President may exercise, in accordance with the provisions of that Act, the authorities of the International Emergency Economic Powers Act [this chapter] with respect to the sanctioned country.

"(2) Exception.—Paragraph (1) does not apply with respect to urgent humanitarian assistance.

"Sec. 1606. Waiver

"The President may waive the requirement to impose a sanction described in section 1603, in the case of Iran, or a sanction described in section 1604(b) or 1605(b), in the case of Iraq and Iran, 15 days after the President determines and so reports to the Committees on Armed Services and Foreign Relations of the Senate and the Committees on Armed Services and Foreign Affairs of the House of Representatives that it is essential to the national interest of the United States to exercise such waiver authority. Any such report shall provide a specific and detailed rationale for such determination.

"Sec. 1607. Reporting requirement

"(a) Annual report.—Beginning one year after the date of the enactment of this Act [Oct. 23, 1992], and every 12 months thereafter, the President shall submit to the Committees on Armed Services and Foreign Relations of the Senate and the Committees on Armed Services and Foreign Affairs of the House of Representatives a report detailing—

"(1) all transfers or retransfers made by any person or foreign government during the preceding 12-month period which are subject to any sanction under this title [this note]; and

"(2) the actions the President intends to undertake or has undertaken pursuant to this title [this note] with respect to each such transfer.

"(b) Report on individual transfers.—Whenever the President determines that a person or foreign government has made a transfer which is subject to any sanction under this title [this note], the President shall, within 30 days after such transfer, submit to the Committees on Armed Services and Foreign Relations of the Senate and the Committees on Armed Services and Foreign Affairs of the House of Representatives a report—

"(1) identifying the person or government and providing the details of the transfer; and

"(2) describing the actions the President intends to undertake or has undertaken under the provisions of this title [this note] with respect to each such transfer.

"(c) Form of transmittal.—Reports required by this section may be submitted in classified as well as in unclassified form.

"Sec. 1608. Definitions

"For purposes of this title [this note]:

"(1) The term 'advanced conventional weapons' includes—

"(A) such long-range precision-guided munitions, fuel air explosives, cruise missiles, low observability aircraft, other radar evading aircraft, advanced military aircraft, military satellites, electromagnetic weapons, and laser weapons as the President determines destabilize the military balance or enhance offensive capabilities in destabilizing ways;

"(B) such advanced command, control, and communications systems, electronic warfare systems, or intelligence collection systems as the President determines destabilize the military balance or enhance offensive capabilities in destabilizing ways; and

"(C) such other items or systems as the President may, by regulation, determine necessary for purposes of this title.

"(2) The term 'cruise missile' means guided missiles that use aerodynamic lift to offset gravity and propulsion to counteract drag.

"(3) The term 'goods or technology' means—

"(A) any article, natural or manmade substance, material, supply, or manufactured product, including inspection and test equipment; and

"(B) any information and know-how (whether in tangible form, such as models, prototypes, drawings, sketches, diagrams, blueprints, or manuals, or in intangible form, such as training or technical services) that can be used to design, produce, manufacture, utilize, or reconstruct goods, including computer software and technical data.

"(4) The term 'person' means any United States or foreign individual, partnership, corporation, or other form of association, or any of their successor entities, parents, or subsidiaries.

"(5) The term 'sanctioned country' means a country against which sanctions are required to be imposed pursuant to section 1605.

"(6) The term 'sanctioned person' means a person that makes a transfer described in section 1604(a).

"(7) The term 'United States assistance' means—

"(A) any assistance under the Foreign Assistance Act of 1961 (22 U.S.C. 2151 et seq.), other than urgent humanitarian assistance or medicine;

"(B) sales and assistance under the Arms Export Control Act [section 2751 et seq. of Title 22];

"(C) financing by the Commodity Credit Corporation for export sales of agricultural commodities; and

"(D) financing under the Export-Import Bank Act [section 635 et seq. of Title 12, Banks and Banking]."

E. Executive Order 12938, Proliferation of Weapons of Mass Destruction

EXECUTIVE ORDER NO. 12938

< Nov. 14, 1994, 59 F.R. 59099 >

PROLIFERATION OF WEAPONS OF MASS DESTRUCTION

By the authority vested in me as President by the Constitution and the laws of the United States of America, including the International Emergency Economic Powers Act (50 U.S.C. 1701 et seq.), the National Emergencies Act (50 U.S.C. 1601 et seq.), the Arms Export Control Act, as amended (22 U.S.C. 2751 et seq.), Executive Orders Nos. 12851 [set out as a note under section 2797 of Title 22, Foreign Relations and Intercourse] and 12924 [set out as a note under this section], and section 301 of title 3, United States Code [section 301 of Title 3, The President],

I, WILLIAM J. CLINTON, President of the United States of America, find that the proliferation of nuclear, biological, and chemical weapons ("weapons of mass destruction") and of the means of delivering such weapons, constitutes an unusual and extraordinary threat to the national security, foreign policy, and economy of the United States, and hereby declare a national emergency to deal with that threat.

Accordingly, I hereby order:

Section 1. International Negotiations. It is the policy of the United States to lead and seek multilaterally coordinated efforts with other countries to control the proliferation of weapons of mass destruction and the means of delivering such weapons. Accordingly, the Secretary of State shall cooperate in and lead multilateral efforts to stop the proliferation of weapons of mass destruction and their means of delivery.

Sec. 2. Imposition of Controls. As provided herein, the Secretary of State and the Secretary of Commerce shall use their respective authorities, including the Arms Export Control Act and the International Emergency Economic Powers Act, to control any exports, to the extent they are not already controlled by the Department of Energy and the Nuclear Regulatory Commission, that either Secretary determines would assist a country in acquiring the capability to develop, produce, stockpile, deliver, or use weapons of mass destruction or their means of delivery. The Secretary of State shall pursue early negotiations with foreign governments to adopt effective measures comparable to those imposed under this order.

Sec. 3. Department of Commerce Controls.

(a) The Secretary of Commerce shall prohibit the export of any goods, technology, or services subject to the Secretary's export jurisdiction that the Secretary of Commerce determines, in consultation with the Secretary of State, the Secretary of Defense, and other appropriate officials, would assist a foreign country in acquiring the capability to develop, produce, stockpile, deliver, or use weapons of mass destruction or their means of delivery. The Secretary of State shall pursue early negotiations with foreign governments to adopt effective measures comparable to those imposed under this section.

(b) Subsection (a) of this section will not apply to exports relating to a particular category of weapons of mass destruction (i.e., nuclear, chemical, or biological weapons) if their destination is a country with whose government the United States has entered into a bilateral or multilateral arrangement for the control of that category of weapons of mass destruction-related goods (including delivery systems) and technology, or maintains domestic export controls comparable to controls that are imposed by the United States with respect to that category of goods and technology, or that are otherwise deemed adequate by the Secretary of State.

(c) The Secretary of Commerce shall require validated licenses to implement this order and shall coordinate any license applications with the Secretary of State and the Secretary of Defense.

(d) The Secretary of Commerce, in consultation with the Secretary of State, shall take such actions, including the promulgation of rules, regulations, and amendments thereto, as may be necessary to continue to regulate the activities of United States persons in order to prevent their participation in activities that could contribute to the proliferation of weapons of mass destruction or their means of delivery, as provided in the Export Administration Regulations, set forth in Title 15, Chapter VII, Subchapter C, of the Code of Federal Regulations, Parts 768 to 799 inclusive.

Sec. 4. Sanctions Against Foreign Persons.

(a) In addition to the sanctions imposed on foreign persons as provided in the National Defense Authorization Act for Fiscal Year 1991 [Pub.L. 101-510, Nov. 5, 1990, 104 Stat. 1485; see Tables for classification], and the Chemical and Biological Weapons Control and Warfare Elimination Act of 1991 [Pub.L. 102-138, Title V, Oct. 28, 1991, 105 Stat. 722; see Tables for classification], sanctions also shall be imposed on a foreign person with respect to chemical and biological weapons proliferation if the Secretary of State determines that the foreign person on or after the effective date of this order or its predecessor, Executive Order No. 12735 of November 16, 1990, knowingly and materially contributed to the efforts of any foreign country, project, or entity to use, develop, produce, stockpile, or otherwise acquire chemical or biological weapons.

(b) No department or agency of the United States Government may procure, or enter into any contract for the procurement of, any goods or services from any foreign person described in subsection (a) of this section. The Secretary of the Treasury shall prohibit the importation into the United States of products produced by that foreign person.

(c) Sanctions pursuant to this section may be terminated or not imposed against foreign persons if the Secretary of State determines that there is reliable evidence that the foreign person concerned has ceased all activities referred to in subsection (a).

(d) The Secretary of State and the Secretary of the Treasury may provide appropriate exemptions for procurement contracts necessary to meet U.S. operational military requirements or requirements under defense production agreements, sole source suppliers, spare parts, components, routine servicing and maintenance of products, and medical and humanitarian items. They may provide exemptions for contracts in existence on the date of this order under appropriate circumstances.

Sec. 5. Sanctions Against Foreign Countries.

(a) In addition to the sanctions imposed on foreign countries as provided in the Chemical and Biological Weapons Control and Warfare Elimination Act of 1991, sanctions also shall be imposed on a foreign country as specified in subsection (b) of this section, if the Secretary of State determines that the foreign country has, on or after the effective date of this order or its predecessor, Executive Order No. 12735 of November 16, 1990, (1) used chemical or biological weapons in violation of international law; (2) made substantial preparations to use chemical or biological weapons in violation of international law; or (3) developed, produced, stockpiled, or otherwise acquired chemical or biological weapons in violation of international law.

(b) The following sanctions shall be imposed on any foreign country identified in subsection (a)(1) of this section unless the Secretary of State determines, on grounds of significant foreign policy or national security, that any individual sanction should not be applied. The sanctions specified in this section may be made applicable to the countries identified in subsections (a)(2) or (a)(3) when the Secretary of State determines that such action will further the objectives of this order pertaining to proliferation. The sanctions specified in subsection (b)(2) below shall be imposed with the concurrence of the Secretary of the Treasury.

(1) Foreign Assistance. No assistance shall be provided to that country under the Foreign Assistance Act of 1961, or any

successor act, or the Arms Export Control Act, other than assistance that is intended to benefit the people of that country directly and that is not channeled through governmental agencies or entities of that country.

(2) Multilateral Development Bank Assistance. The United States shall oppose any loan or financial or technical assistance to that country by international financial institutions in accordance with section 701 of the International Financial Institutions Act (22 U.S.C. 262d).

(3) Denial of Credit or Other Financial Assistance. The United States shall deny to that country any credit or financial assistance by any department, agency, or instrumentality of the United States Government.

(4) Prohibition of Arms Sales. The United States Government shall not, under the Arms Export Control Act, sell to that country any defense articles or defense services or issue any license for the export of items on the United States Munitions List.

(5) Exports of National Security-Sensitive Goods and Technology. No exports shall be permitted of any goods or technologies controlled for national security reasons under the Export Administration Regulations.

(6) Further Export Restrictions. The Secretary of Commerce shall prohibit or otherwise substantially restrict exports to that country of goods, technology, and services (excluding agricultural commodities and products otherwise subject to control).

(7) Import Restrictions. Restrictions shall be imposed on the importation into the United States of articles (that may include petroleum or any petroleum product) that are the growth, product, or manufacture of that country.

(8) Landing Rights. At the earliest practicable date, the Secretary of State shall terminate, in a manner consistent with international law, the authority of any air carrier that is controlled in fact by the government of that country to engage in air transportation (as defined in section 101(10)

of the Federal Aviation Act of 1958 (49 U.S.C. App. 1301(10)).

Sec. 6. Duration. Any sanctions imposed pursuant to sections 4 or 5 of this order shall remain in force until the Secretary of State determines that lifting any sanction is in the foreign policy or national security interests of the United States or, as to sanctions under section 4 of this order, until the Secretary has made the determination under section 4(c).

Sec. 7. Implementation. The Secretary of State, the Secretary of the Treasury, and the Secretary of Commerce are hereby authorized and directed to take such actions, including the promulgation of rules and regulations, as may be necessary to carry out the purposes of this order. These actions, and in particular those in sections 4 and 5 of this order, shall be made in consultation with the Secretary of Defense and, as appropriate, other agency heads and shall be implemented in accordance with procedures established pursuant to Executive Order No. 12851. The Secretary concerned may redelegate any of these functions to other officers in agencies of the Federal Government.

All heads of departments and agencies of the United States Government are directed to take all appropriate measures within their authority to carry out the provisions of this order, including the suspension or termination of licenses or other authorizations.

Sec. 8. Preservation of Authorities. Nothing in this order is intended to affect the continued effectiveness of any rules, regulations, orders, licenses, or other forms of administrative action issued, taken, or continued in effect heretofore or hereafter under the authority of the International Economic Emergency Powers Act, the Export Administration Act, the Arms Export Control Act, the Nuclear Non-proliferation Act [Pub.L. 95-242, Mar. 10, 1978, 92 Stat. 120; see Tables for classification], Executive Order No. 12730 of September 30, 1990, Executive Order No. 12735 of November 16, 1990, Executive Order No. 12924 of August 18, 1994, and Executive Order No. 12930 of September 29, 1994 [set out as notes under this section].

Sec. 9. Judicial Review. This order is not intended to create, nor does it create, any right or benefit, substantive or procedural, enforceable at law by a party against the United States, its agencies, officers, or any other person.

Sec. 10. Revocation of Executive Orders Nos. 12735 and 12930. Executive Order No. 12735 of November 16, 1990, and Executive Order No. 12930 of September 29, 1994 [formerly set out as notes under this section], are hereby revoked.

Sec. 11. Effective Date. This order is effective immediately.

This order shall be transmitted to the Congress and published in the Federal Register.

WILLIAM J. CLINTON

November 12, 1996

NOTICE

CONTINUATION OF EMERGENCY REGARDING WEAPONS OF MASS DESTRUCTION

On November 14, 1994, by Executive Order 12938, I declared a national emergency with respect to the unusual and extraordinary threat to the national security, foreign policy, and economy of the United States posed by the proliferation of nuclear, biological, and chemical weapons ("weapons of mass destruction") and the means of delivering such weapons.

Because the proliferation of weapons of mass destruction and the means of delivering them continues to pose an unusual and extraordinary threat to the national security, foreign policy, and economy of the United States, the national emergency declared on November 14, 1994, and extended on November 14, 1995, must continue in effect beyond November 14, 1996.

Therefore, in accordance with section 202(d) of the National Emergencies Act (50 U.S.C. 1622(d)), I am continuing the national emergency declared in Executive Order 12938.

This notice shall be published in the Federal Register and transmitted to the Congress.

WILLIAM J. CLINTON

THE WHITE HOUSE

F. (EAA) Export Administration Act

UNITED STATES CODE ANNOTATED

TITLE 50 APPENDIX. WAR AND NATIONAL DEFENSE

EXPORT REGULATION

PUB.L. 96-72, SEPT. 29, 1979, 93 STAT. 503

Current through P.L. 104-181, approved 8-6-96

§ 2404. National security controls

(b) Policy toward individual countries

(1) In administering export controls for national security purposes under this section, the President shall establish as a list of controlled countries those countries set forth in section 620(f) of the Foreign Assistance Act of 1961 [22 U.S.C.A. § 2370(f)], except that the President may add any country to or remove any country from such list of controlled countries if he determines that the export of goods or technology to such country would or would not (as the case may be) make a significant contribution to the military potential of such country or a combination of countries which would prove detrimental to the national security of the United States. In determining whether a country is added to or removed from the list of controlled countries, the President shall take into account—

(A) the extent to which the country's policies are adverse to the national security interests of the United States;

(B) the country's Communist or non-Communist status;

(C) the present and potential relationship of the country with the United States;

(D) the present and potential relationships of the country with countries friendly or hostile to the United States;

(E) the country's nuclear weapons capability and the country's compliance record with respect to multilateral nuclear weapons agreements to which the United States is a party; and

(F) such other factors as the President considers appropriate.

Nothing in the preceding sentence shall be interpreted to limit the authority of the President provided in this Act [sections 2401 to 2420 of this Appendix] to prohibit or curtail the export of any goods or technology to any country to which exports are controlled for national security purposes other than countries on the list of controlled countries specified in this paragraph. The President shall review not less frequently than every three years in the case of controls maintained cooperatively with other nations, and annually in the case of all other controls, United States policy toward individual countries to determine whether such policy is appropriate in light of the factors set forth in this paragraph. [....]

(l) Diversion of controlled goods or technology

(1) Whenever there is reliable evidence, as determined by the Secretary, that goods or technology which were exported subject to national security controls under this section to a controlled country have been diverted to an unauthorized use or consignee in violation of the conditions of an export license, the Secretary for as long as that diversion continues—

(A) shall deny all further exports, to or by the party or parties responsible for that diversion or who conspired in that diversion, of any goods or technology subject to national security controls under this section, regardless of whether such goods or technology are available from sources outside the United States; and

(B) may take such additional actions under this Act [sections 2401 to 2420 of this Appendix] with respect to the party or parties referred to in subparagraph (A) as the Secretary determines are appropriate in the circumstances to deter the further unauthorized use of the previously exported goods or technology.

(2) As used in this subsection, the term "unauthorized use" means the use of United States goods or technology in the design, production, or maintenance of any item on the United States Munitions List, or the military use of any item on the International Control List of the Coordinating Committee. [....]

§ 2405. Foreign policy controls

(a) Authority [....]

(2) Any export control imposed under this section shall apply to any transaction or activity undertaken with the intent to evade that export control, even if that export control would not otherwise apply to that transaction or activity. [....]

(6) Before imposing, expanding, or extending export controls under this section on exports to a country which can use goods, technology, or information available from foreign sources and so incur little or no economic costs as a result of the controls, the President should, through diplomatic means, employ alternatives to export controls which offer opportunities of distinguishing the United States from, and expressing the displeasure of the United States with, the specific actions of that country in response to which the controls are proposed. Such alternatives include private discussions with foreign leaders, public statements in situations where private diplomacy is unavailable or not effective, withdrawal of ambassadors,

and reduction of the size of the diplomatic staff that the country involved is permitted to have in the United States.

(b) Criteria

(1) Subject to paragraph (2) of this subsection, the President may impose, extend, or expand export controls under this section only if the President determines that—

(A) such controls are likely to achieve the intended foreign policy purpose, in light of other factors, including the availability from other countries of the goods or technology proposed for such controls, and that foreign policy purpose cannot be achieved through negotiations or other alternative means;

(B) the proposed controls are compatible with the foreign policy objectives of the United States and with overall United States policy toward the country to which exports are to be subject to the proposed controls;

(C) the reaction of other countries to the imposition, extension, or expansion of such export controls by the United States is not likely to render the controls ineffective in achieving the intended foreign policy purpose or to be counterproductive to United States foreign policy interests;

(D) the effect of the proposed controls on the export performance of the United States, the competitive position of the United States in the international economy, the international reputation of the United States as a supplier of goods and technology, or on the economic well-being of individual United States companies and their employees and communities does not exceed the benefit to United States foreign policy objectives; and

(E) the United States has the ability to enforce the proposed controls effectively.

(2) With respect to those export controls in effect under this section on the date of the enactment of the Export

Administration Amendments Act of 1985 [July 12, 1985], the President, in determining whether to extend those controls, as required by subsection (a)(3) of this section, shall consider the criteria set forth in paragraph (1) of this subsection and shall consider the foreign policy consequences of modifying the export controls. [....]

(e) Alternative means

Before resorting to the imposition of export controls under this section, the President shall determine that reasonable efforts have been made to achieve the purposes of the controls through negotiations or other alternative means.

(f) Consultation with Congress

(1) The President may impose or expand export controls under this section, or extend such controls as required by subsection (a)(3) of this section, only after consultation with the Congress, including the Committee on Foreign Affairs of the House of Representatives and the Committee on Banking, Housing, and Urban Affairs of the Senate.

(2) The President may not impose, expand, or extend export controls under this section until the President has submitted to the Congress a report—

(A) specifying the purpose of the controls;

(B) specifying the determinations of the President (or, in the case of those export controls described in subsection (b)(2), the considerations of the President) with respect to each of the criteria set forth in subsection (b)(1), the bases for such determinations (or considerations), and any possible adverse foreign policy consequences of the controls;

(C) describing the nature, the subjects, and the results of, or the plans for, the consultation with industry pursuant to subsection (c) and with other countries pursuant to subsection (d);

(D) specifying the nature and results of any alternative means attempted under subsection (e), or the reasons for imposing, expanding, or extending the controls without attempting any such alternative means; and

(E) describing the availability from other countries of goods or technology comparable to the goods or technology subject to the proposed export controls, and describing the nature and results of the efforts made pursuant to subsection (h) to secure the cooperation of foreign governments in controlling the foreign availability of such comparable goods or technology.

Such report shall also indicate how such controls will further significantly the foreign policy of the United States or will further its declared international obligations.

(3) To the extent necessary to further the effectiveness of the export controls, portions of a report required by paragraph (2) may be submitted to the Congress on a classified basis, and shall be subject to the provisions of section 12(c) of this Act [section 2411(c) of this Appendix]. Each such report shall, at the same time it is submitted to the Congress, also be submitted to the General Accounting Office for the purpose of assessing the report's full compliance with the intent of this subsection.

(4) In the case of export controls under this section which prohibit or curtail the export of any agricultural commodity, a report submitted pursuant to paragraph (2) shall be deemed to be the report required by section 7(g)(3)(A) of this Act [section 2406(g)(3)(A) of this Appendix].

(5) In addition to any written report required under this section, the Secretary, not less frequently than annually, shall present in oral testimony before the Committee on Banking, Housing, and Urban Affairs of the Senate and the Committee on Foreign Affairs of the House of Representatives a report on policies and actions taken by

the Government to carry out the provisions of this section. [....]

(h) Foreign availability

(1) In applying export controls under this section, the President shall take all feasible steps to initiate and conclude negotiations with appropriate foreign governments for the purpose of securing the cooperation of such foreign governments in controlling the export to countries and consignees to which the United States export controls apply of any goods or technology comparable to goods or technology controlled under this section.

(2) Before extending any export control pursuant to subsection (a)(3) of this section, the President shall evaluate the results of his actions under paragraph (1) of this subsection and shall include the results of that evaluation in his report to the Congress pursuant to subsection (f) of this section.

(3) If, within 6 months after the date on which export controls under this section are imposed or expanded, or within 6 months after the date of the enactment of the Export Administration Amendments Act of 1985 [July 12, 1985] in the case of export controls in effect on such date of enactment, the President's efforts under paragraph (1) are not successful in securing the cooperation of foreign governments described in paragraph (1) with respect to those export controls, the Secretary shall thereafter take into account the foreign availability of the goods or technology subject to the export controls. If the Secretary affirmatively determines that a good or technology subject to the export controls is available in sufficient quantity and comparable quality from sources outside the United States to countries subject to the export controls so that denial of an export license would be ineffective in achieving the purposes of the controls, then the Secretary shall, during the period of such foreign availability, approve any license application which is required for the

export of the good or technology and which meets all requirements for such a license.

The Secretary shall remove the good or technology from the list established pursuant to subsection (l) of this section if the Secretary determines that such action is appropriate.

(4) In making a determination of foreign availability under paragraph (3) of this subsection, the Secretary shall follow the procedures set forth in section 5(f)(3) of this Act [section 2404(f)(3) of this Appendix].

(i) International obligations

The provisions of subsections (b), (c), (d), (e), (g), and (h) shall not apply in any case in which the President exercises the authority contained in this section to impose export controls, or to approve or deny export license applications, in order to fulfill obligations of the United States pursuant to treaties to which the United States is a party or pursuant to other international agreements.

(j) Countries supporting international terrorism

(1) A validated license shall be required for the export of goods or technology to a country if the Secretary of State has made the following determinations:

(A) The government of such country has repeatedly provided support for acts of international terrorism.

(B) The export of such goods or technology could make a significant contribution to the military potential of such country, including its military logistics capability, or could enhance the ability of such country to support acts of international terrorism.

(2) The Secretary and the Secretary of State shall notify the Committee on Foreign Affairs of the House of Representatives and the Committee on Banking, Housing, and Urban Affairs and the Committee on Foreign Relations of the Senate at least 30 days before issuing any validated license required by paragraph (1).

(3) Each determination of the Secretary of State under paragraph (1)(A), including each determination in effect on December 12, 1989, shall be published in the Federal Register.

(4) A determination made by the Secretary of State under paragraph (1)(A) may not be rescinded unless the President submits to the Speaker of the House of Representatives and the chairman of the Committee on Banking, Housing, and Urban Affairs and the chairman of the Committee on Foreign Relations of the Senate—

(A) before the proposed rescission would take effect, a report certifying that—

(i) there has been a fundamental change in the leadership and policies of the government of the country concerned;

(ii) that government is not supporting acts of international terrorism; and

(iii) that government has provided assurances that it will not support acts of international terrorism in the future; or

(B) at least 45 days before the proposed rescission would take effect, a report justifying the rescission and certifying that—

(i) the government concerned has not provided any support for international terrorism during the preceding 6-month period; and

(ii) the government concerned has provided assurances that it will not support acts of international terrorism in the future.

(5) The Secretary and the Secretary of State shall include in the notification required by paragraph (2)—

(A) a detailed description of the goods or services to be offered, including a brief description of the capabilities of any article for which a license to export is sought;

(B) the reasons why the foreign country or international organization to which the export or transfer is proposed to be made needs the goods or services which are the subject of such export or transfer and a description of the manner in which such country or organization intends to use such articles, services, or design and construction services;

(C) the reasons why the proposed export or transfer is in the national interest of the United States;

(D) an analysis of the impact of the proposed export or transfer on the military capabilities of the foreign country or international organization to which such export or transfer would be made;

(E) an analysis of the manner in which the proposed export would affect the relative military strengths of countries in the region to which the goods or services which are the subject of such export would be delivered and whether other countries in the region have comparable kinds and amounts of articles, services, or design and construction services; and

(F) an analysis of the impact of the proposed export or transfer on the United States relations with the countries in the region to which the goods or services which are the subject of such export would be delivered.

(k) Negotiations with other countries

(1) Countries participating in certain agreements

The Secretary of State, in consultation with the Secretary, the Secretary of Defense, and the heads of other appropriate departments and agencies, shall be responsible for conducting negotiations with those countries participating in the groups known as the Coordinating Committee, the Missile Technology Control Regime, the Australia Group, and the Nuclear Suppliers' Group, regarding their cooperation in restricting the export of goods and technology in order to carry out—

(A) the policy set forth in section 3(2)(B) of this Act [section 2402(2)(B) of this Appendix], and

(B) United States policy opposing the proliferation of chemical, biological, nuclear, and other weapons and their delivery systems, and effectively restricting the export of dual use components of such weapons and their delivery systems, in accordance with this subsection and subsections (a) and (l) of this section.

Such negotiations shall cover, among other issues, which goods and technology should be subject to multilaterally agreed export restrictions, and the implementation of the restrictions consistent with the principles identified in section 5(b)(2)(C) of this Act [section 2404(b)(2)(C) of this Appendix].

(2) Other countries

The Secretary of State, in consultation with the Secretary, the Secretary of Defense, and the heads of other appropriate departments and agencies, shall be responsible for conducting negotiations with countries and groups of countries not referred to in paragraph (1) regarding their cooperation in restricting the export of goods and technology consistent with purposes set forth in paragraph (1). In cases where such negotiations produce agreements on export restrictions that the Secretary, in consultation with the Secretary of State and the Secretary of Defense, determines to be consistent with the principles identified in section 5(b)(2)(C) of this Act [section 2404(b)(2)(C) of this Appendix], the Secretary may treat exports, whether by individual or multiple licenses, to countries party to such agreements in the same manner as exports are treated to countries that are MTCR adherents.

(3) Review of determinations

The Secretary shall annually review any determination under paragraph (2) with respect to a country. For each such country which the Secretary determines is not meeting the requirements of an effective export control system in accordance with section 5(b)(2)(C) [section 2404(b)(2)(C) of this Appendix] the Secretary shall restrict or eliminate any preferential licensing treatment for exports to that country provided under this subsection.

(l) Missile technology

(1) Determination of controlled items

The Secretary, in consultation with the Secretary of State, the Secretary of Defense, and the heads of other appropriate departments and agencies—

(A) shall establish and maintain, as part of the control list established under this section, a list of all dual use goods and technology on the MTCR Annex; and

(B) may include, as part of the control list established under this section, goods and technology that would provide a direct and immediate impact on the development of missile delivery systems and are not included in the MTCR Annex but which the United States is proposing to the other MTCR adherents to have included in the MTCR Annex.

(2) Requirement of individual validated licenses

The Secretary shall require an individual validated license for—

(A) any export of goods or technology on the list established under paragraph (1) to any country; and

(B) any export of goods or technology that the exporter knows is destined for a project or facility for the design, development, or manufacture of a missile in a country that is not an MTCR adherent.

(3) Policy of denial of licenses

(A) Licenses under paragraph (2) should in general be denied if the ultimate consignee of the goods or technology is a facility in a country that is not an adherent to the Missile Technology Control Regime and the facility is designed to develop or build missiles.

(B) Licenses under paragraph (2) shall be denied if the ultimate consignee of the goods or technology is a facility in a country the government of which has been determined under subsection (j) of this section to have repeatedly provided support for acts of international terrorism.

(4) Consultation with other departments

(A) A determination of the Secretary to approve an export license under paragraph (2) for the export of goods or technology to a country of concern regarding missile proliferation may be made only after consultation with the Secretary of Defense and the Secretary of State for a period of 20 days. The countries of concern referred to in the preceding sentence shall be maintained on a classified list by the Secretary of State, in consultation with the Secretary and the Secretary of Defense.

(B) Should the Secretary of Defense disagree with the determination of the Secretary to approve an export license to which subparagraph (A) applies, the Secretary of Defense shall so notify the Secretary within the 20 days provided for consultation on the determination. The Secretary of Defense shall at the same time submit the matter to the President for resolution of the dispute. The Secretary shall also submit the Secretary's recommendation to the President on the license application.

(C) The President shall approve or disapprove the export license application within 20 days after receiving the submission of the Secretary of Defense under subparagraph (B).

(D) Should the Secretary of Defense fail to notify the Secretary within the time period prescribed in subparagraph (B), the Secretary may approve the license application without awaiting the notification by the Secretary of Defense. Should the President fail to notify the Secretary of his decision on the export license application within the time period prescribed in subparagraph (C), the Secretary may approve the license application without awaiting the President's decision on the license application.

(E) Within 10 days after an export license is issued under this subsection, the Secretary shall provide to the Secretary of Defense and the Secretary of State the license application and accompanying documents issued to the applicant, to the extent that the relevant Secretary indicates the need to receive such application and documents.

(5) Information sharing

The Secretary shall establish a procedure for information sharing with appropriate officials of the intelligence community, as determined by the Director of Central Intelligence, and other appropriate Government agencies, that will ensure effective monitoring of transfers of MTCR equipment or technology and other missile technology.

(m) Chemical and biological weapons

(1) Establishment of list

The Secretary, in consultation with the Secretary of State, the Secretary of Defense, and the heads of other appropriate departments and agencies, shall establish and maintain, as part of the list maintained under this section, a list of goods and technology that would directly and substantially assist a foreign government or group in acquiring the capability to develop, produce, stockpile, or deliver chemical or biological weapons, the licensing of which would be effective in barring acquisition or enhancement of such capability.

(2) Requirement for validated licenses

The Secretary shall require a validated license for any export of goods or technology on the list established under paragraph (1) to any country of concern.

(3) Countries of concern

For purposes of paragraph (2), the term "country of concern" means any country other than—

(A) a country with whose government the United States has entered into a bilateral or multilateral arrangement for the control of goods or technology on the list established under paragraph (1); and

(B) such other countries as the Secretary of State, in consultation with the Secretary and the Secretary of Defense, shall designate consistent with the purposes of the Chemical and Biological Weapons Control and Warfare Elimination Act of 1991 [22 U.S.C.A. § 5601 et seq.].

[....]

(o) Control list

The Secretary shall establish and maintain, as part of the control list, a list of any goods or technology subject to export controls under this section, and the countries to which such controls apply. The Secretary shall clearly identify on the control list which goods or technology, and which countries or destinations, are subject to which types of controls under this section. Such list shall consist of goods and technology identified by the Secretary of State, with the concurrence of the Secretary. If the Secretary and the Secretary of State are unable to agree on the list, the matter shall be referred to the President. Such list shall be reviewed not less frequently than every three years in the case of controls maintained cooperatively with other countries, and annually in the case of all other controls, for the purpose of making such revisions as are necessary in order to carry out this section. During the course of such review, an assessment shall be made periodically of the availability from sources outside the United States, or any of its territories or possessions, of goods and technology comparable to those controlled for export from the United States under this section.

(p) Effect on existing contracts and licenses

The President may not, under this section, prohibit or curtail the export or reexport of goods, technology, or other information—

(1) in performance of a contract or agreement entered into before the date on which the President reports to the Congress, pursuant to subsection (f) of this section, his intention to impose controls on the export or reexport of such goods, technology, or other information, or

(2) under a validated license or other authorization issued under this Act [sections 2401 to 2420 of this Appendix],

unless and until the President determines and certifies to the Congress that—

(A) a breach of the peace poses a serious and direct threat to the strategic interest of the United States,

(B) the prohibition or curtailment of such contracts, agreements, licenses, or authorizations will be instrumental in remedying the situation posing the direct threat, and

(C) the export controls will continue only so long as the direct threat persists. [....]

(r) Expanded authority to impose controls

(1) In any case in which the President determines that it is necessary to impose controls under this section without any limitation contained in subsection (c), (d), (e), (g), (h), or (m) of this section, the President may impose those controls only if the President submits that determination to the Congress, together with a report pursuant to subsection (f) of this section with respect to the proposed

controls, and only if a law is enacted authorizing the imposition of those controls. If a joint resolution authorizing the imposition of those controls is introduced in either House of Congress within 30 days after the Congress receives the determination and report of the President, that joint resolution shall be referred to the Committee on Banking, Housing, and Urban Affairs of the Senate and to the appropriate committee of the House of Representatives. If either such committee has not reported the joint resolution at the end of 30 days after its referral, the committee shall be discharged from further consideration of the joint resolution.

(2) For purposes of this subsection, the term "joint resolution" means a joint resolution of the matter after the resolving clause which is as follows:

"That the Congress, having received on __________ a determination of the President under section 6(o)(1) of the Export Administration Act of 1979 with respect to the export controls which are set forth in the report submitted to the Congress with that determination, authorizes the President to impose those export controls.", with the date of the receipt of the determination and report inserted in the blank.

(3) In the computation of the periods of 30 days referred to in paragraph (1), there shall be excluded the days on which either House of Congress is not in session because of an adjournment of more than 3 days to a day certain or because of an adjournment of the Congress sine die.

(s) Spare parts

(1) At the same time as the President imposes or expands export controls under this section, the President shall determine whether such export controls will apply to replacement parts for parts in goods subject to such export controls.

(2) With respect to export controls imposed under this section before the date of the enactment of this subsection [Aug. 23, 1988], an individual validated export

license shall not be required for replacement parts which are exported to replace on a one-for-one basis parts that were in a good that was lawfully exported from the United States, unless the President determines that such a license should be required for such parts. [....]

§ 2410. Violations [by United States persons....]

§ 2415. Definitions

As used in this Act [sections 2401 to 2420 of this Appendix]—

(1) the term "person" includes the singular and the plural and any individual, partnership, corporation, or other form of association, including any government or agency thereof;

(2) the term "United States person" means any United States resident or national (other than an individual resident outside the United States and employed by other than a United States person), any domestic concern (including any permanent domestic establishment of any foreign concern) and any foreign subsidiary or affiliate (including any permanent foreign establishment) of any domestic concern which is controlled in fact by such domestic concern, as determined under regulations of the President;

(3) the term "good" means any article, natural or manmade substance, material, supply or manufactured product, including inspection and test equipment, and excluding technical data;

(4) the term "technology" means the information and know-how (whether in tangible form, such as models, prototypes, drawings, sketches, diagrams, blueprints, or manuals, or in intangible form, such as training or technical services) that can be used to design, produce, manufacture, utilize, or reconstruct goods, including computer software and technical data, but not the goods themselves;

(5) the term "export" means—

(A) an actual shipment, transfer, or transmission of goods or technology out of the United States;

(B) a transfer of goods or technology in the United States to an embassy or affiliate of a controlled country; or

(C) a transfer to any person of goods or technology either within the United States or outside of the United States with the knowledge or intent that the goods or technology will be shipped, transferred, or transmitted to an unauthorized recipient;

(6) the term "controlled country" means a controlled country under section 5(b)(1) of this Act [section 2404(b)(1) of this Appendix]; [....]

§ 2416. Effect on other Acts [....]

(d) Nonproliferation controls

(1) Nothing in section 5 or 6 of this Act [section 2404 or 2405 of this Appendix] shall be construed to supersede the procedures published by the President pursuant to section 309(c) of the Nuclear Non-Proliferation Act of 1978 [42 U.S.C.A. § 2139a(c)]. [....]

G. Executive Order 12924, Continuation of Export Administration Act

EXECUTIVE ORDER NO. 12924

< Aug. 19, 1994, 59 F.R. 43437 >

CONTINUATION OF EXPORT CONTROL REGULATIONS

By the authority vested in me as President by the Constitution and the laws of the United States of America, including but not limited to section 203 of the International Emergency Economic Powers Act ("Act") (50 U.S.C. 1702) [section 1702 of this title], I, WILLIAM J. CLINTON, President of the United States of America, find that the unrestricted access of foreign parties to U.S. goods, technology, and technical data and the existence of certain boycott practices of foreign nations, in light of the expiration of the Export Administration Act of 1979, as amended (50 U.S.C. App. 2401 et seq.) [section 2401 et seq. of the Appendix to Title 50], constitute an unusual and extraordinary threat to the national security, foreign policy, and economy of the United States and hereby declare a national emergency with respect to that threat.

Accordingly, in order (a) to exercise the necessary vigilance over exports and activities affecting the national security of the United States; (b) to further significantly the foreign policy of the United States, including its policy with respect to cooperation by U.S. persons with certain foreign boycott activities, and to fulfill its international responsibilities; and (c) to protect the domestic economy from the excessive drain of scarce materials and reduce the serious economic impact of foreign demand, it is hereby ordered as follows:

Section 1. To the extent permitted by law, the provisions of the Export Administration Act of 1979, as amended, [section 2401 et seq. of the Appendix to Title 50] and the provisions for administration of the Export Administration Act of 1979, as amended, shall be carried out under this order so as to continue in full force and effect and amend, as necessary, the export control system heretofore maintained by the Export Administration regulations issued under the Export Administration Act of 1979, as amended. The delegations of authority set forth in Executive Order No. 12002 of July 7, 1977, as amended by Executive Order No. 12755 of March 12, 1991 [set out as a note under section 2403 of the Appendix to Title 50]; Executive Order No. 12214 of May 2, 1980 [set out as a note under section 2403 of the Appendix to Title 50]; Executive Order No. 12735 of November 16, 1990 [set out as a note under this section]; and Executive Order No. 12851 of June 11, 1993 [set out as a note under section 2797 of Title 22, Foreign Relations and Intercourse], shall be incorporated in this order and shall apply to the exercise of authorities under this order.

Sec. 2. All rules and regulations issued or continued in effect by the Secretary of Commerce under the authority of the Export Administration Act of 1979, as amended [section 2401 et seq. of the Appendix to Title 50], including those published in Title 15, Subtitle B, Chapter VII, Subchapter C, of the Code of Federal Regulations, Parts 768 through 799, and all orders, regulations, licenses, and other forms of administrative action issued, taken, or continued in effect pursuant thereto, shall, until amended or revoked by the Secretary of Commerce, remain in full force and effect as if issued or taken pursuant to this order, except that the provisions of sections 203(b)(2) and 206 of the Act (50 U.S.C. 1702(b)(2) and 1705) [sections 1702(b)(2) and 1705 of this title] shall control over any inconsistent provisions in the regulations. Nothing in this section shall affect the continued applicability of administrative sanctions provided for by the regulations described above.

Sec. 3. Provisions for administration of section 38(e) of the Arms Export Control Act (22 U.S.C. 2778(e)) [section 2778(e) of Title 22] may be made and shall continue in full force and effect until amended or revoked under the authority of section 203 of the Act (50 U.S.C. 1702) [section 1702 of this title]. To the extent permitted by law, this order also shall constitute authority for the issuance and continuation in full force and effect of all rules and regulations by the President or his delegate, and all orders, licenses, and other forms of administrative actions issued, taken, or continued in effect pursuant thereto, relating to the administration of section 38(e) [section 2778(e) of Title 22].

Sec. 4. Executive Order No. 12923 of June 30, 1994, [formerly set out as a note under this section] is revoked, and that declaration of emergency is rescinded. The revocation of Executive Order No. 12923 shall not affect any violation of any rules, regulations, orders, licenses, and other forms of administrative action under that order that occurred during the period the order was in effect.

Sec. 5. This order shall be effective as of midnight between August 20, 1994, and August 21, 1994, and shall remain in effect until terminated.

WILLIAM J. CLINTON

H. (AECA) Annual Proliferation Report Requirements of the Arms Export Control Act

UNITED STATES CODE ANNOTATED

TITLE 22. FOREIGN RELATIONS AND INTERCOURSE

CHAPTER 39—ARMS EXPORT CONTROL

SUBCHAPTER I—FOREIGN AND NATIONAL SECURITY POLICY OBJECTIVES AND RESTRAINTS

Current through P.L. 104-160, approved 7-9-96 [....]

§ 2751. Need for international defense cooperation and military export controls; Presidential waiver; report to Congress; arms sales policy [....]

HISTORICAL AND STATUTORY NOTES

Revision Notes and Legislative Reports [....]

Annual Report on the Proliferation of Missiles and Essential Components of Nuclear, Biological, and Chemical Weapons

Pub.L. 102-190, Div. A, Title X, § 1097(a)-(f), Dec. 5, 1991, 105 Stat. 1489, as amended Pub.L. 104-106, Div. A, Title XV, §§ 1502(c)(3), 1504(d), Feb. 10, 1996, 110 Stat. 507, 514, provided that:

"(a) Report required.—

(1) The President shall submit to the Committee on National Security and the Committee on International Relations of the House of Representatives and the Committees on Armed Services and Foreign Relations of the Senate an annual report on the transfer by any country of weapons, technology, or materials that can be used to deliver, manufacture, or weaponize nuclear, biological, or chemical weapons (hereinafter in this section referred to as 'NBC weapons') to any country other than a country referred to in subsection (d) that is seeking to acquire such weapons, technology, or materials, or other system that the Secretary of Defense has reason to believe could be used to deliver NBC weapons.

"(2) The first such report shall be submitted not later than 90 days after the date of the enactment of this Act [Dec. 5, 1991].

"(b) Matters to be covered.—Each such report shall cover—

"(1) the transfer of all aircraft, cruise missiles, artillery weapons, unguided rockets and multiple rocket systems, and related bombs, shells, warheads and other weaponization technology and materials that the Secretary has reason to believe may be intended for the delivery of NBC weapons;

"(2) international transfers of MTCR equipment or technology to any country that is seeking to acquire such equipment or any other system that the Secretary has reason to believe may be used to deliver NBC weapons; and

"(3) the transfer of technology, test equipment, radioactive materials, feedstocks and cultures, and all other specialized materials that the Secretary has reason to believe could be used to manufacture NBC weapons.

"(c) Content of report.—Each such report shall include the following:

"(1) The status of missile, aircraft, and other weapons delivery and weaponization programs in any such country, including efforts by such country to acquire MTCR equipment, NBC-capable aircraft, or any other weapon or major weapon component which is dedicated to the delivery of NBC weapons, whose primary use is the delivery of NBC weapons, or that the Secretary has reason to believe could be used to deliver NBC weapons.

"(2) The status of NBC weapons development, manufacture, and deployment programs in any such country, including efforts to acquire essential test equipment, manufacturing equipment and technology, weaponization equipment and technology, and radioactive material, feedstocks or components of feedstocks, and biological cultures and toxins.

"(3) A description of assistance provided by any person or government, after the date of the enactment of this Act [Dec. 5, 1991], to any such country in the development of—

"(A) missile systems, as defined in the MTCR or that the Secretary has reason to believe may be used to deliver NBC weapons;

"(B) aircraft and other delivery systems and weapons that the Secretary has reason to believe could be used to deliver NBC weapons; and

"(C) NBC weapons.

"(4) A listing of those persons and countries which continue to provide such equipment or technology described in paragraph (3) to any country as of the date of submission of the report.

"(5) A description of the diplomatic measures that the United States, and that other adherents to the MTCR and other agreements affecting the acquisition and delivery of NBC weapons, have made with respect to activities and private persons and governments suspected of violating the MTCR and such other agreements.

"(6) An analysis of the effectiveness of the regulatory and enforcement regimes of the United States and other countries that adhere to the MTCR and other agreements affecting the acquisition and delivery of NBC weapons in controlling the export of MTCR and other NBC weapons and delivery system equipment or technology.

"(7) A summary of advisory opinions issued under section 11B(b)(4) of the Export Administration Act of 1979 (50 U.S.C. App. 2401b(b)(4)) [section 2401b(b)(4) of the Appendix to Title 50, War and National Defense] and under section 73(d) of the Arms Export Control Act (22 U.S.C. 2797b(d)) [section 2797b(d) of this title].

"(8) An explanation of United States policy regarding the transfer of MTCR equipment or technology to foreign missile programs, including programs involving launches of space vehicles.

"(d) Exclusions.—The countries excluded under subsection (a) are Australia, Belgium, Canada, Denmark, France, Germany, Greece, Iceland, Israel, Italy, Japan, Luxembourg, the Netherlands, Norway, Portugal, Spain, Turkey, the United Kingdom, and the United States.

"(e) Classification of report.—The President shall make every effort to submit all of the information required by this section in unclassified form. Whenever the President submits any such information in classified form, he shall submit such classified information in an addendum and shall also submit concurrently a detailed summary, in unclassified form, of that classified information.

"(f) Definitions.—For purposes of this section:

"(1) The terms 'missile', 'MTCR', and 'MTCR equipment or technology' have the meanings given those terms in section 74 of the Arms Export Control Act (22 U.S.C. 2797c) [section 2797c of this title].

"(2) The term 'weaponize' or 'weaponization' means to incorporate into, or the incorporation into, usable ordnance or other militarily useful means of delivery." [....]

I. FY 1997 China Report Requirements

NATIONAL DEFENSE AUTHORIZATION ACT FOR FISCAL YEAR 1997

[[Page 110 STAT. 2422]]

Public Law 104-201

104th Congress

An Act

To authorize appropriations for fiscal year 1997 for military activities of the Department of Defense, for military construction, and for defense activities of the Department of Energy, to prescribe personnel strengths for such fiscal year for the Armed Forces, and for other purposes. <<NOTE: Sept. 23, 1996 - [H.R. 3230]>>

Be it enacted by the Senate and House of Representatives of the United States of America in <<NOTE: National Defense Authorization Act for Fiscal Year 1997.>> Congress assembled, [....]

SEC. 1306. PRESIDENTIAL REPORT REGARDING WEAPONS PROLIFERATION AND POLICIES OF THE PEOPLE'S REPUBLIC OF CHINA.

(a) Findings.—The Congress finds that—

(1) the People's Republic of China acceded to the Treaty on the Non-Proliferation of Nuclear Weapons (hereafter in this section referred to as the "NPT") on March 9, 1992;

(2) the People's Republic of China is not a member of the Nuclear Suppliers Group and remains the only major nuclear supplier that continues to transfer nuclear technology, equipment, and materials to countries that have not agreed to the application of safeguards of the International Atomic Energy Agency (hereafter in this section referred to as the "IAEA") over all of their nuclear materials;

(3) on June 30, 1995, the United States and 29 other members of the Nuclear Suppliers Group notified the Director General of the IAEA that the Government of each respective country has decided that the controls of that Group should not be defeated by the transfer of component parts;

(4) a state-owned entity in the People's Republic of China, the China Nuclear Energy Industry Corporation, has knowingly transferred specially designed ring magnets to an unsafeguarded uranium enrichment facility in the Islamic Republic of Pakistan;

(5) ring magnets are identified on the Trigger List of the Nuclear Suppliers Group as a component of magnetic suspension bearings which are to be exported only to countries that have safeguards of the IAEA over all of their nuclear materials;

(6) these ring magnets could contribute significantly to the ability of the Islamic Republic of Pakistan to produce additional unsafeguarded enriched uranium, a nuclear explosive material;

(7) the Government of the People's Republic of China has transferred nuclear equipment and technology to the Islamic Republic of Iran, despite repeated claims by the Government of the United States that the Islamic Republic of Iran is engaged in clandestine efforts to acquire a nuclear explosive device;

(8) representatives of the Government of the People's Republic of China have repeatedly assured the Government of the United States that the People's Republic of China would abide by the guidelines of the Missile Technology Control Regime (hereafter in this section referred to as the "MTCR");

(9) the Government of China has transferred M-11 missiles to the Islamic Republic of Pakistan; and

(10) the M-11 missile conforms to the definition of a nuclear-capable missile under the MTCR.

(b) Sense of the Congress.—It is the sense of the Congress that—

(1) the assistance that the People's Republic of China has provided to the Islamic Republic of Iran and to the Islamic Republic of Pakistan could contribute to the ability of such countries to manufacture nuclear weapons;

(2) the recent transfer by the People's Republic of China of ring magnets to an unsafeguarded uranium enrichment facility in the Islamic Republic of Pakistan conflicts with China's obligations under Articles I and III of the NPT, as well as the official nonproliferation policies and assurances by the People's Republic of China and the Islamic Republic of Pakistan with respect to the nonproliferation of nuclear weapons and nuclear-capable missiles;

(3) the transfer of M-11 missiles from the People's Republic of China to the Islamic Republic of Pakistan is inconsistent with longstanding United States Government interpretations of assurances from the Government of the People's Republic of China with respect to that country's intent to abide by the guidelines of the MTCR;

(4) violations by the People's Republic of China of the standards and objectives of the MTCR and global nuclear nonproliferation regimes have jeopardized the credibility of the MTCR and such regimes;

(5) the MTCR and global nuclear nonproliferation regimes require collective international action to impose costs against and to withhold benefits from any country, including the People's Republic of China, that engages in activities that are contrary to the objectives of those regimes;

(6) the President should explore with the governments of other countries new opportunities for collective action in response to activities of any country, including the People's Republic of China, that aid or abet the global proliferation of weapons of mass destruction or their means of delivery; and

(7) the President should communicate to the Government of the People's Republic of China the sense of the Congress that the stability and growth of future relations between the people, the economies, and the Governments of the United States and the People's Republic of China will significantly depend upon substantive evidence of cooperation by the Government of the People's Republic of China in efforts to halt the global proliferation of weapons of mass destruction and their means of delivery.

(c) Report.—Not later than 60 days after the date of the enactment of this Act, the President shall submit to the Congress a report, in both classified and unclassified form, concerning the transfer from the People's Republic of China to the Islamic Republic of Pakistan of technology, equipment, or materials important to the production of nuclear weapons and their means of delivery. The President shall include in the report the following:

(1) The specific justification of the Secretary of State for determining that there was not a sufficient basis for imposing sanctions under section 2(b)(4) of the Export-Import Bank Act of 1945, as amended by section 825 of the Nuclear Proliferation Prevention Act of 1994, by reason of

the transfer of ring magnets and other technology, equipment, or materials from the People's Republic of China to the Islamic Republic of Pakistan.

(2) What commitment the United States Government is seeking from the People's Republic of China to ensure that the People's Republic of China establishes a fully effective export control system that will prevent transfers (such as the Pakistan sale) from taking place in the future.

(3) A description of the pledges, assurances, and other commitments made by representatives of the Governments of the People's Republic of China and the Islamic Republic of Pakistan to the Government of the United States since January 1, 1991, with respect to the nonproliferation of nuclear weapons or nuclear-capable missiles, and an assessment of the record of compliance with such undertakings.

(4) Whether, in light of the recent assurances provided by the People's Republic of China, the President intends to make the certification and submit the report required by section 902(a)(6)(B) of the Foreign Relations Authorization Act, Fiscal Years 1990 and 1991 (22 U.S.C. 2151 note), and make the certification and submit the report required by Public Law 99-183, relating to the approval and implementation of the agreement for nuclear cooperation between the United States and the People's Republic of China, and, if not, why not.

(5) Whether the Secretary of State considers the recent assurances and clarifications provided by the People's Republic of China to have provided sufficient information to allow the United States to determine that the People's Republic of China is not in violation of paragraph (2) of section 129 of the Atomic Energy Act of 1954, as required by Public Law 99-183.

(6) If the President is unable or unwilling to make the certifications and reports referred to in paragraph (4), a description of what the President considers to be the significance of the clarifications and assurances provided by the People's Republic of China in the course of the

recent discussions regarding the transfer by the People's Republic of China of nuclear-weapon-related equipment to the Islamic Republic of Pakistan.

(7) A description of the laws, regulations, and procedures currently used by the People's Republic of China to regulate exports of nuclear technology, equipment, or materials, including dual-use goods, and an assessment of the effectiveness of such arrangements.

(8) A description of the current policies and practices of other countries in response to the transfer of nuclear and missile technology by the People's Republic of China to the Islamic Republic of Pakistan and the Islamic Republic of Iran.

J. Agricultural Improvement and Reform Act

FEDERAL AGRICULTURE IMPROVEMENT AND REFORM ACT OF 1996

[[Page 110 STAT. 888]]

Public Law 104-127

104th Congress

An Act

To modify the operation of certain agricultural programs. <<NOTE: Apr. 4, 1996 - [H.R. 2854]>>

Be it enacted by the Senate and House of Representatives of the United States of America in Congress assembled, <<NOTE: Federal Agriculture Improvement and Reform Act of 1996.>>

[[Page 110 STAT. 970]]

"SEC. 417. <<NOTE: 7 USC 5677.>> TRADE COMPENSATION AND ASSISTANCE PROGRAMS.

"(a) In General.—Except as provided in subsection (f), notwithstanding any other provision of law, if, after the date of enactment of this section, the President or any other member of the executive branch causes exports from the United States to any country to be unilaterally suspended for reasons of national security or foreign policy, and if within 90 days after the date on which the suspension is imposed on United States exports no other country with an agricultural economic interest agrees to participate in the suspension, the Secretary shall carry out a trade compensation assistance program in accordance with this section (referred to in this section as a 'program').

"(b) Compensation or Provision of Funds.—Under a program, the Secretary shall, based on an evaluation by the Secretary of the method most likely to produce the greatest compensatory benefit for producers of the commodity involved in the suspension—

"(1) compensate producers of the commodity by making payments available to producers, as provided by subsection (c)(1); or

"(2) make available an amount of funds calculated under subsection (c)(2), to promote agricultural exports or provide agricultural commodities to developing countries under any authorities available to the Secretary.

"(c) Determination of Amount of Compensation or Funds.—

"(1) Compensation.—If the Secretary makes payments available to producers under subsection (b)(1), the amount of the payment shall be determined by the Secretary based on the Secretary's estimate of the loss suffered by producers of the commodity involved due to any decrease in the price of the commodity as a result of the suspension.

"(2) Determination of amount of funds.—For each fiscal year of a program, the amount of funds made available under subsection (b)(2) shall be equal to 90 percent of the average annual value of United States agricultural exports to the country with respect to which exports are suspended during the most recent 3 years prior to the suspension for which data are available.

"(d) Duration of Program.—For each suspension of exports for which a program is implemented under this section, funds shall be made available under subsection (b) for each fiscal year or part of a fiscal year for which the suspension is in effect, but not to exceed 3 fiscal years.

"(e) Commodity Credit Corporation.—The Secretary shall use funds of the Commodity Credit Corporation to carry out this section.

"(f) Exception to Carrying Out a Program.—This section shall not apply to any suspension of trade due to a war or armed hostility.

"(g) Partial Year Embargoes.—If the Secretary makes funds available under subsection (b)(2), regardless of whether an embargo is in effect for only part of a fiscal year, the full amount of funds as calculated under subsection (c)(2) shall be made available under a program for the fiscal year. If the Secretary determines that making the required amount of funds available in a partial fiscal year is impracticable, the Secretary may make all or part of the funds required to be made available in the following fiscal year (in addition to any funds otherwise required under a program to be made available in the following fiscal year).

"(h) Short Supply Embargoes.—If the President or any other member of the executive branch causes exports to be suspended based on a determination of short supply, the Secretary shall carry out section 1002 of the Food and Agriculture Act of 1977 (7 U.S.C. 1310).".

K. Ukraine Assistance Limitations

1. FY 1996

FOREIGN OPERATIONS, EXPORT FINANCING, AND RELATED PROGRAMS APPROPRIATIONS ACT, 1996

[[Page 110 STAT. 704]]

Public Law 104-107

104th Congress

An Act

Making appropriations for foreign operations, export financing, and related programs for the fiscal year ending September 30, 1996, and for other purposes. <<NOTE: Feb. 12, 1996 - [H.R. 1868]>>

Be it enacted by the Senate and House of Representatives of the United States of America in Congress assembled, <<NOTE: Foreign Operations, Export Financing, and Related Programs Appropriations Act, 1996.>> That the following sums are appropriated, out of any money in the Treasury not otherwise appropriated, for the fiscal year ending September 30, 1996, and for other purposes, namely: [...]

TITLE II—BILATERAL ECONOMIC ASSISTANCE

For expenses necessary to enable the President to carry out the provisions of the Foreign Assistance Act of 1961, and for other purposes, to remain available until September 30, 1996, unless otherwise specified herein, as follows: [...]

Other Bilateral Economic Assistance [...]

(k) Of the funds made available under this heading, not less than $225,000,000 shall be made available for Ukraine, with the understanding that Ukraine will undertake significant economic reforms which are additional to those which were undertaken in previous fiscal years, and of which not less than $50,000,000 (from this or any other Act) shall be made available to improve energy self-sufficiency and improve safety at nuclear reactors, and of which $2,000,000 should be made available to conduct or implement an assessment of the energy distribution grid that provides recommendations leading to increased access to power by industrial, commercial and residential users, and of which not less than $22,000,000 shall be made available to support the development of small and medium enterprises, including independent broadcast and print media.

[...]

TITLE V—GENERAL PROVISIONS

[...]

Sec. 506. None of the funds appropriated or made available (other than funds for "International Organizations and Programs") pursuant to this Act, for carrying out the Foreign Assistance Act of 1961, may be used, except for purposes of nuclear safety, to finance the export of nuclear equipment, fuel, or technology.

Sec. 507. None of the funds appropriated or otherwise made available pursuant to this Act shall be obligated or expended to finance directly any assistance or reparations to Cuba, Iraq, Libya, North Korea, Iran, Serbia, Sudan, or Syria: Provided, That for purposes of this section, the prohibition on obligations or expenditures shall include direct loans, credits, insurance and guarantees of the Export-Import Bank or its agents.

2. FY 1997

PL 104-164 "To amend the Foreign Assistance Act of 1961 and the Arms Export Control..."

dated: 7-21-96

H.R. 3540 (eas) [Engrossed Amendment Senate]

In the Senate of the United States,

July 26, 1996.

Resolved, That the bill from the House of Representatives (H.R. 3540) entitled "An Act making appropriations for foreign operations, export financing, and related programs for the fiscal year ending September 30, 1997, and for other purposes", do pass with the following

AMENDMENT:

Strike out all after the enacting clause and insert:

That the following sums are appropriated, out of any money in the Treasury not otherwise appropriated, for the fiscal year ending September 30, 1997, and for other purposes, namely:

TITLE I—EXPORT AND INVESTMENT ASSISTANCE

Export-Import Bank of the United States

The Export-Import Bank of the United States is authorized to make such expenditures within the limits of funds and borrowing authority available to such corporation, and in accordance with law, and to make such contracts and commitments without regard to fiscal year limitations, as provided by section 104 of the Government Corporation Control Act, as may be necessary in carrying out the program for the current fiscal year for such corporation: Provided,

That none of the funds available during the current fiscal year may be used to make expenditures, contracts, or commitments for the export of nuclear equipment, fuel, or technology to any country other than a nuclear-weapon State as defined in Article IX of the Treaty on the Non-Proliferation of Nuclear Weapons eligible to receive economic or military assistance under this Act that has detonated a nuclear explosive after the date of enactment of this Act. [...]

Assistance for the New Independent States of the Former Soviet Union [....]

(u) Funds appropriated under this heading may not be made available for the Government of Ukraine if the President determines and reports to the Committees on Appropriations that the Government of Ukraine is engaged in military cooperation with the Government of Libya.

[...]

This Act may be cited as the "Foreign Operations, Export Financing, and Related Programs Appropriations Act, 1997".

Attest:

Secretary.

104th CONGRESS

2d Session

L. Cooperative Threat Reduction Certifications

[Laws in effect as of January 16, 1996]

[Document affected by Public Law 104-106 Section 3131]

[CITE: 22USC5952]

TITLE 22—FOREIGN RELATIONS AND INTERCOURSE

CHAPTER 68A—COOPERATIVE THREAT REDUCTION WITH STATES OF FORMER SOVIET UNION

Sec. 5952. Authority for programs to facilitate cooperative threat reduction

(a) In general

Notwithstanding any other provision of law, the President may conduct programs described in subsection (b) of this section to assist the independent states of the former Soviet Union in the demilitarization of the former Soviet Union. Any such program may be carried out only to the extent that the President determines that the program will directly contribute to the national security interests of the United States.

(b) Authorized programs

The programs referred to in subsection (a) of this section are the following:

(1) Programs to facilitate the elimination, and the safe and secure transportation and storage, of nuclear, chemical, and other weapons and their delivery vehicles.

(2) Programs to facilitate the safe and secure storage of fissile materials derived from the elimination of nuclear weapons.

(3) Programs to prevent the proliferation of weapons, weapons components, and weapons-related technology and expertise.

(4) Programs to expand military-to-military and defense contacts.

(5) Programs to facilitate the demilitarization of defense industries and the conversion of military technologies and capabilities into civilian activities.

(6) Programs to assist in the environmental restoration of former military sites and installations when such restoration is necessary to the demilitarization or conversion programs authorized in paragraph (5).

(7) Programs to provide housing for former military personnel of the former Soviet Union released from military service in connection with the dismantlement of strategic nuclear weapons, when provision of such housing is necessary for dismantlement of strategic nuclear weapons and when no other funds are available for such housing.

(8) Other programs as described in section 212(b) of the Soviet Nuclear Threat Reduction Act of 1991 (title II of Public Law 102-228; 22 U.S.C. 2551 note) and section 5902(b) of this title.

(c) United States participation

The programs described in subsection (b) of this section should, to the extent feasible, draw upon United States technology and expertise, especially from the private sector of the United States.

(d) Restrictions

Assistance authorized by subsection (a) of this section may not be provided to any independent state of the former Soviet Union for any year unless the President certifies to Congress for that year that the proposed recipient state is committed to each of the following:

(1) Making substantial investment of its resources for dismantling or destroying its weapons of mass destruction, if such state has an obligation under a treaty or other agreement to destroy or dismantle any such weapons.

(2) Foregoing any military modernization program that exceeds legitimate defense requirements and foregoing the replacement of destroyed weapons of mass destruction.

(3) Foregoing any use in new nuclear weapons of fissionable or other components of destroyed nuclear weapons.

(4) Facilitating United States verification of any weapons destruction carried out under this chapter, section 5902(b) of this title, or section 212(b) of the Soviet Nuclear Threat Reduction Act of 1991 (title II of Public Law 102-228; 22 U.S.C. 2551 note).

(5) Complying with all relevant arms control agreements.

(6) Observing internationally recognized human rights, including the protection of minorities.

M. United Nations General Assembly Resolution on Coercive Economic Measures

UNITED NATIONS A

General Assembly

Distr.
GENERAL
A/RES/51/22
6 December 1996

Fifty-first session

Agenda item 159

RESOLUTION ADOPTED BY THE GENERAL ASSEMBLY

[without reference to a Main Committee (A/51/L.23)]

51/22. Elimination of coercive economic measures as a means of political and economic compulsion

The General Assembly,

Guided by the principles of the Charter of the United Nations, particularly those which call for the development of friendly relations among nations, and the achievement of cooperation in solving problems of an economic and social character,

Recalling its numerous resolutions in which it called upon the international community to take urgent and effective steps to end coercive economic measures,

Gravely concerned over the recent enactment of extraterritorial coercive economic laws in contravention of the norms of international law and the aims and purposes of the United Nations,

Believing that the prompt elimination of such measures is consistent with the aims and purposes of the United Nations and the relevant provisions of the World Trade Organization,

1. Reaffirms the inalienable right of every State to economic and social development and to choose the political, economic and social system which it deems most appropriate for the welfare of its people, in accordance with its national plans and policies;

2. Calls for the immediate repeal of unilateral extraterritorial laws that impose sanctions on companies and nationals of other States;

3. Calls upon all States not to recognize unilateral extraterritorial coercive economic measures or legislative acts imposed by any State;

4. Requests the Secretary-General to submit to the General Assembly at its fifty-second session a report on the implementation of the present resolution;

5. Decides to include in the agenda of its fifty-second session the item entitled "Elimination of coercive economic measures as a means of political and economic compulsion".

67th Plenary Meeting
27 November 1996

BIBLIOGRAPHY

Amuzegar, J., "Adjusting to Sanctions," *Foreign Affairs,* May/June 1997, pp. 31–41.

Associated Press, "U.S. Raises Ante Against Russia," January 14, 1999.

Bahree, Bhushan, "European Oil Majors March Back to Iran," *The Wall Street Journal,* March 10, 1999.

Baker, John C., *Non-Proliferation Incentives for Russia and Ukraine,* Oxford, UK: Oxford University Press, Adelphi Paper 309, May 1997.

Baruch, Bernard, presentation to the United States Atomic Energy Commission, June 14, 1946; online at http://www.nuclearfiles.org/docs/1946/460614-baruch.html.

Bloomberg News, "European Oil Companies Plan Expansions in Libya," *The New York Times,* April 6, 1999.

Cantigny Conference—see "The Strategy of Sanctions" Conference.

Center for Strategic and International Studies (CSIS), *Unilateral Economic Sanctions: Interim Report of the Steering Committee of the CSIS Project on Unilateral Economic Sanctions,* Washington, D.C., June 10, 1998.

Chow, Brian, *Emerging National Space Launch Programs: Economics and Safeguards,* Santa Monica, Calif.: RAND, R-4179-USDP, 1993.

Chow, Brian G., et al., *The Proposed Fissile-Material Production Cutoff: Next Steps,* Santa Monica, Calif.: RAND, MR-586-1-OSD, 1995.

Day, E., *Economic Sanctions Imposed by the United States Against Specific Countries: 1979 Through 1992,* Washington, D.C.: Congressional Research Service, Report No. 92-631F, August 10, 1992.

Delong, J. V., "Just What Crime Did Columbia/HCA Commit?" *The Wall Street Journal,* August 20, 1997, p. A15.

Director of Central Intelligence, *Report of Proliferation-Related Acquisition in 1997,* Langley, Va., September 17, 1998.

———, *Unclassified Report to Congress on the Acquisition of Technology Relating to Weapons of Mass Destruction and Advanced Conventional Munitions,* Langley, Va., February 9, 1999.

———, *Unclassified Report to Congress on the Acquisition of Technology Relating to Weapons of Mass Destruction and Advanced Conventional Munitions, 1 July Through 31 December 1999,* Langley, Va., August 9, 2000; online at http://www.cia.gov/publications/bian/bian_aug2000.htm.

Eizenstat, Stuart E. (Under Secretary of State for Economic, Business and Agricultural Affairs), "Remarks before the North American Committee of the National Policy Association, Washington, D.C., January 7, 1998.

———, "Testimony Before the Lott Bipartisan Senate Task Force on Sanctions," Washington, D.C., September 8, 1998.

Federal Register, Vol. 64, No. 73, April 16, 1999, p. 18957.

Gertz, B., "Limits to Be Loosened on Supercomputers, Clinton Waits on Sanctioning China," *The Washington Times,* October 5, 1995.

———, "U.S. Helped China Beat Sanctions, Witness Says," *The Washington Times,* June 12, 1998.

Glenn, John (Senator), "Senate Passes Major Nuclear Non-Proliferation Bill," news release, Washington, D.C., April 9, 1992.

Haass, Richard N., ed., *Economic Sanctions and American Diplomacy,* New York: Council on Foreign Relations, 1998.

Hufbauer, G. C., J. J. Schott, and K. A. Elliott, *Economic Sanctions Reconsidered,* 2nd ed., Washington, D.C.: Institute for International Economics, 1990.

Hufbauer G. C., and E. Winston, "'Smarter' Sanctions: Updating the Economic Weapons," paper presented at the Cantigny Conference, Wheaton, Ill., May 8–9, 1997.

Hussain, Syed talat, "US Sanctions Against KRL Raise Old Issues," *The Nation* (Islamabad, Pakistan), May 5, 1998; available as FBIS-TAC-98-125, May 5, 1998.

Jones, Rodney W., et al. (The Carnegie Endowment for International Peace), *Tracking Nuclear Proliferation: A Guide in Maps and Charts, 1998,* Washington, D.C.: The Brookings Institution Press, 1998.

Leitenberg, M., "The Desirability of International Sanctions Against the Use of Biological Weapons and Against Violations of the Biological Weapons Convention," *The Monitor* (Center for International Trade and Security of the University of Georgia, Athens, Ga.), Summer 1997, pp. 23–27.

Morrow, Daniel, and Michael Carriere, "The Economic Impacts of the 1998 Sanctions on India and Pakistan," *The Nonproliferation Review,* Vol. 6, No. 4, Fall 1999.

The Nonproliferation Policy Education Center, "Nonproliferation Policy Reform: Enhancing the Role of Congress," Washington, D.C., June 1996.

Ozga, D. A., "A Chronology of the Missile Technology Control Regime," *The Nonproliferation Review,* Winter 1994, pp. 66–93.

Pape, Robert A., "Why Economic Sanctions Do Not Work," *International Security,* Vol. 22, No. 2, Fall 1997.

Pikayev, A. A., L. S. Spector, E. V. Kirichenko, and R. Gibson (International Institute for Strategic Studies), *Russia, the U.S. and the Missile Technology Control Regime,* New York: Oxford University Press, Adelphi Paper 317, 1998.

The President's Export Council, *Unilateral Economic Sanctions: A Review of Existing Sanctions and Their Impacts on U.S. Economic Interest with Recommendations for Policy and Process Improvement, Executive Summary,* Washington, D.C., June 1997; hereafter called Unilateral Economic Sanctions.

Rennack, Dianne E., *Nuclear, Biological, Chemical, and Missile Proliferation Sanctions: Selected Current Law, Washington, D.C.: Library of Congress,* Congressional Research Service, updated May 27, 1998.

Rennack, Dianne E., with Robert D. Shuey, *Economic Sanctions to Achieve U.S. Foreign Policy Goals: Discussion and Guide to Current Law,* Washington, D.C.: Library of Congress, Congressional Research Service, updated January 22, 1998.

Reuters Ltd., "United States Sees Possible Okay for China Nuclear Deals," September 18, 1997, 8:42 p.m.

Rumsfeld Commission, *Report of the Commission to Assess the Ballistic Missile Threat to the United States, Executive Summary,* Washington, D.C.: U.S. Government Printing Office, July 15, 1998.

Rydell, Randy J., "Giving Nonproliferation Norms Teeth: Sanctions and the NPPA," *The Nonproliferations Review* (Monterey Institute of International Studies, Monterey, Calif.), Vol. 6, No. 2 , Winter 1999.

Sciolino, Elaine, "Clinton Argues for 'Flexibility' Over Sanctions," *The New York Times,* April 28, 1998.

Speier, R. H., "Iran Missile Sanctions," *Proliferation Brief* (Carnegie Endowment for International Peace Non-Proliferation Project, Washington, D.C.), August 27, 1998.

———, "Russia and Missile Proliferation," statement before the U.S. Senate, Subcommittee on International Security, Proliferation, and Federal Services of the Committee on Governmental Affairs, Washington, D.C., June 5, 1997.

"The Strategy of Sanctions" Conference, sponsored by the McCormick Tribune Foundation, the Strategic Studies Institute of the U.S. Army War College, the American Bar Association Standing

Committee on Laws and National Security, and the National Strategy Forum, Cantigny Estate, Wheaton, Ill., May 8–9, 1997; hereafter called the "Cantigny Conference." A Summary of Proceedings, *National Security Law Report* (American Bar Association Standing Committee on Law and National Security, Washington, D.C.), Vol. 19, No. 5, September 1997.

"Turning a Blind Eye," *Defense News,* September 8–14, 1997, p. 26.

Unilateral Economic Sanctions—see The President's Export Council.

USA Engage, publications, online at http://www.usaengage.org.

U.S. Senate, Committee on Foreign Relations, *Foreign Affairs Reform and Restructuring Act of 1997,* Washington, D.C.: Senate Report 105-28, June 12, 1997.

The White House, Office of the Press Secretary, "Easing of Sanctions on India and Pakistan," Washington, D.C.: statement, November 7, 1998.

———, "Fact Sheet on Cooperation on Non-Proliferation and Counterterrorism," Washington, D.C., May 18, 1998.

———,"Text of a Letter from the President to the Speaker of the House of Representatives, the President of the Senate, and the Chairman of the Senate Committee on Foreign Relations and the House Committee on International Relations" (letter dated January 12, 1998), Washington, D.C., January 15, 1998.